T0381011

Seven messages that may change your life

Aspects

of

GOD

This world: its past and future and you

Phil Hinsley

authorHOUSE®

AuthorHouse™
1663 Liberty Drive
Bloomington, IN 47403
www.authorhouse.com
Phone: 833-262-8899

Published by AuthorHouse 02/15/2024

ISBN: 979-8-8230-2243-9 (sc)
ISBN: 979-8-8230-2242-2 (e)

Aspects of God
2023

Introduction

The following seven messages were previously offered as separate articles with different type sizes, some with notes, some without. You will definitely cover some of same ground when these messages are combined, however, each does have its own particular focus and central purpose. I address four church teachings that to both Christians and many non-Christians assume to be core beliefs that have always been accepted as what Christians believe. Which are: we either go to heaven or hell when we die, humans have an immortal soul that goes somewhere when life ends, and lastly, the Triune nature of God. But there is much more that is included that perhaps you haven't thought about.

My wife, Anne, and I, live in a quiet area of Watford and pigeons come to our balcony at our first floor flat for their morning feed, but what gives us pleasure is a pair of white pigeons that come by themselves during the day and if the door is open they'll fearlessly walk in. I take out to them half a biscuit and they'll wait inches away on the balcony rail for me to crush the biscuit and drop it into the tray that used to be for flowers.

Contents

'If you slavishly follow somebody else's ideas, you will be impoverished and impaired. I had certainly found this to be the case in my own life. Blind obedience and unthinking acceptance of authority figures may make an institution work more smoothly, but the people who live under such a regime will remain in an infantile, dependent state. It is a great pity that religious institutions often insist on this type of conformity, which is far from the spirit of their founders, who all, in one way or another, rebelled against the status quo.'

Karen Armstrong
The Spiral Staircase

'Our way of life and understanding of the world may have changed utterly since ancient times, but we flatter ourselves unduly if we think that our behaviour is in any way different, or that human nature has altered much over the millennia.'

Paul Kriwaczek
Babylon

Part 1

So you think you know Jesus?

When Jeffrey Hunter played Jesus in the film 'King of Kings' he had his under arms shaved for the crucifixion scene.

Robert Powell decided that he would never blink when playing the lead role in 'Jesus of Nazareth'

Christian Bale, who played Jesus, in the film 'Mary mother of Jesus', is taught the stories he told by his mother and at the close of the film it's Mary who suggests to the disciples that they should start preaching about her son.

We don't get to see the face of Jesus in 'Ben Hur' but prior to his crucifixion he does get to carry the whole cross while the other two carry just the cross-beam – that happens in almost all the films about Jesus.

The least said about Mel Gibson's 'The Passion of the Christ' the better.

How we learn what's in the Bible is rarely learnt from reading the book itself but through what others say of it and the many films and traditional Christian festivals that focus on particular highlights of the Christian story. We can, and do, assume much that is in fact unbiblical.

What we are shown and what we hear falls far short of what the biblical documents tell us. The resurrection of Jesus is celebrated at Easter, but traditional Christianity ignores or forgets the resurrection of all those who belong to the Messiah at his return and the much later resurrection of the rest of humanity to judgement. Why is that?

Commonly assumed beliefs are:

December 25th is the birthday of Jesus, or some date close to it.

The gospel message is that God loves you and that Jesus loves you (compare that with Mark 1:14-15, Luke 4:43, 5:32).

That Jesus died on a Friday and rose on Sunday morning.

Not only did Jesus pre-exist before his birth; he is God the Son.

Humans have an immortal soul.

When we die, we either go to heaven or to hell.

Some teach that we don't go directly to one of these destinations but wait in some sort of anteroom, perhaps like a five-star hotel, before we receive the call to move blissfully upwards or possible like waiting for the dentist to call our name and then be dragged into everlasting torture.

Tom Wright, in his book, 'Paul A Biography' says, 'I assumed without question, until at least my thirties, that the whole point of Christianity was for people to "go to heaven when they died." It never occurred to my friends and me that, if we were to scour the first century for people who were hoping that their "souls" would leave the present material world behind and "go to heaven," we would discover Platonists like Plutarch, not Christians like Paul. When Paul says, "We are citizens of heaven," he goes on at once to say that Jesus will come *from* heaven not to take us back there, but *to transform the present world* and us with it and this hope for "resurrection," for new bodies within a newly reconstituted creation, doesn't just mean rethinking the ultimate "destination," the eventual future hope. It changes everything on the way as well.

'Paul had always believed that the One God would at the last put the whole world right. The Psalms had said it; the prophets had predicted it; Jesus had announced that it was happening (though in a way nobody had seen coming). Paul declared that it *had* happened in Jesus – and that it *would* happen at his return' (pp.7-8, 406).

Imagine you had a time machine, and you went, not back to the 1920s, as someone said they'd like to do on radio 4 recently, but to Judea in the early part of the first century. When you arrive, providing you can speak Aramaic, which the Jews learned while in their seventy-year captivity in Babylon, you stop people in the street and ask if they know where you can find a man named Jesus Christ.

The person who is the founder of Christianity is always referred to as Jesus Christ so, speaking in Aramaic, you ask around and to your surprise nobody's heard of him. Saddened, you arrive back to the present and invest in a good study Bible and you learn that the name Jesus is from the Greek form of a common Hebrew name, Joshua. He was the leader who took over after Moses died. Jesus would have been known as Joshua bar (son of) Joseph. OK, it would have been pronounced differently than it is in English but there's no point in getting too technical, Yeshua would be closer to his name. The word Christ is again from the Greek (Christos). It's not a name but a title. The Hebrew is Messiah, which means 'the anointed one.' And his mother's name, by the way, was Miriam, not Mary. Elizabeth, the mother of John the Baptist, was known as Elisheba.

Anglicizing these names was a deliberate and effective way of creating a distance from their Jewish roots.

There were many 'anointed ones' in the Old Testament times. All kings and high priests were anointed on taking up their position. We wouldn't say James King or Henry King, unless their surname was King, but rather James the King or Henry the King; better still, King James or King Henry, so, the definite article '*the*' could helpfully be used when speaking of Jesus the Christ or as is often used in the epistles, Christ Jesus or the Messiah Jesus, or Jesus, the anointed one. Plenty of choices.

His birth occurred in the autumn, rather than in December and the visitors who came, perhaps astrologers from Parthia, to give gifts to the child Jesus, arrived up to two years after his birth when they found him in a house. Luke records Jesus being circumcised eight days after his birth and being taken by his parents to the temple twenty-five days later, as the law required a sacrifice to be made (Lev 12:8) and as they then had little money, they were only able to afford two pigeons to be sacrificed. It was then after the visit of the wise men that they escaped to Egypt, and those gifts would have financed their stay there.

It can be confusing and seemingly contradictory to read both Matthew's account and Luke's of the birth of Jesus as Matthew doesn't mention the eight-day-old Jesus being circumcised or the meeting in the temple with Simeon and Anna while Luke doesn't record anything about escaping to Egypt or the Magi. Each of the gospel writers had their own focus on what to include rather than each being a copy of the others, but both accounts are true.

'It was customary for the Magoi to travel with oriental luxury and a large entourage, which included cavalry for protection. The myth of the number "three" (which does not appear in any Bible version) is far from the truth – they rarely travelled in such small numbers' ('The Source New Testament' Dr A. Nyland).

When shopping at Christmas time it's unavoidable to hear the seasonal songs including Harry Belafonte's 'Mary's boy child' which has the moving and influencing line, "man will live for evermore because of Christmas Day." Unfortunately for the apostles and succeeding generations of Christians they never realized this as they believed that repentance and faith was required before immortality was given at the resurrection. But a good tune usually wins over sound theology.

Ivor J. Davidson writes in volume two of his history of the church, 'A Public Faith' 'The earliest evidence for the celebration of December 25 as the festival of the birth of Jesus is to be found in a list of Roman bishops compiled in 354, which mentions the days that were treated as significant in Rome in the year 336.' That date of December 25 was the occasion of a popular pagan feast in honour of the birthday of the sun-god, *Sol Invictus*, "the Unconquered Sun." When the emperor Constantine in 321 declared the first day of the week a public holiday his stated reason was to respect "the venerable day of the Sun." It was the emperor Aurelian who in AD 274 chose Dec 25 as the birthday of the Sun god. Jesus was depicted as Christ Helios, or Jesus as the Sun of Righteousness.

As for what Jesus looked like, of course no one knows, but there are some clues. Judas had to identify Jesus by a kiss, so it wasn't obvious who amongst the disciples was Jesus. The apostle Paul wrote that 'Doesn't nature itself teach you that if a man has long hair, it is shameful to him,' and all films depicting Jesus has him with long hair. Isaiah describes the 'suffering servant' as not having film-star looks, 'he had no beauty or majesty to attract us to him, nothing in his appearance that we should desire him. He was despised and rejected by men, a man of sorrows, and familiar with suffering ...' (Isa 53).

As for his family and occupation, he had four brothers and at least two sisters who at one time thought he was losing his mind and wanted to restrain him. Jesus had the accent of a northerner who worked with stone, metal and wood; he was a skilled worker – a builder. He studied and learned the writings known to us as the Old Testament and quoted from those books often.

John, known as the Baptist, didn't know how to identify who the messiah was. John himself said, 'I didn't know who it would be, but the one who sent me to baptize with water said to me, "When you see the spirit coming down, like a dove, and resting on someone, that's the person who will baptize with the holy spirit." Well, that's what I saw, and I've given you my evidence: he is the son of God' (John 1:31-34).

A dove landing on someone and remaining on them would definitely make that person stand out in a crowd!

Jesus quickly moves away from the Jordan River and into the wilderness where he fasts for forty days. He is now reduced to a state of starvation and Satan (*the* adversary) comes close to gently pushing him over the edge.

Satan's three suggestions are all aimed to grant Jesus an easier and better life, after all, if he is God's son, he should have it all now.

"Use your power to satisfy your hunger – make bread!"

"Throw yourself off this building – you have God's protection!"

"Take control over the world now – turn from God and worship me!"

Jesus answered the adversary by saying, "It is written …" and Satan, knowing the scriptures, didn't argue and as he left angels appeared and took care of Jesus' physical needs.

Jesus had quoted from the book of Deuteronomy (meaning 'second-law giving,' the last book written by Moses). The record of the forty years of the Israelites moving about the wilderness is not an inspiring one. They were rebellious, stubborn, and forgetful. Because conditions were hard, due to their own decision not to enter the promised land when they could of, they were now prepared to turn around and return to Egypt where they thought that they'd be better off. And they were ready to kill Moses to achieve it.

They complained about the lack of food; they questioned whether God was really there for them; and they turned to other gods to worship them. They completely failed to be the people of God because of their lack of trust in God, so out of the 603,550 males, twenty years old and over, that had left Egypt in that great exodus, only two were able to eventually cross over the Jordan River and enter the promised land: They were Joshua and Caleb. They had been positive and enthusiastic that the nation could enter and conquer the land when they returned, with ten others, from spying out the land that they were to go into, but the fears of the other ten who focused on the walled cities and the very tall people they saw won the day and the people chose to return to Egypt with a new leader (see chapter 14 of Numbers if you want to find out what happened next).

Jesus, or Joshua, as he was known, was an Israelite facing the same temptations as they did, but he didn't fail. He quoted scripture back to Satan and trusted God, even when he knew what was ahead for him. The prophet Hosea had written:

'When Israel was a child, I loved him, and out of

Egypt I called my son. The more I called them, the more they went from me; they kept sacrificing to the Baals and offering incense to idols. Yet it was I who taught Ephraim to walk, I took them up in my arms; but they did not know that I healed them. I led them with cords of human kindness, with bands of love. I was to them like those who lift infants to their cheeks. I bent down to them and fed them.'

God was a father to Israel, but they rebelled. Jesus had a father-son relationship with God, and this trust and obedience was the central element of Jesus' teaching in the gospel of John (John 5:19).

Jesus was descended from the most famous of Israel's kings, David. The angel Gabriel had said to Mary, concerning Jesus, "He will be a great man, and he'll be called the son of the Most High. The lord God will give him the throne of David his father, and he shall reign over the house of Jacob forever. His kingdom will never come to an end."

The second psalm has God saying to the King, the Messiah, "You are my son; today I have begotten you, ask of me, and I will make the nations your heritage, and the ends of the earth your possession. You will break them with a rod of iron and dash them in pieces like a potter's vessel."

Jesus had told his disciples, "Don't be afraid,

little flock, your father is delighted to give you the kingdom," and on the night he was betrayed he told them, "You are the ones who have stuck it out with me through the trials I've had to endure. This is my bequest to you: the kingdom my father bequeathed to me! What does this mean? You will eat and drink at my table, in my kingdom, and you will sit on thrones, judging the twelve tribes of Israel."

Some Christians today wonder what that means – it means exactly what it says. When Jesus begins his reign, his people will reign under him ruling over nations, cities, towns and districts. The book of Revelation used psalm 2 in saying that it was still a future event (Rev 2:27, 12:5, 19:15). When will this happen? Many of those living in Judea at that time were looking and waiting for the Messiah to appear and start kicking the Romans out. But they were disappointed, to say the least, when Jesus never used the power he had to take authority to himself and be the king that they wanted. Even John the Baptist had deep concerns that Jesus wasn't doing what psalm 2 said he would do and then when Jesus died a criminal's death his disciples were heartbroken. Their dreams of a powerful new king for Israel were shattered. A week after being welcomed as king, he was dead.

The disciples, while Jesus was alive, were

anticipating him to move into power mode and reestablish the throne of David. So many of the prophets had written of a glorious reign of peace and healing (Isa 9:7, 40:9-10, 52:7, 61:2. Zec 14:4, 16-19. Dan 2:44, 7:27. Joel 2:11. Amos 5:18-20. Mic 4:2-5).

In his last visit with the disciples the resurrected Jesus was asked, "Master, is this the time when you are going to restore the kingdom to Israel?"

"It's not your business to know about times and dates," he replied. "The father has placed all that under his own direct authority. What will happen though, is that you will receive power when the holy spirit comes upon you. Then you will be my witnesses in Jerusalem, in all Judea and Samaria, and to the very ends of the earth."

The holy spirit is the personal presence and mind of God. The human spirit, which returns to God when we die, is our mind and character (see Luke 23:46 & Acts 7:59). This is not our soul. The soul is a living person.

"Your Kingdom come..." This is what Jesus taught his disciples to ask for; and that God's will be done on earth, because there is intensive opposition to it from human and spiritual sources. God's will isn't that planes crash, floods and fires destroy homes and people, and children are murdered. Life is unfair. There are those who try to comfort others when tragedy strikes with statements such as, 'in every bad situation there is something good' or 'inside the shell of sorrow we find the pearl of joy,' these sayings and others like them are said in love but are in denial of the very real evil that exists and has always been here. Isaiah wrote, 'and he will destroy on this mountain the shroud that is cast over all peoples, the sheet that is spread over all nations' (25:7). Paul began his letter to the Galatians by saying, 'Grace to you and peace from God our father and Jesus the Messiah, our Lord, who gave himself for our sins, to rescue us from *the present evil age*, according to the will of God ...'

I never want to miss the trailers when I go to the cinema but the greatest trailer of all I did miss and so did you. All we can do is read about it. It gave a glimpse or preview into that new age where we see Moses and Elijah talking to Jesus about his impending departure (Matt 17:1-9, Mark 9: 2-8, Luke 9:28-36).

The life, death and resurrection of Jesus did not change the grim reality that the age we live in is evil (Gal 1:4) and we're encouraged to look forward to the age to come. When talking of the many things we worry about, Jesus said, "Instead (of worrying), make your top priority God's kingdom and his way of life ..." Speaking of those people of faith who died, the writer of Hebrews says, '...they hadn't received the promise, but they had seen it from far off, and had greeted it, and had recognised that they were strangers and wanderers (or aliens) in the land.'

Jesus spoke in detail of worsening world conditions (Matt 24, Mark 13, Luke 21). But preceding the wars and rumours of wars, famines, earthquakes and persecutions there was also to arise a counterfeit Christianity. This part of his message is obscured by punctuation and quotation marks that were added many centuries later for purposes of clarity but in this case has misrepresented what he said. The disciples had just asked Jesus, "Tell us, when will this be, and what will be the sign that you are going to appear as king, and that the end of the age is upon us?"

"Watch out," replied Jesus, "don't let anyone deceive you. You see there will be several ('many' NRSV) who will come along, using my name, telling you, "I'm the Messiah!" They will fool lots of people." This statement will vary according to what version you're using but the thrust of it is that many will come claiming that they themselves are the Messiah. But there is another way of reading this text that will make it clearer and also making it more impactful in its implication. Let's read it without the quotation marks bracketing the words: I am the Christ. This time from the NIV, 'Watch out that no-one deceives you. For many will come in my name, claiming I am the Christ, and will deceive many.'

Jesus is saying that many will say that he, Jesus, is the Messiah and yet deceive many. This is because false teaching was to set in very quickly and over the years this false teaching, that was proclaiming a different message than the one Jesus brought, would become dominate and his true message would only be held by the few. A counterfeit Christianity that was tightly joined to the state that made its message compulsory and any deviation from it was condemned as heresy and punishable.

The core message of Jesus was the Kingdom of God and that repentance (a radical change of thinking) was a prerequisite for entry into that Kingdom, or Empire, as it could be translated. The kingdom of God was here on earth for a limited time in all the miracles that God did through Jesus while encountering strong opposition from the religious authorities. All his teaching was focused on how to enter that kingdom and what would keep a person out of it. Our attitude and behaviour would either give us access to that kingdom or deny us a place in it.

The last two verses of the book of Acts has, 'Paul lived there (in Rome) for two whole years at his own expense and welcomed everyone who came to see him. He announced the kingdom of God and taught about the Lord Jesus the Messiah, with all boldness and with no one stopping him.'

Alongside the central teaching of the kingdom of God was the teaching of the resurrection. Daniel, writing nearly six hundred years before wrote, 'Many of those who sleep in the dust shall awake, some to everlasting life and some to everlasting contempt.'

"I tell you the truth," Jesus said, "the time is coming – in fact, it's here already! When the dead will hear the voice of God's son, and those who hear it will live … Don't be surprised at this. The time is coming, you see, when everyone in the tombs will hear his voice. They will come out – those who have done good, to the resurrection of life, and those who have done evil, to the resurrection of judgement" (John 5:25, 28).

There will be two resurrections, separated by a thousand years. As John wrote, 'They came to life, and reigned with the Messiah for a thousand years.

The rest of the dead did not come back to life until the thousand years were complete. This is the first resurrection. Blessed and holy is the one who has a share in the first resurrection! The second death has no power over them. They will be priests to God and the Messiah, and they will reign with him for a thousand years' (Rev 20:5-6)

The sequence of resurrections is found in 1 Cor15:22-28. And Revelation 21 tells us that at the end of that thousand years God himself will come to a renewed earth.

That millennium will be, as Peter said on that historic day of Pentecost, a time of restoration (Acts 3:21).

In both old and new testaments death is figuratively spoken of as sleeping. Paul uses the expression 'fallen asleep' repeatably in writing of those who had died. Jesus said, in speaking to his disciples about the death of Lazarus that he had "fallen asleep and I'm going to wake him up," so his disciples said that if Lazarus is sleeping then that's a good sign. Then Jesus told them plainly, "Lazarus is dead" (John 11:11-14).

Strangely, most Christians don't follow these biblical examples of referring to the dead as sleeping but prefer to say the dead person is with the lord or is in heaven looking down on the living. Why is that?

What happened that shifted a clear teaching of death being like a sleep, which a person awakens from at the resurrection to life or the resurrection to judgement, to the teaching of going to heaven?

Greek philosophical speculations happened.

The early church fathers, as they are called, believed that the best of human wisdom was compatible with scripture and even studied the works of Plato and other classical writers *before* they got to the Bible. To be an accepted and respected theologian a man had to know the classical writings of the Greeks and Romans. The teaching of our immortal soul doesn't come from the Bible but Plato, and once that belief is taken for granted, we must come up with supportive beliefs of where that soul goes to after death, and that's what we did.

Everything taught relating to what the dead may experience is false.

The author of the letter to the Hebrews writes, 'just as it is laid down that humans have to die once, and after that comes judgement, so the Messiah, having been offered once and for all to take away the sins of many, will appear a second time. This will no longer have anything to do with sin. It will be in order to save those who are eagerly awaiting him' (Heb 9:27-28).

Jesus said, "celebrate and rejoice; there's a great reward for you in heaven" (Matt 5:12). Let's combine that statement with what Isaiah wrote, twice, 'See, the Lord God comes with might, and his arm rules for him; his reward is with him, and his recompense before him' (Isa 40:10, 62:11. And see Revelation 22:12). These rewards of rulership are given at the resurrection when Jesus returns (see Luke 19:17, Rev 11:18).

It has been often said that Jesus spoke more of hell than any other person in the New Testament. But Jesus never used the word hell because that is an old English word, *Hel* goddess of the dead. The King James Bible uses it but it's not the word Jesus used. He used the word *Gehenna* which is derived from the Hebrew *gehinnom* 'valley of Hinnom,' which is just south of Jerusalem. It was the place where child sacrifice took place and later became the city's rubbish tip and the place to burn things up. Jesus said of that place in speaking of the fate of the wicked, "their worm lives on forever and the fire can never be quenched." Those who teach the ongoing torture of the lost always use this verse to 'prove' that hell (they haven't given up that word) is real, but was Jesus the first to use those words or was he quoting another source?

Jesus was quoting from the very last verse of the book of Isaiah, so let's read that verse, 'And they shall go out and look at the dead bodies of the people who have rebelled against me; for their worm shall not die, their fire shall not be quenched, and they shall be an abhorrence to all flesh.'

Jesus wasn't teaching about immortal worms but maggot infested corpses. The Lutterworth Dictionary of the Bible says, 'Vivid, graphic descriptions of the specific torments of hell are lacking in the Bible but occur in extracanonical literature, and much later are grotesquely expressed in the art and literature of the medieval church and the Renaissance.'

The Bible teaches that the unrepentant wicked will be burnt to ashes. John the Baptist used the metaphor of trees being cut down and being thrown into the fire. He also spoke of gathering corn into the granary and burning up the chaff. Anything that is thrown into a furnace will be totally destroyed. Peter used the example of what happened to Sodom and Gomorrah to point out that what happened to those cities would be the fate of the wicked, which was to be destroyed by fire (2 Peter 2:6).

Jesus did talk of 'weeping and gnashing of teeth," and it's taught that this condition is ongoing as their suffering will be for an eternity yet consider what John wrote in the book of Revelation, 'Then I saw a great white throne and the One that was sitting on it. Earth and sky fled from his presence and no place was found for them. I saw the dead, great and small alike, standing in front of his throne while the books lay open. And another book was open, which is the book of life, and the dead were judged from what was written in the books, according to their deeds.

'The sea gave up all the dead that were in it; Death and Hades (the grave) were emptied of the dead that were in them; and each was judged according to their deeds. Then death and Hades were hurled into the fire. This lake of fire is the second death; and anyone whose name was not found written in the book of life was hurled into the lake of fire' (20:11-15).

If a person demonstrated kindness and mercy in their life, no matter what they understood, God isn't unfair to condemn them to the second death but if a person, no matter what they understood, was unmerciful and cruel they would be thrown into the lake of fire – it is those who are condemned that will weep in great distress and gnash their teeth in rage when they see their fate. But as Peter wrote, 'He (God) does not want anyone to be destroyed. Rather, he wants everyone to come to arrive at repentance.' Paul wrote to Timothy saying, '... This is good, and pleases God our Saviour, who wants all people to be saved and to come to a knowledge of the truth.'

Repentance and faith now, in this age, will mean that you will rule with the Messiah in the age to come (Rev 5:10). Ignoring the good news of the kingdom of God means that you will be resurrected for judgement in the second resurrection.

Apart from the strong influence of philosophical teaching in early church history there was another factor that greatly influenced what was taught and that was antisemitism. This hatred of Jews is well documented throughout the long centuries up to the present day. I was reading a commentary on the book of Revelation by a vicar of Harrogate, Martin Kiddle, which was first published in 1940, and he writes on page 9, 'The Jews particularly, who impaled him, would be forcibly convicted of their unpardonable crime in rejecting Christ: not repentance, as the prophet Zechariah had hoped, but bitter remorse must be their lot.'

Compare that writer's attitude to what is

pardonable and what is not to Peter's response to those who heard his speech on that day of Pentecost – Acts 2: 37-39.

Evidence of antisemitism is seen in a document called *The Didache*, or *Teaching of the Twelve Apostles*. It dates to the late first century or early second century. In it there is an explicit concern to differentiate Christian and Jewish behaviour. When it deals with fasting there is a deliberate move to fast on different days from the Jewish fast days (this is legalism, no matter who is doing it) of Monday and Thursday to Wednesday and Fridays instead. That's why we traditionally have fish & chips on a Friday.

In relation to fasting, Jesus' instruction was not to let anyone know you were doing it! And while you're at it, tidy your hair and wash your face.

The Quartodeciman controversy, please don't stop – it's an important story. This dispute revolved around when to observe Easter. The Eastern church still continued to keep the Passover regardless of what day of the week it happened to fall on, while the Roman custom held that Easter fell on the Sunday following Passover. When Polycarp of Smyrna travelled to Rome in his old age (154 or 155AD) to discuss the conflict with Anicetus, bishop of Rome, they reached no conclusion but parted on good terms and pledged to respect each other's positions.

But by 190 Victor 1, the first Latin-speaking bishop of Rome, called on all churches to follow Rome's lead by observing Easter on the Sunday after Passover. He called synods, regional councils of bishops, in Rome, Palestine and elsewhere to establish the new rule. When congregations in Asia Minor refused to follow his edict, he excommunicated them. They remained unmoved, however, Polycrates, the bishop of Ephesus, wrote to Victor, saying, "I am not scared of threats."

The dispute simmered off and on until it was finally resolved – in favour of Rome – by the Council of Nicaea in 325. Keeping the Passover was considered as Judaism and not Christian. The Christian (so called) authorities blamed the Jews for their crime in failing to recognise the Messiah and in orchestrating his crucifixion. This was early Christian antisemitism.

Rome was beginning to impose uniformity upon all churches. Though condemned by various church councils, the Quartodecimans ('fourteeners' – keeping the Passover on the fourteenth of Nisan, the first month of the Hebrew calendar) were still to be found in many places in the East for several centuries. Eventually it lost out to sheer force of custom, reinforced by the weight of Rome's authority. Rome regarded its right to impress its views on believers throughout the empire.

'It was at this time that conditions rapidly began to deteriorate for Jews living in the Roman Empire, (The Cambridge History of Judaism, vol 4, p.32, quoted in Kegan A. Chandler's 'The God of Jesus') because of Christian theological dogmas that fuelled an antipathy towards Judaism and things Jewish.' The eventual passage of church and state codified ordinances such as the Justinian Code would not only prohibit Jewish worship like the recitation of Jesus' own *Shema* confession (see Mark 12:29) but would strip away even the most basic of civil rights. The anti-Jewish predilections of key figures such as Constantine and Athanasius were emblematic of Gentile theologians of the Roman era. Athanasius industriously removed from Christology every trace of Judaism, particularly, its monotheism.'

The passionate rejection of the Jewish God by the church fathers continued with the leaders of the Reformation in the sixteenth century. The explicit and wanton antisemitism that thrived in the in the Reformation is an often-neglected piece of Protestant history.

The Jews, as both an ethnic and religious group, were considered detestable by the most well-known

Protestant leaders, and so was any theological insight the Jewish heritage had to offer.

John Calvin wrote, 'The Jews' rotten and unbending stiff-neckedness deserves that they be oppressed unendingly and without measure or end and that they die in their misery without the pity of anyone.'

And Martin Luther wrote, 'Such a desperate, thoroughly evil, poisonous, and devilish lot are these Jews, who for these fourteen hundred years have been and still are out plague, our pestilence, and our misfortune.' He went to say, 'What then shall we Christians do with this damned, rejected race of Jews? First, their synagogues should be set on fire, and whatever does not burn up should be covered or spread over with dirt so that no one may ever be able to see a cinder or stone of it. And this ought to be done for the honour of God and of Christianity in order that God may see that we are Christians, and that we have not wittingly tolerated or approved of such public lying, cursing, and blaspheming of His Son and His Christians. Second, their homes should likewise be broken down and destroyed. Thirdly, they should be deprived of their prayer books and Talmud in which such idolatry, lies, cursing, and blasphemy are taught. Fourthly, their rabbis must be forbidden under threat of death to teach any more … they ought not to be protected. You ought not, you cannot protect them, unless in the eyes of God you want to share all their abominations.'

The Jewish Rabbi called Joshua said to his followers, "the time is coming when anyone who kills you will suppose that they are in that way offering worship to God. They will do these things because they haven't known the father, or me. But I have been talking to you about these so that when their time comes, you will remember that I told you about them" (John 16:2-4).

It's not hard to see why Jewish-Christian relations fell apart after the doctrine of the Trinity took its place as a foundational teaching of the church.

On the day of Pentecost (the third of the annual sabbaths given in the law of God) Peter stood up before a large group of Jews and said, "You people of Israel, listen to this. Jesus of Nazareth was a man marked out for you by God through the mighty works, signs and portents which God performed through him right here among you, as you all know. He was handed over in accordance with God's determined purpose and foreknowledge – and you used people outside the law to nail him up and kill him …"

Through this message of Peter many Jews repented and were added to the number of the church. If Peter used terms such as the incarnate God-man who existed alongside two other God-Persons, the Jews would not have lined up to be baptised. Amongst the serious questions and debates that the apostles had to deal with there is no mention of Jesus being God himself. When Jesus became, for many, God, the separation between Jews and Christians deepened even more. To Christians God became a Trinity and heresy – making a choice for yourself – became a crime and Judaism became a form of infidelity because of their monotheism.

Will Durant in his 'The Story of Civilization' vol 3: Caesar and Christ p.595-599, writes, 'Christianity did not destroy paganism; it adopted it. The Greek mind, dying, came to a transmigrated life in the theology and liturgy of the church; the Greek language, having reigned for centuries over philosophy, became the vehicle of Christian literature and ritual ... Other pagan cultures contributed to the syncretistic result. From Egypt came the idea of a divine trinity ... and the mystic theology that made Neoplatonism and Gnosticism and obscured the Christian creed ... Christianity was the last great creation of the ancient pagan world.'

One of the most referred to texts in the New Testament that is used to prove Jesus is God is John 8:58. Breaking into a long hostile exchange where Jesus actually told his critics that their father was the devil because their behaviour was closer to the devil than it was to Abraham and then Jesus said to them, "I'm telling you the solemn truth, before Abraham existed, I Am." In a rage they picked up stones to throw at him, but he escaped from them.

Many might remember what God said to Moses at the burning bush, "I am who I am," and see Jesus making the claim that he was the one who spoke to Moses, yet the two statements are very different. While the Greek phrase *egō eimi* in John 8:58 does mean "I am," the Hebrew phrase in Exodus actually means "to be" or "to become." In other words, God is saying, "I will be what I will be."

The phrase "I am" *egō eimi*, occurs many other times in the NT, and is often translated as "I am he" or some equivalent. "I am" was a common way of designating oneself, such as the following examples will show:

The blind man: "egō eimi" John 9:9

Paul of Tarsus: "egō eimi: 1Tim 1:15

Judas Iscariot: "egō eimi" Matt 26:25

John the Baptist "egō eimi" John 1:27

Though this is the same words that Jesus used no one argues that these men were quoting Exodus, much less claiming to be God. The truth is that "egō eimi" is not any sort of divine name, it's simple the Greek for "I am he" or "I am the man." Neither the words 'he' or 'the man' are actually in the text, but the translators understand that they are implied by his use of the simple phrase "egō eimi." Trinitarian translators have even followed this model with Jesus' other sayings, such as John 8:24, "I told you that you would die in your sins; that's what will happen to you if you don't believe that *I am* the one."

When Jesus spoke to the Samaritan woman at the well, she'd said, "I know that the Messiah is coming, the one they call 'the anointed' and when he comes, he'll tell us everything."

"I'm the one, the one speaking to you right now," said Jesus. The Greek in Jesus' answer is "egō eimi," it means, "I'm the Messiah you' re talking about."

Regarding what Jesus said about Abraham, "Your father Abraham celebrated the fact that he would see my day. He saw it and was delighted." Paul was to write in his letter to the Galatians that the gospel was announced to Abraham in advance. He was looking ahead, as the writer of Hebrews says, 'to the city that has foundations, the city of which God is the designer and builder.' Jesus didn't actually physically exist in Abraham's time; rather he 'existed' in the mind of God as His plan (*logos*). Jesus existed in God's foreknowledge. God's plan for saving mankind existed long before Abraham lived.

When the resurrected Jesus identified himself to Mary near to the tomb, she turned and spoke in Aramaic, "Rabbouni!" (which means 'teacher) "Don't cling to me," said Jesus. "I haven't yet gone up to the father (the 1984 NIV has 'returned' but the Greek is 'ascended,' the 2011 edition has now changed it to 'ascended') but go to my brothers and say to them, "I'm going up to my father and your father – to my God and your God."

'But are trinitarians not monotheists?' (asks Eric H.H. Chang in his book 'The Only True God') 'As trinitarians we argued that we are monotheists, not polytheists, because our faith is in one God in three persons. We closed our eyes (and ears) to a fact that should have been perfectly obvious: If the Father is God, and the Son is God, and the Spirit is God, and all three are coequal and eternal, then the conclusion is inescapable that there are three Gods. So how did we manage to maintain that we still believe in one God? There was only one way: the definition of the word: "God" had to be changed – from a "Person" to a divine "Substance" (or "Nature") in which the three persons share equally.'

'Jewish Christianity always insisted on the historic fact that the Messiah and the Lord Jesus of Nazareth was not a divine being, a second God, but a human being among human beings' (Hans Küng, *Christianity*, p.97).

The traditional Easter observance of commemorating the death of Jesus on a Friday and his resurrection on the Sunday is a foundational teaching of the church. Mark records that Jesus rose early on the first day of the week, but we'll come back to that text later.

Earlier we spoke of travelling back in time to find the man called Jesus and discovered that wasn't even his name. Now, we'll go back in time again to that historic week when Jesus died and see what the people of Judea themselves would have been observing and find out if the chronology of the Friday – Sunday tradition remains strong.

The first event of significance in Israel's calendar is the Passover which looked back to when the Israelites were slaves in Egypt and the last plague was about to happen. They were instructed to put the blood of a lamb on the sides and top of their door frames. They had kept the lamb in their homes for four days – from the 10th day of the first month (Nisan) to the 14th. It was to be killed as the sun was going down. That same night they were to roast and eat the meat along with bitter herbs and unleavened bread. None of the bones of the lamb were to be broken and they were to eat it quickly and be dressed and ready for immediate departure.

On the same night, about midnight, a destroying angel would pass every house and if there was no blood on the door frame he would enter and kill the firstborn, human and animal, but if the angel saw the blood he would pass over that home. This was a night to be commemorated throughout their generations.

A day is reckoned, for the Israelites, from sunset to sunset – not midnight to midnight as we do. After they had observed the Passover, that next day, beginning at sunset, would be the first of the annual sabbaths, which is called 'The Lord's Feast of Unleavened Bread' and it lasted for seven days; The first day they held a sacred assembly and all regular work stopped and the last day would be the same. The day before that special day was known as the preparation day, just as Friday was the preparation day for the weekly sabbath.

The weekly sabbaths were holy days and the annual sabbaths were holy days.

John records (John 19:31) that the day of the crucifixion was the day of preparation and the Jews didn't want the bodies left hanging on the cross during the sabbath, especially because that sabbath was a day of great solemnity or 'a very special day.'

Most of us have been taught that that preparation day was a Friday because the regular Saturday sabbath was the next day, yet John calls it a 'very special one.' It's much more likely that John was referring to the First Day of Unleavened Bread, and not just a weekly sabbath.

If that 'special day' was on a Thursday, the day before would be a prep' day and the day after that special sabbath would also be a prep' day. That week had two prep' days and two sabbaths – the first of the annual sabbaths and the weekly sabbath. The Passover of that week would have been on the Tuesday evening, the same night Jesus was arrested. The following day, Wednesday, was when he was crucified at 9am and died about 3pm. He was entombed just before the sun went down.

Jesus said that he (the son of man, see Daniel 7:13) "will be in the heart of the earth for three days and three nights." Modern scholars rightly tell us that in Greek a day may mean just a portion of a day, so with that reckoning one can (only with some difficulty) fit three days between Friday sunset and Sunday morning but not three nights. We must remember that Jesus employed the example of Jonah who was in the giant fish for three days and three nights and in Hebrew a day was a day and a night was a night.

So, counting from, and including Wednesday night, three days and three nights, Jesus rose as the sun was setting on that weekly sabbath.

Now back to what Mark wrote: 'Having risen in the morning on the first day of the week …' (Mark 16:9) Mark's gospel ends at verse 8; verses 9-20 were written later and it's not known if Mark intended to end at verse 8 or what he then wrote was lost. The other gospel accounts say that by the time the women arrived at the tomb it was still quite dark, and the tomb was empty.

Two details about the crucifixion.

First; because of the enormous amount of paintings and films of the crucifixion it's virtually impossible to think of it without picturing a hill and the three crosses on its summit. 'The Robe' was the first film made in CinemaScope and in the crucifixion scene it looks like it takes place about a mile outside the city where just a small group of devoted people had managed to climb the rocky hill to see it.

We're presented with this hill yet there is not one word of a hill in the telling of that event in scripture. The thinking behind public executions would be that they would act as a deterrent. A public square would be an obvious choice or a place like a busy junction would serve its purpose. Jesus, and the others, were executed outside the city wall so the major arterial route into and out of the city would be an ideal spot. A place where seeing the long drawn out and painful death of criminals was unavoidable. As usual large crowds would gather to see the spectacle.

At school, in Barry, I used to sing the hymn titled, 'There is a green hill far away,' good as that hymn is, the picture it portrays is pure tradition. The executions were done on ground level where people would have to walk past.

Secondly, the four gospels, factual and historical as they are, were not written as history is written in our time. Each gospel writer chose and selected a particular perspective and focus. Each gospel is different, not because they contradict each other but that their aim was different.

A few examples may help:

A Roman centurion pleads with Jesus to heal his dying servant and when Jesus intends to go to the Roman's home, he tells Jesus that it's not necessary as he is a man under authority and knows that Jesus has only to say the word and his servant will be healed.

In another account it's not the centurion himself but Jewish elders who were sent by the Roman to speak to Jesus on his behalf. And when Jesus came near to the house the Roman sent some friends of his to say that Jesus doesn't need to be there personally, and to give Jesus his reasons for saying this.

Another example is when Jesus stepped out from a boat and a man possessed by many demons and dangerously violent met him and was healed. Two accounts speak only of one man, but Matthew's account says there were two of them. Each writer made a choice of what to include and what to leave out. It's a matter of focus, not contradiction.

Matthew, Mark and Luke write of the darkness from midday until about 3pm on the day of the crucifixion but John doesn't mention the darkness at all. One film of John's gospel doesn't show the darkness just because it's not written by John!

The last example is again about the crucifixion:

All four accounts say that two others were crucified with Jesus. Matthew, Mark and Luke mention Simon, who was enlisted to carry Jesus' cross (the crossbeam), but John selects not to mention Simon.

Luke says, 'When they reached the place called The Skull, there they crucified him and the criminals, one on his right, the other on his left …'

Mark has, 'They offered him wine mixed with myrrh, but he did not take it. Then they crucified him and shared his clothes by casting lots to decide what each should take.'

Matthew writes the same as Mark but differs from Luke in that the criminals are crucified at the same time as Jesus, yet Matthew has, 'When they had crucified him they shared out his clothing by casting lots, and then, sitting down, they guarded him there. And they placed above his head the charge against him; it read: 'This is Jesus, the King of the Jews.' *Then* they crucified two bandits with him, one on his right, one on his left.' We might notice here that sharing the clothing, casting lots and guarding him took a little time, while Luke implies that the three of them were crucified at the same time.

In the Greek of John's gospel, the part where it says, '...where they crucified him and with him two others, one on either side, Jesus being in the middle,' we see that clearly there were three crosses. But what we just read isn't what the Greek says. The word *one* in John's sentence isn't in the Greek text, so we should read it as, '... where they crucified him and with him two others on either side.' Two were crucified at the same time as Jesus and then, after the soldiers cast their lots for his clothes and began guarding them, two others were crucified either side of Jesus. There were five executions that day.

When they came to break the legs of the condemned men, they broke the legs of the first two then came to Jesus and saw that he was dead already – if there were only three crosses then they would have had to go around Jesus to get to the third man. Young's Literal Translation and E.W. Bullinger's Companion Bible both write of two others, either side of Jesus.

The ancient Israelites failed to become the children of God because of their hardheartedness and rebellion while Jesus, a Jew from the tribe of Judah, a descendant of King David, proved by his obedience and what he willingly suffered, that he was truly the son of God. But he was more than the most faithful son of Israel – he won what Adam lost. Adam represented mankind in choosing to go their own way. Jesus obeyed his father and pleased him in all he did. Adam sinned – he died – we all sin – and we all die.

Everything hinged on the Messiah's obedience *as a man*.

Paul puts it this way, '… just as sin came into the world through one human being, and death through sin, and in that way, death spread to all humans, in that all sinned … So then, just as through the trespass of one person the result was condemnation for all people, even so, through the upright act of one person, the result is justification – life for all people. For just as through the disobedience of one person many received the status of 'sinner', so through the obedience of one person many will receive the status of 'in the right.'

'While we were still weak, at that very moment he died on behalf of the ungodly. It's a rare thing to find someone who will die on behalf of an upright person – though I suppose someone might be brave enough to die for a good person. But this is how God demonstrates his own love for us, the Messiah died for us while we were still sinners.

'How much more, in that case – since we have been declared to be in the right by his blood – are we going to be saved by him from God's coming anger! When we were enemies, you see, we were reconciled to God through the death of his son; if that's so, how much more, having already been reconciled, shall we be saved by his life. And that's not all. We even celebrate in God, through our Lord Jesus the Messiah, through whom we have now received this reconciliation.

'It all comes from God. He reconciled us to himself through the Messiah, and he gave us the ministry of reconciliation. This is how it came about: God was reconciling the world to himself in the Messiah, not counting their transgressions against them, and entrusting us with the message of reconciliation. So, we are ambassadors, speaking on behalf of the Messiah, as though God were making his appeal through us. We implore people on the Messiah's behalf to be reconciled to God. The Messiah did not know sin, but God made him to be sin on our behalf, so that in him we might embody God's faithfulness to the covenant' (Rom 5:12, 18-19,6-11. II Cor 5:18-21. A better translation for verse 21 would be 'He made him who did not know sin to be a sin *offering* on our behalf, so that, through union with him, we would become the righteousness of God.' This verse then would be in full agreement with the first letter of John where he writes, 'He is himself a sacrifice to atone for our sins, and not only ours but the sins of the whole world' 2:2.

Paul further explains to the Colossians what God through Jesus has accomplished.

'… giving joyful thanks to the Father, who has qualified you to share in the inheritance of his holy people in the kingdom of light. For he has rescued us from the dominion of darkness and brought us into the kingdom of the Son he loves, in whom we have redemption, the forgiveness of sins.'

He goes on to write.

'Once you were alienated from God and were enemies in your minds because of your evil behaviour. But now he has reconciled you by Christ's physical body through death to present you holy in his sight, without blemish and free from accusation – if you continue in your faith, established and firm, and do not move from the hope held out in the gospel' (Col 1:12-13, 21-23a).

The former Pharisee, Saul, now known as Paul, stood in chains before king Agrippa II, great-grandson of Herod the Great, and spoke of his persecution of Christians and the authority given him from the chief priests to pursue God's people wherever they were. He told the king that when he was close to Damascus he saw a very strong bright light which caused him to fall to the ground blinded. He then heard a voice who identified himself as Jesus, the man whose followers Paul had wanted to destroy. "I've appeared to you," Jesus said, "for this reason: to appoint you as my servant... I shall rescue you from the people and from the nations to whom I send you to open their eyes, so that they may turn from darkness to light, from the dominion of Satan to God, and receive forgiveness of sins and a share in the inheritance of those who are sanctified by faith in me."

Paul was in shock – there was so much to think about; he believed he was serving God by his zealous attacks on the servants of Jesus only now to learn that he had been in the dark, serving Satan. It was going to take some time before he would be ready to do the work he was called to do – there was a considerable amount to unlearn.

The following is from the book 'The Only True God' by Eric H.H. Chang, p.303. 'Paul was as monotheistic as any monotheist, as is perfectly clear from his letters (Rom 16:27; I Cor 8:6, 8:4; Rom 3:30; Eph 1:3,3:14, 4:6; I Tim 1:17,2:5, etc). As

44

apostle to the Gentiles, Paul saw his mission as being that of bringing Gentiles into "the commonwealth of Israel" through faith in Jesus [the] Christ (Eph 2:12); they thereby become members of the "Israel of God" (Gal 6:16.

'But within a hundred years, the church had evolved from being under dedicated Jewish leadership to becoming a predominantly Gentile church under Gentile leaders. *A quantum shift had taken place*. The church was now composed of people from a polytheistic background who lacked the ardent commitment to monotheism which was characteristic of the Jews. It soon became apparent that the Gentile church was not particularly averse to adding one or two more persons to the Godhead, while nominally acknowledging the monotheistic character of the faith and the Scriptures (both Old and New) that they had inherited from the Jewish church.

'The Gentile church proceeded boldly with the process of the deification of Christ in spite of the fact that they could not find one verse in their New Testament which plainly stated that Jesus is God. The fact that trinitarianism could find nothing in the NT that supported them is hardly surprising given the fact that all except one (i.e. Luke) of the writers of the New Testament were Jews. Little wonder that the Nicene Creed, which had become determinative for the (Gentile) Christian Church, and in which Jesus is raised to full deity so as to be coequal with the Father, does not quote a single verse in support of this new dogma.'

In the first letter of John he writes, 'My children, I am writing these things to you so that you may not sin. If anyone does sin, we have one who pleads our cause before the father – namely, the Righteous One, Jesus the Messiah. *He is the sacrifice which atones for our sins* – and not ours only, either, but those of the whole world.'

And Paul wrote to the Roman Christians saying, '… for there is no distinction, since all have sinned and fall short of the glory of God; they are now justified by his grace as a gift, through the redemption that is in the Messiah Jesus, whom God put forward *as a sacrifice of atonement by his blood*, effective through faith.'

The Day of Atonement, (the fifth of seven annual sabbaths in Israel) when many rituals had to be followed exactly and sacrifices made to restore a right relationship between the people of Israel and God – there was no forgiveness without the shedding of blood (Heb 9:22, Matt 26:28-29) This had to be done each year as well as the daily sacrifices. These laws of sacrifices, writes the author of the letter to the Hebrews, are a shadow of the good things that are coming, not the actual form of the things themselves. Thus, it is unable to make worshippers perfect through the annual round of the same sacrifices which are continually being offered … but, as it is, the sacrifices serve as a regular annual reminder of sins, since it's impossible for the blood of bulls and goats to take sins away.

'That's why, when the Messiah comes into the world, this is what he says: You didn't want sacrifices and offerings.

Instead, you've given me a body.

You didn't like burnt offerings and sin-offerings.

Then I said, 'Look here I am!

This is what it says about me in the scroll, the book.

I've come, O God, to do your will. (Heb10:5-7, quoting Psalm40: 7-9, Greek-Septuagint 39:7-9)

'But now the Messiah has come, as the high priest of all the blessings that were to come. He has passed through the greater, the more perfect tent, not made by human hands… taking with him not the blood of goats and bull calves, but his own

47

blood, having won an eternal redemption' (1Peter 1:19).

The blood sacrifices, given as commandments to the nation of Israel are now obsolete. Yet what the Day of Atonement pictured and pointed to (the word *atonement* means 'covered), just as the Passover does, goes beyond one nation's escape from slavery to encompass the whole world in its significance. Jesus won a victory that's difficult to fully comprehend. None of the ancient Israelites in the times when they kept those seven annual festivals had any idea that these special days would contain a deep meaning for the liberation of the whole world – from the Passover to the Last Great Day (see John 7:37) or, if we have the eyes to see it, from the violent death of Jesus on the cross, when he took our punishment and the iniquity of all of us was laid on him, to the time of the great white throne judgement after the thousand year reign of the Messiah on earth (Rev 20:11).

Jesus is the way to God and isn't the destination, which is God himself, Jesus is the means, not the end (1Tim 2:5).

Jesus didn't have a 'death wish.' He suffered intense emotion and trauma in the garden before his arrest as he dreaded what was going to happen to him. It wasn't his will to be tortured and die. He asked for an alteration in God's plan, but he was committed to God's objective and was strengthened to fulfil his Father's will (Rom 8:32).

In one of the many times when Israel were rebellious against Moses and God they said, "Why have you brought us up out of Egypt to die in the wilderness? There's no food and water, and we detest this 'manna.'" Then the Lord sent poisonous snakes among the people and many people died from their bites. Then the people came to Moses and said, "We've sinned by speaking against the Lord and you; pray to the Lord to take away the snakes from us." So, Moses prayed for the people. And the Lord said to Moses, make a poisonous snake and set it on a pole; and everyone who is bitten shall look at it and live." So, Moses made a bronze snake and put it upon a pole; and whenever a snake bit someone, that person would look at the bronze snake and live' (Numbers 21:4-9).

Fast forward 1,280 years or so…

Nicodemus, a ruler in Judea, came to Jesus during the night and said, "Rabbi, we know that you are a teacher who's come from God. Nobody can do these signs that you're doing, unless God is with him."

After recording some of the conversation

between them John continues his narration, 'So, just as Moses lifted up the snake in the desert, in the same way the son of man must be lifted up, so that everyone who believes in him may share in the life of God's new age. This, you see, is how much God loved the world: enough to give his only, special son, so that everyone who believes in him should not be lost but should share in the life of God's new age' (John 3:1,14-16).

Ezekiel wrote to a rebellious people, '... I will judge you, O house of Israel, all of you according to your ways, says the Lord God. Repent and turn from all your transgressions; otherwise iniquity will be your ruin. Cast away from you all the transgressions that you've committed against me and get yourselves a new heart and a new spirit! Why will you die, O house of Israel? For I have no pleasure in the death of anyone, says the Lord God. Turn, then, and live' (Ezek 18:30-32).

The message of Jesus, who was the greatest prophet, continued that theme, "Repent for the Kingdom of God is close at hand," Just as John the Baptist did (Matt 3:2,4:17).

A lawyer with a questionable motive asked Jesus, "Teacher, what must I do to inherit eternal life?" He said to him, "What's written in the law? What's your reading of it?" He replied, 'You shall love the Lord your God with all your heart, with all your soul, with all your strength, and with all your mind, and your neighbour as yourself.' Jesus said to him, "You've answered right, do this and you shall live" (Luke 10:25-28, Deut 6:5, Lev 19:18). The 'Shema' (Mark 12:29-30) was banned by Justinian in AD529.

During an argumentative encounter with some closed-minded religious people Jesus said to them, "When you've lifted up the son of man, then you'll know that I am he and that I do nothing of my own accord. But as the Father has taught me, so I speak; he who sent me is with me, and hasn't left me to myself, for I always do what pleases him. If you remain in my word, you're truly my disciples; you'll come to know the truth, and the truth will set you free" (John 8:28-32).

Free from teaching born from philosophical reasoning and antisemitism.

The message of Jesus was to proclaim the Kingdom (or Empire) of God and call sinners to repentance (Luke 4:43, 5:32, 19:10). That is the gospel. But there's more. Due to the strong antisemitism that was existing from the earliest times in the church the festivals that God gave to ancient Israel were looked on as being just Jewish traditions that were not relevant to New Testament Christians and were soon replaced by our major holy periods of Christmas and Easter which had its origins in pagan celebrations. Paul Kriwaczek, author of 'Babylon' writes, 'The goddess Ishtar of Nineveh, mother, virgin and whore, whose planet was Venus, and whose symbol was an eight-pointed star, was famed throughout the Near East.' Eostre was the Saxon mother goddess – the source of all things and the bringer of new life who also represented fertility and rebirth. This is where we get our word Easter from.

By jettisoning those Old Testament festivals, the worldwide Christian community has lost an understanding that history is like an arrow that moves towards a target called the Kingdom of God. History does have direction and meaning. Our present age is seen as being both evil and dark (Gal 1:4, 1 Col 1:13) and many Christians find it very difficult to answer the question of suffering while non-Christians see the suffering and evil in the world as proof that God either doesn't exist or if he did then he's gone away and hasn't the power to do anything about the evil in the world. Yet, those redundant Jewish feasts, as many would see them, provide the outline of God's plan for humanity in a far more profound way than Easter or Christmas can.

Those annual festivals are found in Leviticus 23 and in Israel's long history there were often periods when they were replaced by the pagan festivals of the nations around them as well as those kept in the land of Canaan when Israel took over their towns and cities.

By the time of Jesus these seven special times were being observed but covered over with many traditions of the elders that weren't commanded in the writings of Moses and when some of the legalistically minded Pharisees came into the church they taught that Christians needed to be circumcised to demonstrate that they were obedient to God's commands – this early controversy caused the apostle Paul, a former Pharisee himself, to spend much of his time refuting this wrong teaching. He wrote and taught that 'no-one will be declared righteous in his (God's) sight by observing the law; rather, through the law we become conscious of sin.' As John wrote, 'Everyone who sins breaks the law, in fact, sin is lawlessness' (1 John 3:4).

'All who rely on observing the law are under a curse... Clearly no-one is justified before God by the law,' Paul wrote to the Galatians, but God commanded circumcision so how were Christians to obey that law?

Moses had written to the rebellious Israelites, 'Circumcise your hearts, and don't be stiff-necked any longer.' And later he wrote, 'The Lord your God will circumcise your hearts and the hearts of your descendants, so that you may love him with all your heart and with all your soul, and live.'

To the Roman Christians, Paul wrote, 'circumcision is circumcision of the heart, by the spirit, not by the written code. Such a man's praise isn't from men, but from God.' To the Galatians he wrote, 'For in Christ Jesus neither circumcision nor uncircumcision has any value. The only thing that counts is faith expressing itself through love.'

The Israelites were commanded to keep the Passover as a perpetual reminder of being liberated from slavery in Egypt. There is much significant ritual associated with observing this special evening but what did Paul teach concerning the Passover? '… for Christ (or Messiah), our Passover lamb, has been sacrificed, therefore let us keep the festival, not with the old bread leavened with malice and wickedness, but with the unleavened bread of sincerity and truth (1 Cor 5:7-8).

In Paul's second letter to the Corinthians (5:21)

we read, 'God made him who had no sin to be a sin offering for us, so that in him we might become the righteousness of God.'

The bloody daily and annual sacrifices that Israel was commanded to keep were a continual reminder of sins, yet, as the writer of the letter to the Hebrews plainly says, 'It's impossible for the blood of bulls and goats to take away sins... Day after day every priest stands and performs his religious duties; again and again he offers the same sacrifices, which can never take away sins. But when this priest (see 9:11) had offered for all time one sacrifice for sins, he sat down at the right hand of God, and since that time he waits for his enemies to be made his footstool, for by one sacrifice he has made perfect for ever those who are being made holy (10:11-14).

The old covenant became obsolete, as Jeremiah wrote, 'I will put my laws in their minds and write them on their hearts... (Jer 31:31-34, Heb 8:7-13). We may not see ourselves as enemies of God needing reconciliation yet that is what the death of Jesus accomplished. Sin entered the world through one man, Adam, and death came to all because all of us have sinned. As Paul wrote, 'God presented Christ as a sacrifice of *atonement*, through the shedding of his blood (Rom 3:25).

The Day of Atonement is the only day where fasting is commanded. It is the fifth of the annual holy days and Leviticus 16 goes into great detail of what was to be done on that day but it comes down to two goats – one is sacrificed and the other was to represent all the sins of the Israelites and then be led out to a remote place far away and released. The ritual was to show how Israel was to be reconciled to God – by dumping all their sins on the head of an animal!

That law, as it says in Hebrews, is only a shadow of the good things that are coming – not the realities themselves (10:1).

The reality was and is what Jesus did, and through trust in him as our atonement we can be reconciled to God. As quoted before, John wrote, 'He is the atoning sacrifice for our sins, and not only for ours but also for the sins of the whole world' (1John 2:2).

Amongst all the differing teachings coming from a multitude of Christian churches we should remember the clear teaching Paul gave to Timothy: 'For there is one God and one mediator between God and mankind, the man Christ Jesus who gave himself as a ransom for all people (1 Tim 2:5).

After Jesus, as King, has ruled this world for a

thousand years, God himself will make his home here on earth. As humans these are realities that we can hardly grasp any more than being changed from mortal to immortal and where death no longer exists, but that is what is promised.

'Now may the God of peace, who
through the blood of the

eternal covenant brought back from
the dead our Lord Jesus,

that great shepherd of the sheep,
equip you with everything good

for doing his will, and may he work
in us what is pleasing to him,

through Jesus Christ, to whom be
glory for ever and ever.'

Hebrews 13:20-21

There was little interest in Hebrew writings by now. According to the hectoring sermons being preached by a new generation of intolerant Christian clerics, the Jews were not a people with an ancient wisdom to be learnt from: they were instead, like the pagans, the hated enemies of the Church. A few years earlier, the preacher John Chrysostom had said that: 'the synagogue is not only a brothel … it also is a fen of robbers and a lodging for wild beasts … a dwelling of demons … a place of idolatry'. St Chrysostom's writings would later be reprinted with enthusiasm in Nazi Germany.

The spread of Christianity … is a story of forced conversion and government persecution. It is a story in which great works of art are destroyed, buildings are defaced and liberties are removed. It is a story in which those who refused to convert were outlawed and, as the persecution deepened, were hounded and even executed by zealous authorities. The brief and sporadic Roman persecutions of Christians would pale in comparison to what the Christians inflicted on others – not to mention on their own heretics.

Catherine Nixey
The Darkening Age pp.133,99

Part 2

The Failure of the Church

Theologians in all ages have looked out admiringly upon the material universe and... demonstrated the power, wisdom, and goodness of God; but we know of no one who has demonstrated the same attributes from the history of the human race.

James A. Garfield

On the morning of July 2, 1881 James Abram Garfield, the president of the United States, and his Secretary of State James Blaine, walked into the Baltimore and Potomac train station. Moments after they had entered the waiting room Charles Guitean shot the president twice. The first shot passed through his right arm, but the second entered his back four inches to the right of his spinal column, broke two of his ribs and grazes an artery. The bullet did not hit any vital organs as it continued its trajectory to the left, finally coming to rest behind his pancreas.

Garfield's Secretary of War, Robert Todd Lincoln, Abraham Lincoln's only surviving son, quickly took charge and sent for Dr D. Willard Bliss who was confident that the president could not hope to find a better physician. "If I can't save him," he told a reporter, "no one can."

According to his biographer, Candice Millard,[1] that far from preventing or even delaying the president's death, his doctors very likely caused it. Bliss was condemned by the international medical community particularly because of the repeated, unsterilized probing of the president's wound by fingers and instruments searching for the bullet.

"None of the injuries inflicted by the assassin's bullet were necessarily fatal," wrote Arpad, a New York surgeon who had recently been in Europe studying the "Listerian method of wound treatment," and would write the first American surgical textbook based on that method. To the physicians of his generation, Gerster continued, "Garfield's death proved with certainty that, as the poet Thomas Gray had written more than a century earlier, 'ignorance is Bliss.'"

---

[1] *Destiny of the Republic- A Tale of Madness, Medicine and the Murder of a President.*

In the summer of 1876 the United States held its Centennial Exhibition in Philadelphia. Congressman James Garfield, his wife, Lucretia, and their six children walked through the fair which had fourteen acres of exhibits. He was born into extreme poverty in a log cabin in rural Ohio. He had a love of learning and became a professor of ancient languages, literature and mathematics. He paid for his first year of collage by working as a carpenter.

Among the inventors at the fair was a young Scotsman named Alexander Graham Bell. His invention was "a new apparatus operated by the human voice." He had missed the official deadline for registering and so his invention was not listed in the fair's programme. After much difficulty in getting it set up the judges were amazed as they understood that Bell's voice, quoting Shakespeare's words travelled clearly about a hundred yards away. The telephone had worked.

A short distance away Joseph Lister struggled to convince his audience of experienced and admired physicians and surgeons of the critical importance of antisepsis – preventing infection by destroying germs.

Very few of those who listened to Lister's believed what he said and none of them seriously considered putting his theory into practice – it just meant extra work – they scoffed at the idea of germs and thought it would be ridiculous to set up a system for destroying what they thought did not exist. Most American doctors simply shrugged off Lister's findings, uninterested and unimpressed. Dr Samuel Gross, the president of the Medical Congress regarded antisepsis as useless, even dangerous, "Little, if any faith, is placed by any enlightened or experienced surgeon on this side of the Atlantic in the so-called carbolic acid treatment of Professor Lister," he wrote.

When Alexander Graham Bell heard that President Garfield had been shot, he knew that, in the case of a gunshot wound, "no one could venture to predict the end so long as the position of the bullet remained unknown." It distressed him to think of Garfield's doctor blindly searching with knife and probe for the bullet. He reasoned that "science should be able to discover some less barbarous method." Had Garfield been shot fifteen years later, the bullet in his back would have been quickly found by x-ray images and the wound treated with antiseptic surgery. He might have been back on his feet within weeks. Had he been able to receive modern medical care, he likely would have spent no more than a few nights in hospital.

Even had Garfield simply been left alone, he almost certainly would have survived. Lodged as it was in the fatty tissue below and behind his pancreas, the bullet itself was no continuing danger to the president. "Nature did all she could to restore him to health," a surgeon would write just a few years later, "She caused a capsule of thick, strong, fibrous tissue to be formed around the bullet, completely walling it off from the rest of the body and rendering it entirely harmless."

For one doctor in particular, this national crisis was a rare and heady coming together of medicine and political power – an opportunity for recognition he would never see again. Although ten different doctors had examined Garfield at the train station, as soon as the patient reached the White House, Dr Willard Bliss made it perfectly clear that he was in charge. Bliss's complete confidence in his position convinced his most determined competitors that he had been given full authority over Garfield's case. Bliss led other doctors to believe that the president had chosen to trust his case, and his life, solely to him and they were all dismissed.

This marriage of arrogance and wilful ignorance is seen in the records of the early church where individuals seeking positions of authority would undermine the teachings of the apostles and in spite of repeated warnings that this would occur false teaching did gain the upper hand. Just as an infection can become dangerous so unsound teaching can lead to a deviation from the truth that will misrepresent what has been originally taught. This was a real problem for the writers of the New Testament. The former Pharisee and apostle, Paul wrote to his assistant Timothy about sound teaching[2] 'for the time will come when people will not put up with sound doctrine...' the word *sound* literally means 'healthy' and that unhealthy teaching was already there in Paul's time.

The historian William Reade wrote in his 'The Martyrdom of Man' The church diverged in discipline and dogma more and more widely from its ancient form, till in the second century the Christians of Judea, who had faithfully followed the customs and tenets of the twelve apostles, were informed that they were heretics. During that interval a new religion had arisen. Christianity had conquered paganism and paganism had corrupted Christianity... The single Deity of the Jews had been exchanged for the Trinity, which the Egyptians had invented, and which Plato had idealised into a

---

[2] 1Tim 1:10; 2Tim 1:13; 4:3; Titus 1:9; 1:13; 2:2,8.

philosophic system. The man who had said, "Why call me good? There is none good but one, that is God," had now himself been made a god, or the third part of one.'[3]

'There has always been,' according to the late John Stott, in his commentary on 1 Timothy & Titus, pp.109-113, [an] 'unremitting struggle between truth and error.' His comments on 1 Tim 4:1 are helpful, first the verse; 'Now the Spirit expressly says that in the later times some will depart from the faith, giving heed to deceiving spirits and doctrines of demons.' The key statement, Stott writes, is that 'in spite of the church's role as the guardian of the truth some will abandon the faith. When will this Christian apostasy take place? In the later times, Paul replies, but he quickly slips from the future tense into the present (3-6), indicating his belief that the 'later times' have already begun, 'later times' and 'the last days' both denote the Christian era, which Jesus inaugurated at his first coming and will consummate at his second.'

Jesus himself said that "Then many false prophets will rise up and deceive many."[4] This is spiritual sepsis on a worldwide scale. 'Paul looks

---

[3] Quoted from Kegan A. Chandler's 'The God of Jesus In Light of Christian Dogma.'p.132

[4] Matt 24:11.

beneath the surface appearance' Stott continues, 'of people being taken in by false teaching and looks beneath. He explains to Timothy the underlying spiritual dynamic.

'The first cause of error is diabolical. There is the Holy Spirit and evil spirits or demons. False teachers teaching under the influence of deceiving spirits. We tend,' Stott goes on to say, 'not to take this fact sufficiently seriously. Scripture portrays the devil not only as the tempter, enticing people into sin, but also as the deceiver, seducing people into error. Often, he does both together, as when in the Garden of Eden he prevailed upon our first parents to doubt and then to disobey God's word. No wonder Jesus called him, "a liar and the Father of lies."[5] And the apostles regularly attributed human error to devilish deceit.[6] There is not only a spirit of truth but also a spirit of falsehood, who is able to delude, drug, be with and even blind people.[7]

'Secondly, error has a human cause. The devil does not usually deceive people direct, 'demon inspired doctrines' gain an entry into the world and the church through human agents. Paul wrote, 'Yes, and all who desire to live godly in Christ Jesus

---

[5] John 8:44

[6] 2 Cor 2:11; Eph 6:11; 2 Thes 2:9; 1 John 2:18; Rev 13:14.

[7] 1 John 4:6; 2 Tim 2:26; Gal 3:1; 2 Cor 4:4.

will suffer persecution, but evil men and impostors will grow worse and worse, deceiving and being deceived'.[8]

'The false teaching in Ephesus consisted of a false asceticism which led eventually to the monastic system of living: 'They forbid people to marry and order them to abstain from certain foods (3a). Marriage and food relate to the two most basic appetites of the human body. They are natural appetites too, although both can be abused by degenerating into lust and greed. Yet some have taught that sex and hunger are themselves unclean appetites, that the body itself is a nasty encumbrance (if not actually evil) and the only way to holiness is abstinence, the voluntary renunciation of sex and marriage, and, since eating cannot be given up altogether, then at least the renunciation of meat.

'This unbiblical teaching, held by the Essenes, came to be mingled with the dualism of Greek philosophy, and especially with the emergence of "Gnosticism," which is a modern designation for a category of ancient religions that preached the soul's salvation from the material world through the enlightenment of secret knowledge. Tertullian, one of the early church fathers, regarded virginity

---

[8] 2 Tim 3:12-13. John Stott

as always higher and holier than marriage,' as did Augustine. In his view sex and procreation were seen as negative activities that trapped immortal souls in the bondage of inherited corruption.

The various Christian Gnostic sects actively blended mystical Platonic, Egyptian and eastern philosophies with Jewish and Christian teaching. This toxic mixture was strongly influential on the early church fathers.

The *International Standard Bible Encyclopaedia* reveals that 'the Greek, Platonic idea that the body dies, yet the soul is immortal ... is utterly contrary to the Israelite consciousness and is nowhere found in the Old Testament' (Vol. 1. p.812).

This teaching was a spiritual infection that grew in many directions and made its home in early church thinking.

In the Hebrew Bible, God is not viewed as having imbued the empty body of Adam with a pre-existing soul. Rather, Genesis 2:7 says, "And the Lord God formed man out of the dust of the ground and breathed into his nostrils the breath of life, and man became a living soul." Adam was a soul. A soul is a person. Humans are mortal. When a person dies, they remain in that state of death until the resurrection; either the first, at the time of the Messiah's return, or the second, a thousand years later, to face judgement.

Both Jesus and Paul used the term 'sleep' for those who had died.[9] When a person dies, they do not go to another place. It was one of Plato's teachings that the soul migrates and is immortal. Immortality is given as a gift from God for those who are in Christ.[10]

For the many who believe that the wicked suffer in torment for eternity and for those who have heard that this is what Christianity teaches; they have rejected the Bible. Eternal suffering for the lost is not a biblical teaching. Its defenders say that Jesus spoke about 'hell' more than any of the writers of the New Testament, yet if you were actually one of the many who listened to Jesus speak you would never have heard that word 'hell' spoken by him. That is because it is not a Hebrew or Greek word – it's British!

The English word 'hell' comes unchanged from Old English (cf. Old Norse Hel, goddess of the dead). The King James Version uses the word 'hell' to translate the Hebrew *Sheol* and the Greek *Hades*. Both mean death and the grave.

---

[9] John 11:11-14; 1 Cor 15: 18,20,51.
[10] Rom 6:23: 1 Cor 15:53-54.

What word then did Jesus use in speaking of the fate of those who would rebel against God? And where did all those lurid and graphic descriptions of the horrors of hell come from?

The word Jesus used was *Gehenna* which is derived from the Hebrew *Gehinnom*, 'Valley of Hinnom.' It is a valley south-west of Jerusalem that had a horrific history.

Throughout the history of Israel we read of their continual rebellion against God's laws and although many prophets were sent to warn them that their behaviour would end in captivity and deportation there was no radical changes in their worship of the gods that were worshipped in Canaan and the nations close to them. They worshipped with a zeal that outshone any residual memories that might be retained of being rescued from slavery in Egypt and taken to their present fertile land. They rejected the very laws that would have made them the greatest nation on earth and chose gods of the earth and sky instead.

Part of these demon inspired religions was child sacrifice. The location for these murders was the Valley of Hinnom. This valley was so defiled by these atrocities that it remained uncultivated and became a place to burn the city's rubbish and the bodies of executed criminals. In the time of

Jesus this public incinerator was always alight and infested with maggots which feasted on animal and human remains dumped there.

Jesus assumed his hearers would understand what was meant by Gehenna – as the very worst place to end up in.

Those who believe in everlasting torment have a number of texts they would turn to in establishing the truth, as they would see it, of the orthodox teaching on hell and their favourite section would be when Jesus talked about "Their worm does not die, and the fire is not quenched."[11] These words are often spoken with the volume tuned up and if printed it is seen with bright red letters against a dark background and just in case we missed the point there would be paintings of humans in extreme mental and physical distress as they were tortured by the constant burning and having wicked things done to them by gleeful demons. It is also taught that despite the ongoing pain these humans would never die because they had been given indestructible bodies so that the suffering would never end.

Those words of Jesus concerning worms and fire did not originate with Jesus – he was quoting

---

[11] Mark 9:44,46,48.

the last verse of the book of Isaiah. This is what it says:

"And they shall go forth and look upon the corpses of the men who have transgressed against me. For their worm does not die, and their fire is not quenched. They shall be an abhorrence to all flesh."

Isa 66:24. NKJV

These are corpses being fed on by invertebrates – they are not living people. They were rebels (v4). Even though these rebels are dead the false teachers continue to teach that these rebels live forever in dreadful pain. Millions of people have been misled into believing a teaching that would make God infinitely crueller than anything Isis has done. Canon Dr Michael Green has written in a letter to me that the orthodox teaching of hell owes more to the writing of Virgil and Dante than scripture. Other non-biblical sources do speak of eternal suffering such as 4 Maccabees and 1Enoch.

Here though is what the Bible teaches as the fate of the wicked: '[God] condemned the cities of Sodom and Gomorrah by burning them to ashes and made them an example of what is going to happen to the ungodly.'[12] 'In a similar way, Sodom and Gomorrah and the surrounding towns gave

---

[12] 2 Peter 2:6. NIV

themselves up to sexual immorality and perversion. They serve as an example of those who suffer the punishment of eternal fire' (Jude 7).

The fires that destroyed those cities have long been extinguished but the emphasis is focused on the total elimination of those people; reduced to ashes will do that. The people of those ancient cities are not still suffering; and they stand as an example of the future destiny of those who rebel against God.

Paul wrote that the wages of sin is death (not life in hell)[13] and the 'weeping and gnashing of teeth' spoken of by Jesus[14] will be experienced when the death sentence is announced to the unrepentant and they then realise that their choices in life have brought them to this end which will be permanent and everlasting. There will be others who rise in the second resurrection who lived better lives of helping others and showing kindness and mercy. The lives they lived – and the lives we lead – will have an important bearing on their, and our, judgement. Peter also wrote, 'For it is time for judgement to begin with the family of God; and if it begins with us, what will the outcome be for those who do not

---

[13] Rom 6:23.
[14] Matt 13:42,50.

obey the gospel of God?[15] The warnings of Jesus are not to be ignored or taken lightly: "If you forgive men their trespasses, your heavenly Father will also forgive you, but if you do not forgive men their trespasses, neither will your Father forgive your trespasses."[16]

The writer of the book of Hebrews underlines the importance of not falling away or abandoning or letting go or forgetting or hardening our hearts from trusting God, 'for if we sin wilfully after we have received the knowledge of the truth, there no longer remains a sacrifice for sins, but a certain fearful expectation of judgement and fiery indignation which will devour the adversaries,'[17]

Paul warned the Galatians, 'Do not be deceived. God is not mocked; for whatever a man sows, that he will also reap.'[18]

Malachi writes, 'For behold, the day is coming. Burning like an oven, and all the proud, yes, all who do wickedly will be stubble, and the day which is coming shall burn them up.'[19] But that is not God's will, as Peter wrote, 'The Lord is not slack

---

[15] 1 Peter 4:17
[16] Matt 6:14-15.
[17] Heb 10: 26-27.
[18] Gal 6:7.
[19] Mal 4:1a.

concerning his promise, as some count slackness, but is longsuffering (patient) towards us, not willing that any should perish but that all should come to repentance.'[20]

Whatever happens there is always someone that will say. "It was God's will." If it is a load of money that has fallen into your lap then that is a comfortable concept to believe in but if it is the tragic loss of a child, then either God is the one to blame or he just does not exist.

The pastor at Bridgetown Church in Portland, Oregon makes some helpful comments:

'One of the – if not *the* – primary objections that people have to the idea of God is this: *If there's a God and he's all loving and all powerful, why is there evil in the world?* Philosophers call this the "problem of evil," and it's a source of unbelief for millions of people.

Note that: *millions.*

We just can't find a way to reconcile what we see on the news every day … with the idea of a Creator God who is "compassionate and gracious."

But what's strange is the Scripture writers have little or nothing to say about the problem of evil,

---

[20] 2 Peter 3:9.

at least not in the philosophical sense. They don't debate its nature or theorize about its origins or have a crisis of faith over a tsunami.

Why not?

Because evil was *assumed*.

Take, for example, Jesus' central prayer: "Your Kingdom come, your will be done, on earth as it is in heaven."

Notice that Jesus *assumed* that God's will was *not* done on earth. Hence, his prayer.

For Jesus, heaven is the place where God's will is done *all* the time. Earth, on the other hand, is the place where God's will is done *some* of the time. Because on earth, there are other "wills" at play. God isn't the only one with a will – an agenda for what he wants to see happen in the world, and the capacity to carry it out.

Human beings have a measure of free will as well.

And make sure you're paying attention here: *so do spiritual beings*.

You could even argue the nature has a "will" of its own.

That's a lot of wills…

God's will.

My will.

My friends', families, co-workers,' neighbours,' and a few other billion human beings' wills.

Satan and his demonic armada's will.

Even nature's will.

All living in God's good *free* world. Some under God's life-giving authority, others in flat-out rebellion.

To clarify, it's not that God's will is weak – on an even playing field with all the other wills. As if we, God, and Satan are all equal players in a game for the world. It's that in the universe God has chosen to actualize, love is the highest value, and love demands a choice, and a choice demands freedom. So God has chosen to limit his overwhelming capacity to override any "will" stacked against him, in order to create space for real, genuine freedom for his creatures, human and nonhuman. And evil is the by-product of that freedom that God built into the fabric of the universe. Put simply, God is incredibly good, but the world is a terrifyingly free, dangerous, beautiful place to call home.'[21]

The sin of misrepresenting God gets into

[21] John Mark Comer. 'God has a name' pp.108-110

our DNA – it is in our spiritual bloodstream; it becomes part of us. One elderly Christian man who was presented with the biblical evidence that the traditional teaching on hell was wrong and that the burden of carrying that message to others could be lifted from his shoulders just said, "I can't do it". 'Hell' has become so deeply lodged in our understanding that our minds reject the very thought of changing a belief that has been held for centuries and continues to be taught by church teachers that we hold in high regard.

The picture most people have of heaven is quite similar to the ancient belief that good and noble souls find their rest and peace in the delightful Fields of Elysium which would be equal to the idea of paradise – pleasant and pastoral, where one would continue to enjoy all that was enjoyed while in their physical body.

Our old friend Plato passed on what he had learned from the Egyptians concerning our immortal souls and added that all human souls had previously existed in a higher, more perfect sphere of life where they once had all knowledge. Upon incarnating into human forms in the world, all but a residual, innate knowledge had dissipated; humanity was forced to learn all over again.[22]

---

[22] Chandler. p.65.

But what does ancient Greek philosophies have to do with what Christians believe today?

The immortality teaching came into the church through the early church fathers who greatly admired Plato. For example, Eusebius of Caesarea calls Plato "the only Greek who has attained the hight of [Christian] truth," and Augustine describes, "the utterance of Plato, the most pure and bright in all philosophy, scattering the clouds of error." There is a greater amount of synthesis between ancient philosophic understanding and Christianity than we have realised.

Just as in the case of the attempt to find scriptures to back up the teaching on hell the same is done in defence of going to heaven. We will look at a couple of examples: Jesus said to one of the other men who were crucified with him, "I tell you the truth, today you will be with me in paradise."[23] This certainly looks like Jesus and the repentant criminal were later on that same day in paradise, yet when Jesus spoke to Mary identifying himself after his resurrection, he said to her, "Do not hold on to me, for I have not yet ascended (the 1984 edition NIV has *returned* but the Greek is *ascended*. The NIV has now corrected that error) to the Father. Go instead to my brothers and tell them,

---

[23] Luke 23:43.

'I am returning [ascending] to my Father and to your Father, to my God and your God,'" Jesus died on the cross and was brought back to life only after being three days and nights in the tomb, so he was not in heaven the same day he died.

Looking again at Luke 23:43, we need to remember that full stops and commas only came many centuries later. The Greek text was in all capitals without breaks. As Jesus spoke in Aramaic (at the time of Jesus Aramaic was the vernacular language of the Jews) and that in turn was written in Greek and we read it in English so we can perhaps take a fresh look at what Jesus actually said. The highly respected Bible expositor Leon Morris writes in his commentary on Luke that the *today* in "I tell you the truth, today you will be with me ..." 'is occasionally taken with the preceding words,'[24] which would change the line to, "I tell you the truth today, you will be with me ..." This would make it consistent with the rest of scripture that says that the next moment of consciousness after death is the resurrection. There is no intermediate body between death and the resurrection spoken of in scripture (see 1 Corinthians 15: 42-44).

"I desire to depart," wrote Paul, "and be with

---

[24] Tyndale New Testament Commentaries. p.329.

Christ, which is better by far ..."[25] A doctrine should not be based on one verse but all the verses that relate to the subject being studied. Yes, when Paul died, he died in the sure hope of the resurrection as he writes in the third chapter of his letter, "I want to know Christ and the power of his resurrection and the fellowship of sharing in his sufferings, becoming like him in his death, and so, somehow, to attain to the resurrection from the dead." His focus is not going to heaven but to experience the resurrection. In another place he says what he looked forward to, "Now there is in store for me the crown of righteousness, which the Lord, the righteous judge, will award to me on that day – and not only to me, but also to all who have longed for his appearing."

'On that day' is shorthand for the time when the Messiah returns – the same time as the first resurrection.

"Heaven is in fact never used in the Bible for the destination of the dying."[26]

"Blessed are the meek (those with humility) for they shall inherit the earth." All the promises concerning the future of this world speak of

---

[25] Phil 1:23. 3:10-11. 2 Tim 4:8.
[26] J.A. Robinson. 'In the End God' p. 104

restoration and healing; of health and security; of peace and perfect government – this is the good news – the Kingdom or Empire of God is coming! Liberation is yet future.

"Rejoice and be glad," Jesus said, "because great is your reward in heaven."[27]

If someone had a reward for you kept in their home, it does not mean that you have to travel to that person's home to receive it. It could be that when that person visits you, they will bring your reward to you – where you are. Twice in the book of Isaiah and again in the book of revelation we read that "Your Saviour comes. See, his reward is with him." That will happen 'on that day' when he appears.

Do not be led astray by those who say that the dead go to heaven, or some other location. Jesus will be here on earth soon – there is no need for us to be in heaven; our battle ground is here, and this is where the need is. When our personal battle is finished then we will rest until that voice will be heard – the trumpet will sound and the dead in Christ will be raised, immortal and imperishable – to begin the great work under Christ of restoration, "as he promised long ago through his holy prophets."[28]

---

[27] Matt 5:12. Isa 40:10; 62:11; Rev 22:12.
[28] Acts 3:21.

John wrote about 'those who are trying to lead you astray' and alerts them to the dangerous doctrine concerning who Jesus really was – his nature and his relationship with his Father. This was to be expected as Peter wrote, 'there were also false prophets among the people (in Old Testament times), just as there will be false teachers among you. They will secretly introduce destructive heresies…'[29] There is a real and dark intelligence that has worked against God and humanity from the beginning. John ends his first letter with, 'We know that we are the children of God, and that the whole world is under the control of the evil one.' Jesus called him, "the prince of this world," and Paul wrote of the 'god of this age blinding the minds of unbelievers, so that they cannot see the light gospel …'of the

Just about every branch of a divided Christianity can track their foundational teachings back to the creeds written, and enforced, in the 4th and 5th centuries. Some teachers say that as the Bible is such a big book and open to all interpretations the best and safest way to remember the essential truths is to know and be familiar with one or more of the creeds and that knowledge will protect each

29 John 2:26; 2 Peter 2:1; 1 John 5:19; John 14:30; 2 Cor 4:4.

Christian from the many false teachings that have sprung up in every century since the church began.

That sounds like good, sound and healthy advice until you start reading how many of these creeds themselves caused more divisions and splits among the eastern and western factions of the church. This ecclesiastical history is replete with violence, threats and coercion by both the state and church leadership. The common man and woman did not have a say in any of those bitter disputes except to face severe punishments if they did not agree; that applied to their bishops first and then to their congregations who followed their leaders.

Unity was the prize, but it was never achieved, yet long after those fierce disputes have been mostly forgotten evangelical church leaders of our time claim that the litmus test of who is a true Christian and who is not is the question of agreement with one or more of the creeds that were written by various bishops under the oversight of the Roman emperor.

The creeds remain vitally important in laying down the core beliefs of Christianity. The reformation did not change that orthodox position. A church pastor named Guy A. Davies wrote, 'Evangelism in its best and most consistent form is an expression of the Reformed faith. And it is worth stressing that the reformers had no wish to reject the theological heritage of the church and start again from scratch. They saw themselves as defenders of the catholic tradition that had been corrupted by the Roman Catholic Church of their day. The reformers held to the ancient Trinitarian creeds and the teachings of the church fathers, especially Augustine, with his emphasis on the sovereignty of grace. Of course, they taught that the Holy Spirit speaking in scripture is the supreme authority, but they were catholic in outlook, holding to the faith confessed by the church throughout the ages.'

In contrast to this trust in the creeds *The Westminster Confession of Faith*, a famous standard set forth by Reformed Christianity, has this to say about the authority of the councils:

1V. All synods or councils, since the apostles' times, whether general or particular, may err; and many have erred. Therefore they are not to be made the rule of faith, or practice; but to be used as a help in both.[30]

Chapter XXX1, Of Synods and Councils,
Westminster Confession of Faith, 1646

How many Reformed Christians today are aware that one of their most cherished foundational

---

[30] Quoted in 'The God of Jesus' pp.29-30

documents states that many of the councils *have* erred in their deliverance of the rule of faith?

Renowned Catholic scholar Graham Greene makes this observation of Protestants today:

'Our opponents sometimes claim that no belief should be held dogmatically which is not explicitly stated in Scripture... But the Protestant churches have themselves accepted such dogmas as the Trinity, for which there is no precise authority in the Gospels.'

At the time of the Reformation the Protestant Church took over the doctrine of the Trinity without serious examination, but why did this dogma not receive the same scrutiny as, say, the Catholic doctrines of transubstantiation or the primacy of the Pope? On this issue, one modern scholar writes,

'Protestant forms of Christianity, following the motto of *sola scriptura*, insist that all legitimate Christian beliefs (and practices) must be found in, or at least based on, the Bible. That's a very clear and admirable principle. The problem is that Protestant Christianity was not born in a historical vacuum and does not go back to the time that the Bible was written. Protestantism was and is a reformation of an already fully developed form of Christianity: Catholicism. When the Protestant

Reformation occurred just five hundred years ago, it did not reinvent Christianity from scratch, but carried over many of the doctrines that had developed within Catholicism over the course of the previous thousand years and more. In this sense, one might argue that the Protestant Reformation is incomplete, that it did not fully realise the high ideals that were set for it.[31]

On his last night with his disciples Jesus prayed to his Father saying, "This is eternal life, that they may know you, the only true God, and Jesus [the] Christ whom you have sent." The Athanasian Creed (late fifth century) states that Jesus is 'true God from true God,' yet we have just read that Jesus said, "Father ... you, the only true God."[32]

There were many laws and statutes given to ancient Israel, but which one was the most important?

This question was asked of Jesus by one of the teachers of the law. "The most important one," Jesus answered, "is this: 'Hear O Israel, the Lord our God, the Lord is one. Love the Lord your God with all your heart and with all your soul and with all your mind and with all your strength.' The second

---

[31] Jason David BeDuhn, 'Truth in translation.'pp.163-164..

[32] John 17:1a, 3a.

is this: 'Love your neighbour as yourself.' There is no commandment greater than these."

Instead of Jesus taking this opportunity to give a new understanding about his own relationship to his Father, which would have made the controversial arguments of later centuries unnecessary, he simply quoted the famous passage from the book of Deuteronomy.[33] Jesus was a Jew who stood firmly in the monotheistic theology of his forefathers.

The *Shema* (from the first word, *Shema*, "Hear") was the confession of faith given to the nation of Israel, which included the tribe of Judah, (technically, not all Israelites were Jews; only those who were descended from Judah, a son of Jacob. After their return from Babylonian captivity the Southern tribes of the nation of Judah, plus Benjamin and Levi, were collectively known from that time onwards as Jews) from which Jesus was descended. According to Jewish tradition, the *Shema* should be recited morning and evening as a part of prayer.

By means of the *Shema* Judaism has affirmed its belief in one God over against both ancient polytheism and Christian Trinitarianism. Jesus was not a Trinitarian. 'We find that despite the solidified

---

[33] Deut 6:4.

status of the Trinity doctrine, major internal disagreements over the increasingly complicated dogma continued into the sixth century, even to the point that the death penalty had to once again be asserted for denial of the Trinity by the violent emperor Justinian (in AD 530) ... not only was the Trinity imposed by Justinian here, but so was the dreadful banning of the *Shema*, the biblical statement of faith claimed by Jesus himself (Mark 12:28). Jewish citizens in the empire were now considered lower than animals; "correct" profession of certain Christian ideas became a fundamental requirement for full participation in the benefits of society. Thus the triune God was once again pressed more firmly into ecumenical acceptance "by the sword of civil government."[34] The passionate rejection of the Jewish God by the church fathers continued with the leaders of the Reformation in the 16th century. The explicit and wanton antisemitism that thrived in the Reformation is an often-neglected piece of Protestant history. The Jews, as both an ethnic and religious group, were considered detestable by the most well-known Protestant leaders, and so was any theological insights the Jewish heritage had to offer.

---

[34] Thomas Jefferson, quoted in Kegan A. Chandler's 'The God of Jesus' p.234.

So strong was this antisemitism that the seven festivals that Jesus, the apostles, and the early church kept were rejected and replaced by rebranded pagan festivals which has resulted in the plan of saving humanity being lost and substituted by long established religious festivals that neither answer the big questions we face or inform us to what the future holds.

John Calvin reveals his attitude towards the Jews as, "rotten and unbending stiffneckedness deserves that they be oppressed unendingly and without measure or end and that they die in their misery without the pity of anyone."

And Martin Luther writes, "Such a desperate, thoroughly evil, poisonous, and devilish lot are the Jews, who for these fourteen hundred years have been and still are our plague, our pestilence, and our misfortune." Luther's 'On the Jews and their lies,' suggests what Christians should do with the Jews, which amounts to destroying them.

Truly, the deity of Jesus closed the door firmly on the Jewish world of Jesus.

If the apostle Peter had stood up on the day of Pentecost and preached an incarnate God-man who existed alongside two other God-persons, do we think for a moment that the Jews would have lined up in droves to be baptized in his name without serious questions or outright rejection? Peter preached, "Jesus of Nazareth was a man, accredited by God through miracles which God did through him!"[35]

The apostle Paul wrote, 'For there is one God and one mediator between God and man, the man Christ [Messiah] Jesus.'[36]

There are many verses Trinitarians would turn to clearly show how obvious and plain the teaching of the Trinity is. It is beyond the scope of this chapter to answer all the texts presented in that cause, but I can recommend 'One God & One Lord' written by John A. Lynn, Mark H. Graeser and John W. Schoenheit of the 'Spirit and Truth Fellowship'. I will limit myself to just two examples:

1 John 5:20

'And we know that the Son of God has come and has given us an understanding, that we may know him who is true; and we are in him who is true, in his Son Jesus Christ. This is the true God and eternal life.'

NKJV

John Stott, a Trinitarian, writes on this verse:

---

[35] Acts 2:22.
[36] 1 Tim 2:5.

'The final sentence of verse 20 runs: 'He is the true God and eternal life.'(NIV) To whom does he refer? Grammatically speaking. It would normally refer to the nearest preceding subject, namely *his Son Jesus Christ*. If so, this would be the most unequivocal statement of the deity of Jesus Christ in the New Testament, which the champions of orthodoxy were quick to exploit against the heresy of Arius. Luther and Calvin adopted this view. Certainly it is by no means an impossible interpretation. Nevertheless, 'the most natural reference' (Westcott) is to *him who is true*. In this way the three references to 'the true' are to the same person, the Father, and the additional points made in the apparent final repetition are that it is this one, namely the God made known by Jesus Christ, who is both *the true God* and *eternal life*. As he is both light and love (1:5; 4:8), so he is also life, himself the only source of life (Jn. 5:26) and the giver of life in Jesus Christ (11). The whole verse is strongly reminiscent of John 17:3, for there as here eternal life is defined in terms of knowing God, both Father and Son.'

The second important verse is John 8:58

'Jesus said to them, "Most assuredly, I say to you, before Abraham was, I AM."'

NKJV

Here it is; the great I AM statement, written in capitals for emphasis. It should be remembered that all the Greek text was in capitals, not just that phrase. The Greek for 'I am' is *ego eimi*, which is used twice already in this chapter, verse 24, "I told you that you would die in your sins; if you do not believe that I am he (*ego eimi*), you will indeed die in your sins."

V. 28: "When you have lifted up the Son of Man, then you will know that I am the one (*ego eimi*) I claim to be.

C. K. Barrett[37] writes, *Ego eimi* ["I am"] does not identify Jesus with God, but it does draw attention to him in the strongest possible terms. "I am the one – the one you must look at, and listen to, if you would know God."

The phrase "I am" occurs many other times in the New Testament and

is often translated as "I am he" or some equivalent ("I am he" – Mark 13:6; Luke 21:8; John 13:19; 18:5,6,8. "It is I" – Matt 14:27; Mark 6:50; John 6:20. "I am the one I claim to be" – John 8:24 and 28). It is obvious that these translations are quite correct, and the phrase is translated as "I am" only in John 8:58. If the phrase in John 8:58

---

[37] *The Gospel according to John.*

were translated "I am he" or "I am the one," like all the others, it would be easier to see that Jesus was speaking of himself as the Messiah of God (as indeed he was), spoken of throughout the Old Testament.

"I am" (*ego eimi*) was a common way of designating oneself, and it did not mean you were claiming to be God.

The argument is made that because Jesus was "before Abraham" Jesus must have been God. There is no question that Jesus figuratively 'existed' in Abraham's time, however, he did not actually physically exist as a person; rather he existed in the mind of God as His plan for the redemption of man. A careful reading of the context of the verse shows that Jesus was speaking of 'existing' in God's foreknowledge. Verse 56 is accurately translated in the King James Version, which says, "Your father Abraham rejoiced to see my day: and he saw it and was glad." This verse says that Abraham 'saw' the day of Christ, which is normally considered by theologians to be the day when Christ conquers the earth and sets up his Kingdom. That would fit in with what the book of Hebrews says about Abraham: 'For he was looking forward to the city with foundations, whose architect and builder is God.'[38]

In order for the Trinitarian argument that Jesus' "I am" statement makes him God, his words must be equivalent with God's "I am" words in Exodus 3:14. However, the two statements are very different. While the Greek phrase in John does mean "I am," the Hebrew phrase in Exodus actually means "to be" or "to become." In other words God is saying "I will be what I will be." Thus the "I am" in Exodus is actually a mistranslation of the Hebrew text, so the fact that Jesus said "I am" did not make him God.

Frank Stagg, writing on the subject of the Holy Spirit[39] makes several important points on how we understand God's Spirit:

'In the OT, "the Spirit of God" does not imply a person separate from God. In Ps 139:7, Spirit is a synonym for God (cf. Isa 31:3). In Gen 1:1ff., there is an interchange between "God" and "the Spirit of God".… The Spirit of God is God acting in the created world. The "Spirit of God," "his Spirit," "thy Spirit," and "Holy Spirit" are all references to God himself, with no implications of plurality or division. Such usage does not undercut monotheism,

---

[38] Heb 11:10.
[39] Lutterworth Dictionary of the Bible. pp.384-385. & The Holy Spirit Today.

foundational to OT theology… The Holy Spirit is not a separate person within deity.

'In the NT, the Holy Spirit represents the presence of God, active and powerful in revealing, convicting of sin, judging, guiding, empowering, comforting, enlightening, teaching, restraining, and otherwise. Every step in the Christian life may be attributed to the work of the Holy Spirit, from conversion (John 3:6) to such maturity as reflects "the fruit of the Spirit" (Gal 5:22).

The Holy Spirit is personal in the NT, but not a person separate from God. The oneness of God is as firm in the NT as it is in the OT. Jesus himself affirmed the oneness of God, building the love commandment upon Deut 6:4 (Mark 12:29). The oneness of God is explicit in Paul and other NT writers (Rom 3:30; 1 Cor 8:6; Gal 3:20; Eph 4:6; 1 Tim 1:17; Jas 2:19; Jude 25; John 17:3). The Holy Spirit is not a third God nor one-third of God. The Holy Spirit is God himself, present and active within his world. Significantly, "Spirit of God," "Spirit of Christ," and "Christ" are interchanged in Rom 8:9-11… "Baptized with the Holy Spirit" (Acts 1:5), for the Holy Spirit to "come upon" someone (Acts 1:8), and to be "filled with the Holy Spirit" (Acts 2:4) are interchangeable. These are stylistic differences, not theological distinctions.'

After the death of President Garfield his doctor, D. Willard Bliss said that he died not from a massive blood infection, but as a result of a broken backbone. He insisted, moreover, that the care he had given the president had been not only adequate, but exemplary. In a document titled "Statement of the Services Rendered," Bliss and the few surgeons he had allowed to work with him argued that "he should receive, as he merits, the sympathy and goodwill (as well as the lasting confidence) of every patriotic citizen for the great skill, unequalled devotion and labour performed in this notable case, which … secured to the distinguished patient the perfection of surgical management."

To the astonishment of the members of Congress, Bliss confidently presented them with a bill for $25,000 – more than half a million dollars in today's currency. While caring for the president, Bliss said, he had lost twenty-three pounds, and his health was 'so greatly impaired as to render him entirely unable to recover or attend to his professional duties.'

Congress agreed to pay Bliss $6,500, and not a penny more. Bliss, outraged, refused to accept it, bitterly complaining that it was 'notoriously inadequate as a just compensation.'

Seven years later, Bliss would die quietly at his home following a stroke, having never recovered his health, his practice, or his reputation.

Today, the dangers of infection and the risk of septicaemia are understood, and precautions are taken that were not realised or believed in earlier times. The majority of the medical experts were wrong, and it took some difficulty for them to come to a better understanding.

In earlier centuries the church leaders, both Catholic and Protestant, understood that to burn people to death was better than allowing the contagion of their heretical beliefs to contaminate healthy Christians.

Jesus did all he could in teaching his disciples so that they would not deviate from his message. But he knew what was ahead of them when he said, "All this I have told you so that you will not go astray (he had just told them that "If the world hates you, keep in mind that it hated me first. If you belonged to the world, it would love you as its own. As it is, you do not belong to the world, but I have chosen you out of the world. That is why the world hates you."). They (the church leadership) will put you out of the synagogue; in fact, a time is coming when anyone who kills you will think he is offering a service to God. They will do such things because they have not known the Father or me."[40]

Church leaders from many church communities have sentenced heretics to death – they did this because they did not know the Father or his Son. Some of those who are guilty of this are well known names who have millions following in their footsteps and holding the same mindsets. They are quick to point the finger at other fellowships that they disagree with but are unable to see their own faults.

The deep divisions and splits among Christians will not be solved in this age as each denomination is fully convinced of their own rightness. The churches have within them devoted and faithful Christians who rightly rely on the grace and love of God to continue day by day in honouring God, but there is not one of us that has not been deceived to one degree or another. Did we, or do we, believe that we have an immortal soul? Did we, or do we believe that the lost suffer an eternity of pain as a just punishment from God? Did we, or do we believe that the saved go to heaven to receive their reward? Did you, or do you believe that God exists

---

[40] John 15:18; 16:1-3.

as in three persons? Did you, or do you believe that the church is the kingdom of God? Did you, or do you believe that Jesus pre-existed before his birth? I was taught all these things. How was I to know what was correct?

The church has failed to answer the important questions of why there is so much suffering in the world and to ask the question: will that suffering continue to exist alongside our ecclesiastical divisions? We cannot answer because we are infected with a counterfeit Christianity (it is important to know that the many sincere people who do their best to follow Jesus are not counterfeit Christians but the message they have been given is) that has corrupted the true message that Jesus brought. We have substituted the resurrection with going to heaven and replaced the Kingdom of God with our own personal salvation. We have endorsed eternal torture while God intends to end all torture. We have claimed to have immortality while denying our mortality – if it were not for the resurrection, we would all remain dead. We deny that Satan has this world in its grip and so God is blamed for all the evil there is here. Can we face the biblical text that says, '... Satan, who leads the whole world astray,[41] and believe it? This encompasses all of us without exception.

Rather than call Jesus the second man or the last Adam, as Paul did,[42] in contrasting the first son of God (see Luke 3:36) and his disobedience with the second son of God and his perfect obedience we have made Jesus into a God rather than the son who submitted totally to his Father and loved his Father as the only true God.

This chapter cannot answer all the questions that could be asked for those who do want to know what the Bible really teaches, and there is no perfect bible translation, for example, check the history of 1John 5:7 in the KJV and Mark 16:9 to the end of that chapter. We need to question, 'seek, ask and knock,' in other words, collect the evidence as we move forwards and be careful whom we believe. "Let every matter be established by the testimony of two or three witnesses (Matt 18:16). Be aware though; the majority of church leaders are Trinitarians so consider as well, the case of the non-Trinitarians.

Paul said to the Thessalonians concerning those who had, in his words, 'fallen asleep,'[43] that he did

---

[41] Rev 12:9

[42] 1 Cor 15:45,47; Rom 5:19

[43] 1 Thes 4:13.

not want them to be ignorant. The doctors who treated President Garfield were ignorant of some vitally important aspects of treatment, and so can we, no matter how devoted, faithful and dedicated we may be.

Jesus said, "Take heed that no one deceives you, for many will come in my name saying I am the Christ and will deceive many."[44]

> Many have come, *in his name*,
> and have deceived many.

The antidote to this spiritual septicaemia is the willingness to look again at what we always thought was true and the courage to make those needed changes no matter what the cost.

'Therefore, since we have these promises, dear friends, let us purify ourselves from everything that contaminates body and spirit, perfecting holiness out of reverence for God.'

2 Corinthians 7:1 T N I V

---

[44] Matt 24:5,11.

To oppose another man's religion, to repress their worship – these were not, clerics told their congregations, wicked or intolerant acts. They were some of the most virtuous things a man might do. The Bible itself demanded it. As the uncompromising words of Deuteronomy instructed: 'And you shall overthrow their alters, and break their pillars, and burn their groves with fire; and you shall hew down the graven images of their gods, and destroy the names of them out of that place.'

The Christians of the Roman Empire listened. And as the fourth century wore on, they began to obey.

The Darkening Age *Catherine Nixey*

Part 3

In the beginning Sinai 862 BC

He had been an extraordinary runner but now he was walking. He had been travelling for over a month. The heat was almost unbearable; forcing him to find whatever shelter there was during the hottest part of the day.

He had a statement to make before he was ready to die and it could only be done at a mountain range due south.

He was perplexed and broken hearted. That day on Mount Carmel had ended so well. 450 prophets of Baal had prayed and shouted for most of the day and nothing had happened. He had prayed for less than 20 seconds and fire came down from heaven. The people who witnessed this miracle cried, "The Lord, he is God! The Lord, he is God!" At his order the prophets of Baal were seized and taken down to a brook and executed.

This incredible event would, he believed, be the turning point where the nation would return to the God of their fathers and eradicate all Baal worship from the land. God had given convincing proof that Baal was a non-existing god and was clearly discredited. What he felt would happen – must happen – didn't.

The day after the Baal prophets were killed he received a message from king Ahab's wife, Jezebel, saying that by the next day he'd be as dead as those prophets of hers were. Nothing was going to change. Darkness continued to reign. His hopes were crushed. He wanted to die.

He wasn't afraid to die but not at the hand of Jezebel. He finally reached the mountain; his destination – Horeb – the mountain of God.

He spent that night in a cave.

Then came the voice,

"What are you doing here Elijah?"

The first war on earth went
completely unrecorded.

No one knows when it happened
or how long it lasted.

The war destroyed our solar system.

The only physical evidence that this devastation occurred are the craters that bombarded our planets and moon leaving them lifeless. Earth, with all its vast and abundant life, ended in total ruin and darkness.

This was a war between spiritual beings that have far greater power than humans. The first humans were created long after that war had ended. In older translations of the Hebrew scriptures Adam and Eve were instructed to replenish the world just as Noah and his family were to do after the great flood.

Verse one of Genesis says, 'In the beginning God created the heavens and the earth.' But verse two describes a world of darkness and ruin, of chaos and desolation. It became that way; it was not made that way. Our world is much older than many Christians have been taught.

Two prophets of the Old Testament, Isaiah and Ezekiel, reveal something that was not included in the Genesis account.

Ezekiel first: He begins by speaking of the pride and blasphemy of the ruler of Tyre but then moves to talk of a being that is more than human; more than a man.

'You were the model of perfection, full of wisdom and perfect in beauty. You were in Eden, the garden of God; every precious stone adorned you...your settings and mountings (Meaning of the

Hebrew is uncertain) were made of gold; on the day you were created they were prepared.

'You were anointed as a guardian cherub (not a chubby baby!) for so I ordained you. You were on the holy mount of God; you walked among the fiery stones. You were blameless in your ways from the day you were created till wickedness was found in you.... your heart became proud on account of your beauty, and you corrupted your wisdom because of your splendour.'

As Ezekiel spoke of the king of Tyre, Isaiah begins with a charge against the king of Babylon before moving from the human to the non-human: 'How you have fallen from heaven, O morning star, son of the dawn. You have been cast down to the earth, you who once laid low the nations. You said in your heart, "I'll ascend to heaven; I'll raise my throne above the stars of God; I'll sit enthroned on the mount of assembly, on the utmost heights of the sacred mountain. I'll ascend above the tops of the clouds; I'll make myself like the Most High."

Christopher J. H. Wright cautions, in a footnote to his commentary on Ezekiel, '...the Old Testament does not engage in speculation about the origins or the 'life story' of Satan, in these texts or elsewhere. The only relevant point that we may take from reflecting on such passages is that, if the fall of those created angels whom we refer to as Satan and his hosts is in some way mirrored in the fall of human beings, then it must have likewise involved an over-reaching hubris and arrogant aspirations after divine status and autonomy.'

J. Alec Motyer, in his commentary on Isaiah, sees it as an imaginative trip to Sheol, the abode of the dead, saying that the dead are alive and that there is a continuation of the person but in a different place. He relates the failed heavenly coup to the Canaanite myth of Ishtar.

You, the reader, may make up your own mind.

This super-being, having been created both perfect in beauty and wisdom, became corrupted by pride and his attempt to usurp God himself brought him and those angelic hosts who followed him to a dramatic change in their nature – from being angels they became demons and from being a 'Shining One' to the enemy of God and the adversary of humans; especially those who are called of God.

Jesus called the devil, "the father of lies" and the reason that his opponents were unable to grasp the truth was that they "belonged to their father, the devil, and want to carry out their father's desire. He was a murderer from the beginning, not holding to the truth, for there's no truth in him. When he lies, he speaks his native language, for he's a liar and the father of lies. Yet because I tell the truth, you don't believe me. Can any of you prove me guilty of sin? If I'm telling the truth, why don't you believe me? He who belongs to God hears what God says. The reason you don't hear is that you don't belong to God."

We either belong to God or to the devil. John Stott writes in his commentary on the letters of John, 'There are only two groups. There are not three. Nor is there only one …Our parentage is either divine or diabolical. The universal fatherhood of God is not taught in the Bible, except in the general sense that God is the Creator of all. But in the intimate, spiritual sense God is not the father of all people, and not all people are his children.'

David Jackman in 'The Message of John's Letters' writes, 'He affirms, in common with the rest of the Bible, that the devil is a created being, a highly superior spiritual intelligence, who chose to rebel against God's authority, to seek to usurp his throne and to set himself up as a rival ruler of the universe. In his rebellion evil finds its origin. The devil was the first sinner, and sinners today, without Christ, are his posterity.'

The apostle Paul wrote, 'For such men are false apostles, deceitful workmen, masquerading as apostles of [the] Christ. And no wonder, for Satan himself masquerades as an angel of light. It is not surprising, then, if his servants masquerade as servants of righteousness. Their end will be what their actions deserve.'

The power of this dark entity is in deceiving humans: 'Eve was deceived by the serpent's cunning,' This was achieved through a clever distortion of what God had said and a misrepresentation of God's nature. This continues to happen today. All mankind has been deceived and led astray. This has resulted in a counterfeit Christianity that appeared to be motivated less by faith than a hatred of anything and anyone that was not like itself. As Jesus predicted, "All this I've told you so that you'll not go astray. They'll put you out of the synagogue; in fact, a time is coming when anyone who kills you will think he is offering a service to God. They'll do such things because they've not known the Father or me."

Tragically, men, women and children have been lynched, burned, drowned and killed through other means by church authorities claiming to be disciples of Jesus, but because they were servants of the devil, they acted in a way completely alien to the teaching of the one they called Lord.

They were deceived into doing such terrible

deeds because they were part of a world controlled by the enemy. Jesus and his true followers worked and lived in enemy territory that was in the grip of an unseen malignant force. Jesus had prayed to his Father on behalf of the disciples: "I've given them your word and the world has hated them, for they're not of the world any more than I'm of the world. My prayer isn't that you take them out of the world but that you protect them from the evil one." Jesus called this age, 'adulterous and sinful' and 'wicked and godless'.

Jesus cured all who were brought to him and amongst those who suffered from severe disabilities many came because they were infected and seriously affected by demons. When they were driven out of the person Jesus wouldn't allow the demons to speak because they knew who he was. There're many Christians who consider that the Devil and demons have been invented as a cover for our human responsibility for doing wrong and blaming all evil on outside entities. They clearly existed during the time of Jesus and there's no reason to think that they're any less in number than then.

"No-one can come to me," Jesus said, "unless the Father who sent me draws him, and I'll raise him up at the last day. This enabling is initiated by God himself; not by man, and that group, that belonged to him, however scattered they may be, aren't immune to the anguish and pain of living in this world and have needed to endure patiently knowing that waiting and sometimes suffering is part of the Christian's calling.

Slavery takes many forms: individuals with addictions, groups bonded together for an evil purpose, people ruled over by tyrants, within a family home, or in a community, as Paul wrote, 'Don't you know that when you offer yourself to someone to obey him as slaves, you are slaves to the one whom you obey – whether you're slaves to sin, which leads to death, or to obedience, which leads to righteousness? But thanks be to God that, through you used to be slaves to sin, you wholeheartedly obeyed the form of teaching to which you were entrusted. You've been set free and have become slaves to righteousness.'

One biblical writer observed, 'I saw the tears of the oppressed – and they had no comforter; power was on the side of their oppressors … this is the evil in everything that happens under the sun: The same destiny overtakes all. The hearts of men are full of evil and there is madness in their hearts while they live and afterwards they join the dead.'

What was true three thousand years ago, when

that was written, is true today. The kingdoms of this age belong to him who rebelled so long ago. 'We all followed the ways,' as Paul wrote, 'of this world and of the ruler of the kingdom of the air, the spirit who is now at work in those who are disobedient ... gratifying the cravings of our sinful nature and following its desires and thoughts. Like the rest, we were by nature objects of wrath. But because of his great love for us, God, who is rich in mercy, made us alive in [the]Christ even when we were dead in transgressions.'

In the vividly colourful and highly symbolic book of Revelation the writer John tells us that 'there was war in heaven. Michael and his angels fought against the dragon, and the dragon and his angels fought back, but he was not strong enough, and they lost their place in heaven. The great dragon was hurled down – that ancient serpent called the devil, or Satan, who leads the whole world astray. He was hurled to the earth, and his angels with him.'

Since then he's been actively pursuing the destruction of those whose minds have been opened and their spiritual blindness taken away and preparing minds to reject the good news of the kingdom. This would be in fulfilment of what Isaiah wrote, 'You'll be ever hearing but never understanding; you'll be ever seeing but never perceiving. For this people's heart has become calloused; they hardly hear with their ears, and they've closed their eyes. Otherwise they might see with their eyes, hear with their ears, understand with their hearts and turn, and I would heal them.' The evil one offered Jesus rule over the nations if only Jesus would acknowledge him as master, "I'll give you all their authority and splendour, for it has been given to me and I can give it to anyone I want to. So, if you worship me it'll all be yours."

How did the enemy become the ruler of the world?

Luke, in his genealogy of Jesus, traces his line back to the first man, Adam, who was 'the son of God.' God's son Adam was without sin up until the time he deliberately chose to disobey his Father. He had been given authority to rule over the earth and all that lived on it. Everything was good, but this serpent like being cunningly deceived the woman into thinking that God didn't mean what he said and in fact, God was lying and didn't want her to reach her full potential; She was taken in by this lie and did what she was told not to do. But Adam wasn't deceived. He made the decision to go against what he had been commanded to do and therefore God told him that from then onwards he would live under the curse of a difficult life ending in death.

Adam was made in the likeness of God and to have a close relationship with his creator but now man was alienated and separated from God because of sin, which can be understood as missing the mark, falling short and trespassing. The apostle John wrote that sin is the breaking of the law, in fact, he says, sin is lawlessness. Paul wrote, 'death reigned from the time of Adam to the time of Moses, even over those who did not sin by breaking a command, as did Adam, who was a pattern of the one to come.'

There was to be a second Adam; another son of God.

'The judgement followed one sin (Adam's) and brought condemnation, but the gift followed many trespasses and brought justification. For if, by the trespass of the one man, death reigned through that one man, how much more will those who receive God's abundant provision of grace and the gift of righteousness reign in life through the one man (the second Adam), Jesus [the] Christ.

'Consequently, just as the result of one trespass was condemnation for all men, so also the result of one act of righteousness was justification that brings life for all men. For just as through the disobedience of the one man the many were made sinners, so also through the obedience of the one man the many will be made righteous.'

'So it is written, "The first man Adam became a living being"; the last Adam, a life-giving spirit. The spiritual did not come first, but the natural, and after that the spiritual.'

The first man lost his rule over the earth through disobedience. The second Adam qualified for rule over the earth through obedience. That rule begins at his appearing and the first resurrection. Paul wrote, 'Now there is in store for me the crown of righteousness, which the Lord, the righteous judge, will award to me on that day – and not only me, but also to all who have longed for his appearing.' It's at his 'appearing' that the god of this world will be removed. That event is still future.

Central to the old covenant was the sacrificial system. Without the spilling of blood there was no forgiveness; this was to show the seriousness of sin and the cost of reconciliation.

The day of Atonement was one of seven annual days commanded to be kept as a 'sacred assemble'. The weekly day of rest was also termed as a 'sacred assemble' just as the annual days were. These days were, and still are today, significant as they point to what had happened in the history of Israel and what would happen in relation to the coming Messiah when sin and death will be finally dealt with. There were many rules that had to be carefully observed in keeping that day from the high priest bathing himself and putting on special clothes to what exactly to do with the blood of the atoning sacrifice. There were two male goats for a sin offering, a ram for a burnt offering and a bull as a sacrifice for himself and his family. Only one of the goats was to be slaughtered and its blood sprinkled within the Holy Place – the only time in the year the high priest could enter it – then he was 'to lay both hands on the head of the live goat and confess over it all the wickedness and rebellion of the Israelites – all their sins – and put them on the goat's head. He shall send the goat away into the desert in the care of a man appointed for the task. The goat will carry on itself all their sins to a solitary place; and the man shall release it in the desert.'

The special clothes the high priest had on were then taken off and he had another bath and then put his regular service clothes back on and sacrificed the ram as a burnt offering to make atonement for himself and the people. Even the man that took the goat into the desert had to wash his clothes and bath himself when he got back and before he entered the camp (or city).

This was all done to cleanse the people; then they would be clean from all their sins.

Of course, carrying out a ritual correctly doesn't change the participant's heart because they are done outwardly and as the writer of Hebrews puts it, 'The law is only a shadow of the good things that are coming – not the realties themselves. For this reason, it can never, by the same sacrifices repeated endlessly year after year, make perfect those who draw near to worship. If it could, would they not have stopped being offered? For the worshippers would have been cleansed once for all, and would no longer have felt guilty for their sins. But these sacrifices are an annual reminder of sins, because it is impossible for the blood of bulls and goats to take away sins.'

Towards the end of the life of Moses there was a great need for the Israelites to remember what had happened to them so he wrote, 'Ask now about the former days, long before your time, from the day God created man on earth; ask from one end of the heavens to the other. Has anything so great as this ever happened, or has anything like it ever been heard of? Has any other people heard the voice of God speaking out of fire, as you have, and lived?

'Has any god ever tried to take for himself one nation out of another nation, by miraculous signs and wonders, by war, by a mighty hand and an outstretched arm, or by great and awesome deeds, like all the things the Lord your God did for you in Egypt before your very eyes?

'You were shown these things so that you might know that the Lord is God; besides him there is no other. From heaven he made you hear his voice to discipline you. On earth he showed you his great fire and you heard his words out of the fire. Because he loved your forefathers and chose their descendants after them, he brought you out of Egypt by his Presence and his great strength, to drive out before you nations greater and stronger than you and to bring you into their land to give it to you for your inheritance, as it is today.'

Moses was aware of the human condition and so to warn the Israelites not to become puffed up with pride he wrote, 'After the Lord your God has driven them out before you don't say to yourself, "The Lord has brought me here to take possession of this land because of my righteousness." No, it's because the wickedness of these nations that the Lord is going to drive them out before you…God will drive them out to accomplish what he promised to your fathers, to Abraham, Isaac and Jacob. Understand then, that it's not because of your righteousness that God is giving you this good land to possess, for you're a stiff-necked people.'

True to their nature the people of Israel did forget.

'The Lord said to Moses, "Now the day of your death is near. Call Joshua and present yourselves at the Tent of Meeting where I'll commission him" ….and the Lord said to Moses, "You're going to rest with your people and these people will soon prostitute themselves to the foreign gods of the land they're entering. They'll forsake me and break the covenant I made with them. On that day I'll become angry with them and forsake them; I'll hide my face from them and they'll be destroyed. Many disasters and difficulties will come on them, and on that day they'll ask, 'haven't these disasters come on us because our God isn't with us?' "And I'll certainly hide my face on that day because of all their wickedness in turning to other gods."

God gave Moses a song that the leadership had to teach the people in reinforcing the vital warning against forgetting their God. It contains the lines, 'They've acted corruptly towards him; to their shame they're no longer his children, but a warped and crooked generation. Is this the way you repay the Lord, O foolish and unwise people? Is he not your Father, your Creator, who made you and formed you?' – there's no evidence of them ever singing it. At that time Moses said to the Levites, who were responsible for teaching the people, "Take this book of the law and place it beside the ark of the covenant of the Lord. There it'll remain as a witness against you, because I know how rebellious and stiff-necked you are. If you've been rebellious against the Lord while I'm still alive and with you, how much more will you rebel after I die!"

Israel served the Lord throughout the lifetime of Joshua and the elders who out lived him and had experienced everything the Lord had done for Israel but after that generation died another generation grew up who knew neither the Lord or what he had done. They then served other gods and while God raised up leaders to rescue them they didn't remain faithful for long and they progressively became more corrupt than their fathers.

With just a few exceptions the history of Israel went from bad to worse ending in national defeat and deportation, first for the northern kingdom of Israel and later the southern kingdom of Judah.

All through this turbulent period individual prophets addressed the matter of paganism and the rejection of God's covenant. Along with predictions of the downfall of the two nations a message of hope and restoration was given which was centred on a descendant of King David who would bring greatness and righteousness to Israel – this would be a kingdom that never ended. Isaiah wrote, 'In love a throne would be established; in faithfulness a man will sit on it – one from the house of David – one who in judging seeks justice and speeds the cause of righteousness.' A new covenant would replace the old. Jeremiah wrote, "It'll not be like the covenant I made with their forefathers when I took them by the hand to lead them out of Egypt, because they broke my covenant, though I was a husband to them. This is the covenant that I'll make with the house of Israel after that time: I'll put my law into their minds and write it on their hearts. I'll be their God and they'll be my people."

When Stephen, a follower of Jesus, was arrested and brought before the Sanhedrin what he said held the interest of all who listened to him. He traced the dealings between God and Israel beginning with Abraham through the exodus and the Israelites refusal to obey God and their turning to the pagan deities of that time. Stephen talked of David, who enjoyed God's favour and laid the plans for a great temple that Solomon, his son, would build. Then Stephen ended his speech in a way that turned his audience from respectful agreement to furious rage. This is what he said:

"You stiff-necked people, with uncircumcised hearts and ears. You're just like your fathers:

you always resist the holy spirit – was there ever a prophet your fathers didn't persecute? They even killed those who predicted the coming of the righteous one, and now you've betrayed and murdered him – you who have received the law that was put into effect through angels but have not obeyed it."

Refusing to hear any more they rushed at him and dragged him out and through the city gate where they stoned him to death. A young man named Saul looked after their outer clothes while they rolled up their sleeves and grabbed some stones.

The writer of this account uses the same expression found in both testaments in describing a persons' death: "he fell asleep".

That young man, Saul, better known as Paul, was later to write of himself, 'circumcised on the eighth day, of the people of Israel, of the tribe of Benjamin, a Hebrew of Hebrews; regarding the law, a Pharisee; as for zeal, persecuting the church, as for legalistic righteousness, faultless.' He thought that through a diligent study of the law and meticulous practice of its precepts he would earn righteousness and be justified by what he accomplished. 'The law,' he said, 'is holy, and the commandment is holy, righteous and good,' but he came to see that the very commandment that was intended to bring life actually brought death. 'Is the law sin?' He asks, 'certainly not, indeed I wouldn't have known what sin was except through the law.'

Paul saw beneath the outward physical display of obedience to the condition of his heart. 'We know,' he went on to say, 'that the law is spiritual; but I'm unspiritual, sold as a slave to sin. I don't understand what I do. What I want to do I don't do but what I hate I do, and if I do what I don't want to do, I agree that the law is good – it comes down to the sin living in me, because I know that nothing good lives in my sinful nature.'

He said that the sinful mind is hostile to God – it doesn't submit to God's laws, nor can it and those controlled by the sinful nature can't please God; so, no-one can be declared righteous in God's sight by observing the law because it's through the law we become conscious of sin.

The law is good and holy but humans aren't.

How then can sinful humans become righteous?

After saying that all (Jews and Gentiles) are condemned as lawbreakers Paul goes on to say, 'But now a righteousness from God, apart from the law, has been made known, to which the law and the prophets (Old Testament) testify. This righteousness from God comes through faith in

Jesus[the]Christ to all who believe. There's no difference, for all have sinned and fall short of the glory of God ... God presented him as a sacrifice of atonement, through faith in his blood.'

'You see, at just the right time, when we were still powerless (to save ourselves from being condemned) Christ (the Messiah) died for the ungodly ... God demonstrates his own love for us in this: While we were still sinners, Christ died for us. Since we've now been justified by his blood, how much more shall we be saved form God's wrath through him. For if, when we were God's enemies, we were reconciled to him through the death of his son, how much more, having been reconciled, shall we be saved through his life.'

An integral part of the Christian message is reconciliation. The ministry of the church was, in Paul's words. 'the ministry of reconciliation – that God was reconciling the world to himself in Christ, not counting men's sins against them and he has committed to us the message of reconciliation. Because of this we're Christ's ambassadors, as though God were making his appeal through us. We implore you on 'the Anointed One's' behalf: Be reconciled to God. He made him who had no sin to be a sin offering for us, so that in him we might become the righteousness of God.'

Paul contrasts the old covenant, specifically, the ten commandments, as letters written on stone – letters, because of what they reveal to our conscience, condemn us, but the new covenant, through God's spirit, gives life. Paul goes on to say that the ministry that brought death came with glory because the face of Moses shone. The account in Exodus says that when Moses came down from Mount Sinai with the ten commandments engraved on stone in his hands, he wasn't aware that his face was radiant because he had spoken with the Lord and when the others saw him they were afraid to come near him so Moses put a veil over his face and only took it off when he talked with the Lord. That radiance did eventually fade.

'If the ministry,' Paul continued, 'that condemns men is glorious, how much more glorious is the ministry that brings righteousness... we're not like Moses, who'd put a veil over his face to keep the Israelites from gazing at it while the radiance was fading away. Their minds were made dull, because to this day the same veil remains when the old covenant is read. It hasn't been removed because it's only in and through the Messiah that it's taken away.'

Paul, under arrest at the time, was given permission to speak directly to King Agrippa

(Agrippa II, Marcus Julius Agrippa and his sister, Bernice). He took this special opportunity to share his story: "King Agrippa, I consider myself fortunate to stand before you today as I make my defence against the accusations of the Jews, and especially so because you're well acquainted with all the Jewish customs and controversies.

The Jews all know the way I've lived in my own country and also in Jerusalem. They've known me a long time and can say, if they're willing, that according to the strictest sect of our religion I lived as a Pharisee. It's because of my hope in what God has promised our fathers that I'm on trial today. This is the promise our twelve tribes are hoping to see fulfilled as they earnestly serve God day and night. It's because of this hope that the Jews are accusing me. Why should any of you consider it incredible that God raises the dead?

I too was convinced that I ought to do all that was possible to oppose the name of Jesus of Nazareth, and that's just what I did in Jerusalem. On the authority of the chief priests I put many of the saints in prison, and when they were put to death I cast my vote against them. Many a time I went from one synagogue to another to have them punished, and I tried to force them to blaspheme. In my obsession against them I even went to foreign cities to persecute them.

On one of my journeys I was going to Damascus with the authority and commission of the chief priests and about noon as I was on the road I saw a light from the sky brighter than the sun blazing around me and my companions. We all fell to the ground and I heard a voice saying to me in Hebrew, "Saul, Saul, why do you persecute me? It's hard for you to fight against your own conscience."

"Who are you, Lord?" I asked.

"I'm Jesus, the one you're persecuting. Now get up. I've appeared to you to appoint you as a servant and as a witness of what you've seen of me and what I'll show you. I'll rescue you from your own people and from the Gentiles. I'm sending you to them to open their eyes and turn them from darkness to light and from the power of Satan to God, so that they may receive forgiveness of sins and a place among those who are sanctified by faith in me."

So then, King Agrippa, I wasn't disobedient to the vision from heaven. First to those in Damascus, then to those in Jerusalem and in Judea, and to the Gentiles also, I preached that they should repent and turn to God and prove their repentance by their deeds.

That's why the Jews seized me in the temple courts and tried to kill me. But I've had God's help to this very day, and so I stand here and testify to small and great alike. I'm saying nothing beyond what the prophets and Moses said would happen – that the Messiah would suffer and, as the first to rise from the dead, proclaim light to his own people and to the Gentiles.

"proclaim light"

Paul was later to write, 'You're all sons of the light and sons of the day. We don't belong to the night or to the darkness.'

Jesus said, "For judgement I've come into the world, so that the blind will see and those who see will become blind."

The Pharisees that were with him heard him say this and asked, "What? Are we blind too?"

Jesus replied, "If you were blind, you wouldn't be guilty of sin; but because you claim you can see, your guilt remains."

Later he said, "You're going to have the light just a little while longer. Walk while you have the light, before darkness overtakes you. The man who walks in the dark doesn't know where he's going. Put your trust in the light while you have it, so that you may become sons of the light."

Isaiah had written, 'We look for light, but all is darkness, for brightness, but we walk in deep shadows.' A little later he writes, 'Arise, shine, for your light has come, and the glory of the Lord rises upon you. See, darkness covers the earth and thick darkness is over the peoples, but the Lord rises upon you and glory appears over you. Nations will come to your light, and kings to the brightness of your dawn.'

"from the power of Satan to God."

'The god of this age has blinded the minds of unbelievers,' as Paul wrote to the Corinthians, 'so that they can't see the light of the good news of the glory of the Messiah, who is the image of God... for God who said, "Let light shine out of darkness," made his light shine in our hearts to give us the light of the knowledge of the glory of God in the face of the Messiah.'

Jesus faced the hatred of the religious orthodoxy of his time who witnessed the good he did and attributed it to the devil and so Jesus said to those who had no excuse for what they said, "Any kingdom divided against itself will be ruined, If Satan is divided against himself how can his kingdom stand? Now if I drive out demons by Beelzebub, by whom do your followers drive them out? So, then they'll be your judges, but if I drive out demons by the finger of God, then the kingdom of God has come to you … he who isn't with me is against me and he who doesn't gather with me, scatters. Men will have to give account on the day of judgement for every careless word they've spoken. For by your words you'll be acquitted, and by your words you'll be condemned." The Pharisees saw the kindness and power of God in the healings that Jesus did and because they said it was from the devil there was no forgiveness for them.

"…so that they may receive forgiveness of sins and a place among those who are sanctified by faith in me."

John writes, 'He came to that which was his own, but his own did not receive him. Yet to all who received him, to those who believed in his name, he gave the right to become children of God – children born not of natural descent, nor of human decision or a husband's will, but born of God.'

When Peter spoke publicly, on the day of Pentecost, to many who had seen Jesus die he ended by saying, "Therefore let all Israel be assured of this: God has made this Jesus, whom you crucified, both Lord and Christ."

When the people heard this, they were cut to the heart and said to Peter and the other apostles, "Brothers, what shall we do?"

Peter replied, "Repent and be baptised, every one of you, in the name of Jesus the Messiah for the forgiveness of your sins and you'll receive the gift of the holy spirit ..."

A short time later a man who was crippled from birth was placed near a gate in the temple area so he could beg from those who were entering the temple. He saw two men about to go through the gate and asked them for money. The men looked at him and he looked at them expecting to get what he had asked for and one of the men said to him, "Silver or gold I don't have, but what I have I give you. In the name of Jesus [the] Christ of Nazareth, walk."

Taking him by the right hand, he helped him up. Instantly the man's feet and ankles became strong – he jumped to his feet and began to walk. He then went with the two men into the temple courts walking, jumping and praising God. He was recognised as the same man who used to sit begging at the gate and they were amazed and astonished at what had happened to him.

The beggar held on to the two men who then saw people rushing to them to get a better look and one of the men said, "Men of Israel, why does this surprise you? And why do you stare at us as if by our own power or godliness we had made this man walk? The God of Abraham, Isaac and Jacob, the God of our fathers, has glorified his servant Jesus. You handed him over to be killed, and you disowned him before Pilate, though he had decided to let him go. You disowned the holy and righteous one and asked that a murderer be released to you. You killed the author of life, but God raised him from the dead. We're witnesses of this. By faith in the name of Jesus this man whom you see and know was made strong. It's Jesus' name and the faith that comes through him that has given this complete healing to him, as you can all see.

Now, brothers, I know that you acted in ignorance, as did your leaders, but this is how God fulfilled what he had foretold through all the prophets, saying that his Messiah would suffer. Repent then, and turn to God so that your sins may be wiped out, that times of refreshing may come from the Lord and that he may send the Messiah, who has been appointed for you – even Jesus. He must remain in heaven until the time comes for God to restore everything, as he promised long ago through his holy prophets. Moses said, 'The Lord your God will raise up for you a prophet like me from among your own people; you must listen to everything he tells you. Anyone who doesn't listen to him will be completely cut off from his people.'

Indeed, all the prophets from Samuel on have foretold these days. And you're heirs of the prophets and of the covenant God made with your fathers. He said to Abraham, 'Through your offspring all peoples on earth will be blessed. When God raised up his servant he sent him first to you to bless you by turning each of you from your wicked ways."

While they were speaking to the people the temple guard and the Sadducees came and arrested them but many who heard the message believed.

Owning a Bible, reading it or even preaching from it doesn't mean that our minds have been opened to understand it.

The two downhearted disciples on their way home had lost the hope that they had that Israel was going liberated from the Romans and their nation would achieve greatness. They shared each other's deep disappointment. Unaware of who he was, Jesus joined them on their long walk.

"What are you talking about," Jesus asked.

"Are you the only visitor to Jerusalem that doesn't know what's been happening?"

"What things?"

"About Jesus of Nazareth – he was a prophet, powerful in what he said and what he did. The chief priests had him sentenced to death and he was crucified. We had hoped that he was going to restore Israel – this was just three days ago and some of our women who went to his tomb said they saw angels who said he was alive! Some of the disciples went to have a look and said that the tomb was empty."

"You really can't see it. Don't you understand? Didn't the Messiah have to suffer these things and then enter his glory?" Starting with Moses and then all the prophets, he explained all the texts that spoke of him.

As they neared where their home was they saw that this man wanted to keep walking but they strongly felt the need to hear more from him so they urged him to stay with them and he agreed.

When they sat to eat, the stranger took the bread and gave thanks for it and then he shared it with them. At that moment, they recognised who he was and he disappeared.

"Wasn't our hearts glowing," they said to

each other, "while he talked to us and *opened* the scriptures to us?"

Later that day the disciples were shocked and frightened to see a dead man with them in a locked room. "Why are you in such a state and full of disbelief? Look at me. Look at my hands and feet. Touch me, if you like – I'm real." They still couldn't believe what was in front of them when he said, "You got anything to eat?" Unable to barely speak they gave him a piece of broiled fish and watched with widened eyes and open mouthed as he ate it.

As they slowly began to settle he said, "This is what I told you before. Everything must be fulfilled that was written about me in the Law of Moses, the Prophets and the Psalms." They he *opened* their minds so that they could understand the scriptures. "This is what is written: The Messiah will suffer and rise from the dead on the third day, and repentance and forgiveness of sins will be preached in his name to all nations, beginning at Jerusalem. You're witnesses of what has happened."

The unseen enemy who lies and deceives wasn't successful in drawing Jesus from his mission but his aims of distorting and misrepresenting both God and Jesus continue.

Jesus warned his disciples what would precede

his return, and the end of this age. There would be wars and rumours of wars, nation against nation and kingdom against kingdom, famines and earthquakes in different places. These would be a constant in world history as well as persecution but he began with the words, "Be careful that no-one deceives you because many will come in my name (representing him) saying I'm the Messiah (stating that Jesus is the Christ) and will deceive many." This would be a counterfeit message. "Many false prophets will appear and deceive many people," Jesus told his disciples.

Paul reinforced the warning of active deception in a letter to Timothy, 'For the time will come when men will not put up with sound doctrine, instead, to suit their own desires, they'll gather around them a great number of teachers to say what their itching ears want to hear. They'll turn their ears away from the truth and turn aside to myths.' He'd alerted the church leadership that after he's gone savage wolves will come among them and won't spare the flock. Even from their own ranks men will get up and distort the truth, to draw away disciples after them.'

The records of the early church clearly show how widespread that distortion went. Antisemitism also played a major part in divorcing the Jewish roots from Christianity. An early example of this is found in the *Didache*, or *Teaching of the twelve apostles*, written in the late first or early second century. Its concern is differentiating between Christian and Jewish behaviour. Fasting is to be observed on different days from the Jewish fast days of Monday and Thursday. They, the believers, would fast on Wednesday and Friday instead. The reason for this hostility to the Jews was that they were regularly depicted as responsible for the death of Jesus and complicit in the persecution meted out to his faithful followers.

Another issue to arise later was the question of the date of Easter. This controversy was called the *Quartodeciman* question. The word Easter, which isn't a biblical word, comes from *Eostur*, the Norse word for 'Spring'. The Babylonian goddess known in various locations as Astarte, Ishtar and the Queen of heaven, mentioned in Jeremiah 44, was a goddess of love and fertility, and a goddess of war. The Hebrews devotion to this goddess involved the whole family in worship and making cakes in her image as Jeremiah wrote condemning the practice. The churches in Asia Minor were known as 'fourteeners' as they observed on the same night as the Passover which was on the 14th Nisan, regardless of which day of the week it fell on. They were maintaining a practice that the apostle John kept. The Roman custom, also held in some parts of Asia Minor observed this day on the Sunday following Passover, that is, the Sunday following the first full moon after the Spring equinox. Eusebius tells us that when Polycarp, bishop of Smyrna, visited Anicetus, Rome's bishop, around 155, the two discussed the issue but reached no agreement. Anicetus followed the principle assumed by his predecessors that the Lord's resurrection was celebrated every Sunday rather than just once a year. They parted on good terms and agreed to respect each other's position. A generation after Anicetus had agreed to disagree with his Asian brethren, one of his successors aroused considerable opposition by attempting to impose uniformity of practice not only in Rome but also upon the churches in Asia. Victor, bishop of Rome threatened to excommunicate any communities that refused to comply. Polycrates, bishop of Ephesus, opposed him and was supported by Irenaeus who called it an abuse of authority that would needlessly divide the churches. The excommunication order was countermanded but in the long-term Victor's position would win.

At the Council of Nicaea, 325, it was stipulated that Easter should be celebrated everywhere as a Sunday festival. Nevertheless, those who continued

John's tradition continued to exist in Rome for some time, and there were further protests against the Sunday *Pascha* (in memory of the death and resurrection of Jesus) by Eastern churchmen in the fourth century. Though condemned by various church councils, Quartodecimans were still to be found in many places in the East for several centuries.

Kegan Chandler writes in his illuminating book 'The God of Jesus In Light of New Testament Theology,' 'The passionate rejection of the Jewish God by the Church Fathers continued with the leaders of the Reformation in the 16th century. The explicit and wanton antisemitism that thrived in the Reformation is an often-neglected piece of Protestant history, but it is perhaps a key to unlocking the mystery of how certain staunchly Catholic doctrines could carry on through the flames of 16th century scepticism. The Jews, as both an ethnic and religious group, were considered detestable by the most well-known Protestant leaders, and so was any theological insight the Jewish heritage had to offer. Undoubtedly, the perpetual rejection of the Jewish perspective on the identity of God during the Reformation maintained the exegetical darkness in which Christians had been groping for centuries.

'John Calvin reveals his attitude towards the Jews thus: "[The Jews] rotten and unbending stiffneckedness deserves that they be oppressed unendingly and without measure or end and that they die in their misery without the pity of anyone." And Martin Luther writes, "Such a desperate, thoroughly evil, poisonous, and devilish lot are these Jews, who for these fourteen hundred years have been and still are our plague, our pestilence, and our misfortune."' Luther's hostility wasn't restricted only to Jews. The Anabaptists, who rejected infant baptism and were convinced that the separation of church and state should be allowed, faced opposition from all sides. In Luther's preface to his commentary on Paul's letter to the Galatians he writes, 'Who cannot see here in the Anabaptists, not men possessed by demons, but demons themselves possessed by worse demons?'

Chandler adds, 'Many of today's western Christians will undoubtedly be shocked at the words of their denominational founders. Many Christians around the world today feel, especially in light of the Holocaust, a special duty to support or protect the Jewish people. But Luther concludes his own terrible plan for the Jews by boldly declaring that they "ought not to be protected. You ought not, you cannot protect them, unless in the eyes of God you want to share all their abomination.'"

The biblical teaching of an earthy millennial reign of God, which was held by Irenaeus and other church leaders was, in time, replaced by the traditional teaching that at death the saved go to heaven and that God's rule on earth is fulfilled by the church. Ask, if you dare, someone that believes that a dead person lives in heaven, 'with what body do they have?' There are only two bodies: our human, physical and mortal body and the glorified and powerful spiritual body that we'll receive at the resurrection. There is no intermediate body between the physical and spiritual. The dead are 'awakened' at the time of the resurrection. Our soul, which is our life, isn't a separate entity that lives on after death.

"What about when Jesus said to the thief on the cross, 'I tell you the truth, today you will be with me in paradise,'?"

What we read in English was written in Greek and originally spoken in Aramaic. There were no full stops and commas or verses and chapters in the original documents. Jesus didn't go immediately to paradise at his death (paradise: a Persian word that means *garden*), that will only become a reality when God's Kingdom is here on earth. Neither did

Jesus ascend to his Father when he died; John 20:17. So, what did Jesus really say to the repentant thief?

The dying man asked Jesus to remember him when he came into his kingdom and Jesus reassured him by saying, "Today, I'm speaking the truth to you, you'll be with me in that kingdom."

"What about the verse that says, 'great is your reward in heaven'?" That's true, our reward is in heaven but Jesus says, "I'm coming soon. My reward is with me, and I'll give to everyone according to what he's done." Isaiah had written, 'See, your Saviour comes. See, his reward is with him.'

Peter writes of an incorruptible inheritance that is reserved in heaven for you but this glory and honour will be given when Jesus appears or is revealed. As Paul puts it, 'we'll all be changed – in a flash, in the twinkling of an eye, at the last trumpet. The trumpet will sound, the dead will be raised imperishable, and we'll be changed.'

That applies to those whom God has chosen to reign on earth under Jesus. Being chosen isn't by merit but as a gift, yet the position in God's government is based on what each individual did with what they'd been given. The first resurrection is called the better resurrection because those with Jesus then will be restoring the world. The rest of the dead will wait for a thousand years until awoken by the second resurrection – then comes judgement. What a person did in their lives is so important, and that record will be taken into account, but no-one can be saved by their own efforts. If their names are in the book of life they'll live, if not they'll be destroyed. Moses wrote, 'For the Lord your God is a consuming fire, a jealous God.' This same line is written to New Testament readers in the book of Hebrews.

"That servant who knows his master's will and doesn't get ready or doesn't do what his master wants will be beaten with many blows. But the one who doesn't know and does things deserving punishment will be beaten with few blows. From everyone who has been given much, much will be demanded; and from the one who has been entrusted with much, much more will be asked."

The biblical text that 'the wages of sin is death,' or as in other texts, 'eternal destruction', was replaced by the condemned suffering eternal torment which can be found only in non-biblical literature. The teaching of *Gehenna* misleadingly translated as *Hell* in our Bibles, describes a location outside of Jerusalem which became a public incinerator for the waste of the city to be burned up. The word *Gehenna* is derived from a Hebrew word meaning '*valley of Hinnom*'. The fire that is written about in context of the fate of those who rebel against God is compared to a furnace that consumes all that is thrown into it and is reduced to ashes. Peter wrote of God condemning 'the cities of Sodom and Gomorrah by burning them to ashes, and made them an example of what is going to happen to the ungodly.'

"What about the verse, 'their worm doesn't die and the fire isn't quenched?" Jesus was quoting from the last verse in Isaiah which talks of the decomposing dead bodies of those who rebelled against God. One highly regarded Bible scholar writes, '…and it is their endless lot to live the life of corruption (*their worm will not die*) under the endless antagonism of divine holiness, i.e. the unquenched *fire*. On the lips of Jesus, these words are used to express the burning 'life' of Gehenna.' But none of that exposition is found in the Isaiah text or in the use of it made by Jesus. To picture the dead on a burning rubbish tip becoming food for invertebrates is given as a graphic warning of the utter ruin for those who rebel against God. Jesus assumed his hearers would understand what was meant by Gehenna.

God does punish, disciplines and corrects but never tortures – this is what the enemy of mankind does and all torture will be eradicated in the kingdom of God.

The teaching that humans are mortal and will only attain to immortality at the resurrection at the time of Jesus' return was rejected in favour of the Greek philosophical concept of our immortality. The early church fathers were strongly influenced by philosophy which embraced the study of logic; in the words of Augustine (354-430) dialectic was the 'discipline of disciplines' because 'it teaches how to teach and how to learn.' Peter Abelard (1079-1142) loved to learn. In his autobiography, History of my Calamities' he presents himself as a complete egotist. He was driven by ambition and had to be the greatest philosopher in the world, 'for so I rated myself.' He wrote that he had been 'seduced by so great a love to be educated in the bosom of Minerva.' goddess of learning. Abelard wanted to be thought of as the next Aristotle. He insisted that his students 'arm' themselves with the writings of Aristotle because logic is the art of scholastic warfare, they needed, he told them, to be armed with dialectical reasonings.' The concept of our immortal soul comes from Plato.

Back in the first century the apostle Paul wrote to Timothy of those who are 'always learning but never able to acknowledge the truth.'

On that day of Pentecost when Peter addressed the people there, he said that Jesus of Nazareth was a man accredited by God, and Paul wrote, 'For since death came through a man, the resurrection of the dead came through a man,' and to Timothy he wrote, 'For there is one God and one mediator between God and men, the man Messiah Jesus.' To say that Jesus was a man descended from king David whose beginning was his miraculous birth in Bethlehem arouses great agitation among those who dogmatically hold that Jesus was God. This was not even a debating point until several centuries later.

After the resurrection Jesus said to a tearful Mary, "Don't hold on to me, because I've not yet ascended (the NIV has *'returned'* – later versions have changed it to ascend – the Greek is *ascended* as the KJV has, as well as the NKJV, NRSV and the NEB) to the Father. Go instead to my brothers and tell them, I'm ascending (not, *'returning'*) to my Father and your Father, to my God and your God." The critics of Jesus said he made himself equal with God but Jesus himself never said that he was equal with God.

Jesus said, "No one has ever gone into heaven except the one who came from heaven – the Son of Man." The Jews wouldn't have taken these words to mean that Jesus was God made flesh. It was common for them to say something 'came from heaven' if God were its source. God is the source of Jesus as he was God's plan (*Logos*) and then God directly fathered Jesus. God sent Jesus into the world and he sends his disciples into the world but his disciples weren't incarnated with Jesus before they were born; they were sent just as Jesus was. The Messiah was expected to be a descendent of David, not God the Son.

Questioning the most important and fundamental teaching of traditional Christianity is guaranteed to provoke the quick response of the live issue of heresy which led to the death of many in past centuries who couldn't accept a teaching not found, explained or defended in the scriptures.

Jesus said in his prayer for the disciples, "This is eternal life: that they may know you, the only true God, and Jesus [the] Christ, whom you've sent."

The writer of Hebrews, speaking of the Messiah as our continuing high priest, wrote, 'For the Anointed One hasn't entered the holy places made with hands, which are copies of the true, but into heaven itself, now to appear in the presence of God for us.' This writer also wrote, 'In bringing many sons to glory, it was fitting that God, for whom and through whom everything exists, should make the author of their salvation perfect through suffering.

Both the one who makes men holy and those who are made holy are of the same family ... during the days of Jesus' life on earth, he offered up prayers and petitions with loud cries and tears to the one who could save him from death and he was heard because of his reverent submission. Although he was a son, he learned obedience from what he suffered and once made perfect he became the source of eternal salvation for all who obey him.'

God is God, and Jesus has many titles but he is still subject to God, his Father. Jesus will reign until he has put all his enemies under his feet... when he has done this, then the Son himself will be made subject to him who put everything under him, so that God may be all in all.

"What are you doing here, Elijah?"

The question was gently asked of the servant of God. Elijah was broken by the realisation that the nationwide Baal worship was not going to end. The wound done to it on Mount Carmel would soon heal and it would be back to business as usual. Elijah felt it wasn't worth living anymore and answered, "I've been zealous for the Lord God Almighty. The Israelites have rejected your covenant, broken down your altars and killed your prophets. I'm the only one willing to speak out publicly and now they're trying to kill me."

God still had some work for him to do and he sent him back but not before he encouraged him with the fact that seven thousand, of his fellow Israelites had not bowed down to Baal or had kissed his image.

From being active in the front line the time had come for Elisha to take up the mantle from Elijah. Everyone knew this was going to happen but Elisha didn't want it to happen so he stayed close to Elijah even though he had been told to stay where he was. Elisha's response was to tell Elijah that he wasn't going to leave him; he repeated his unwillingness to leave him as they walked through Bethel and passed Jericho and stopped at the Jordan where Elijah rolled up his cloak and hit the water with it, then they both walked across on dry ground. Elijah asked Elisha what he could do for him before he's taken away, and Elisha asks for a double share of the spirit that was in Elijah, as Elisha looked to Elijah as his father.

"You've asked a difficult thing," Elijah replied, "yet if you see me when I'm taken from you, it'll be yours – if you don't then you won't."

As they walked alone talking a fiery chariot and horses drove them apart and a whirlwind took Elijah up into the sky.

"My father, my father," Elisha cried, "the chariots and horsemen of Israel!" And that was the last he saw of him but the same power that was with Elijah was now with Elisha.

That wasn't the end of Elijah. After being carried a great distance he was set down in a place where he could find the rest he sought. He was aware of what was happening in Israel and Judah and sometime later he wrote a letter to king Jehoram, son of Jehoshaphat, which can be read in the second book of chronicles.

God always has a people, even though they might be small enough to be overlooked. They're his 'little flock' "Don't be afraid, little flock, for your Father has been pleased to give you the kingdom."

Zechariah had written, 'The Lord their God will save them on that day as the flock of his people. They'll sparkle in his land like jewels in a crown. How attractive and beautiful they'll be.'

All the disputes, conflicts and divisions that are live issues among many Christian groups and fellowships will only be settled *on that day*. At present, many maintain a discrete and hostile distance between each other. Some members would feel content if this or that group would just disappear and leave so that the others could have a better access to those who need saving without ever noticing how mistaken they themselves may be on important theological issues. It would be unthinkable to consider that they may be as wrong as those they'd want to eliminate. Each is firmly convinced over their own rightness in handling the word of God. Such sectarian hatred, let alone well-mannered antagonism, is still with us.

An overview of the coercion and threats that litter the pages of church history and its failure to preach and to live a message that bears comparison with New Testament teaching could lead, and has led, to some concluding that the church project has done more harm than good and its failure to bring peace to the world has discredited its very existence. Those, who like Elijah, have become perplexed and depressed over the state of the world and the ineffectiveness of the church in changing the world wonder why the world hasn't become a better place need to remember to pray, as Jesus instructed, for God's kingdom to come because it's not here yet and for his will to be done on earth as it is in heaven because it's not yet. Sometime in the future all things in heaven and on earth will be brought together under one head, the Anointed One. That day is still ahead of us.

Worldwide liberation will come with the return of the King.

In the bestseller 'Is Paris Burning?' written by Larry Collins and Dominique Lapirre, they write of the time the liberation of Paris was first announced, 'Within minutes, his (Charles Collingwood, a CBS reporter assigned to the allied armies) dramatic description of the liberation was ringing into millions of homes. Two New York papers made over their late editions to carry it verbatim under huge headlines. In Mexico City the newspaper *Excelsior* blinked the words PARIS ESTA LIBERTADA from its light tower, and all the city's papers published extras. In Perón's Buenos Aires 1,800 miles south, for the first time since 1939, cheering crowds dared to chant, "*Democracia, sí. Axis, no.*" Quebec broke out the French tricolor, and Mayor Lucien Borne asked his fellow citizens to ignore their wartime "Brown-out" and illuminate their homes at night. From Washington F.D.R called the news "an ebullient passage of total victory," and from his hospital bed General John J. Pershing called it "a great step on the road to victory."

'In New York, Lily Pons, in a USO uniform, sang

the "Marseillaise" for 20,000 excited Americans at the Rockefeller Center while 32 French sailors in pompons raised the tricolor. London went wild. People kissed and danced in the streets of Soho, on Picadilly Circus, around Nelson's colomn in Trafalgar Square. To hard pressed London, the news was a happy prelude to V-E Day, which, it seemed, could not now be far off. Anthony Eden interrupted a banquet marking the Franco-English Civil Affairs Agreement to propose a joyous toast to his French counterpart. The king himself sent a warm cable of congratulations to De Gaulle.

'In the general euphoria that followed the BBC flash, no one paid any attention to SHAEF's awkwardly phrased denials of the story. All day and night, the BBC announcement and Collingwood's broadcast, carried across the Atlantic by the Yankee Doodle Network, went on and on like a long-playing record.

And it was all a ghastly mistake.

In a distinctly unliberated Paris where the men of General von Choltitz, more menacing with each passing hour, were still very much present, the news was greeted with fury and stupefaction.' It was a taped announcement made by Collingwood just in case liberation came before he was able to broadcast it. So it was made and sent to London ready for instant relay to all America. London's censors assumed it had been cleared in the field and passed it on to CBS.'

It's premature for Christians to celebrate the great victory over this world before it has happened.

The often-seen ecstatic celebration of Christians crying out for more of the spirit bears comparison with the Baal worship on Mount Carmel including pleas that fire would descend, than the quiet and patient trust exhibited by God's people who don't attempt to impose, enforce, intimidate or control what others think.

The apostle John made a statement that answers that important question of why is the world such a place of suffering and division. He wrote, 'We know that we're the children of God, and that the whole world is under the control of the evil one.' We shouldn't lay all the evils of this world at the feet of the enemy because its power is limited to lies and misrepresentation. Our own sins have caused pain and injustice around the world. James wrote, 'each one is tempted when, by his own desire, he's dragged away and enticed. Then, after desire has conceived, it gives birth it sin; and sin, when it's full grown, gives birth to death ... submit yourselves to God. Resist the devil (with his deceptions and self-centredness) and he'll run from you. Come near to God and he'll come near to you.'

In one of the last messages that Jesus gave to his disciples he said, "And I confer on you a kingdom, just as my Father conferred on me, so that you may eat and drink at my table in my kingdom and sit on thrones, judging the twelve tribes of Israel. Simon, Simon, Satan has asked to sift you (plural) as wheat, but I've prayed for you (singular), Simon, that your faith may not fail and when you've turned back, strengthen your brothers."

Great promises of ruling under the king but also warnings of unfaithfulness and neglecting the high calling that's been given. As humans, singly or collectively, we do not have the power or authority to eject Satan from controlling this world, neither can we bring peace to the world. Jesus didn't pray for the world but for those chosen out of this world yet commissioned to go into the world.

It's natural for a mother to what the best for her boys and the mother of James and John is no exception. "What do you want?" Jesus asked her when she, kneeling, asked a favour of him.

"Grant that one of these two sons of mine may sit at your right and the other at your left in your kingdom." All the disciples knew his kingdom was coming and that there would be top jobs to be given out and they sometimes openly talked about what position they'd like to get. But now the mother of these brothers got in first and the others were angry about it.

Turning to the brothers, Jesus said, "You don't know what you're asking. Can you drink the cup I'm going to drink?"

"Yes, we can," they quickly answered.

"You will drink from my cup, but to sit at my right or left isn't for me to grant. These places belong to those for whom they've been prepared by my Father."

Then he taught all of them about being a servant and not to desire to be number one so that others can serve them. "The son of man didn't come to be served, but to serve, and to give his life as a ransom for many."

The followers of Jesus are compared to strangers and aliens looking forward to a country and a city that has been prepared for them – for here they don't have an enduring city but are looking for the city that is to come. These individuals stretch all the way back to the beginning, down all the centuries to our own time. Dead or alive, they're all waiting still. 'These were all commended for their faith, yet none of them received what had been promised. God had planned something better for us so that only together with us would they be made perfect.'

"Peace I leave; my peace I give you. I don't give to you as the world gives. Don't let your hearts be troubled and don't be afraid. You heard me say, 'I'm going away and I'm coming back to you.' If you loved me, you'd be glad that I'm going to the Father, because the Father is greater than I. I've told you now before it happens, so that when it does happen you'll believe. I'll not speak with you much longer because the prince of this world is coming. He has no hold on me, but the world must learn that I love the Father and that I do exactly what my Father has commanded me."

Seven letters were written to churches in what is now western Turkey. They were written to warn and encourage Christians experiencing what has been common for followers of Jesus up to the present time. They expose our weaknesses and the need of repentance. At the end of each letter there is a promise to those who are faithful to the end.

To Ephesus: "To him who overcomes, I'll give the right to eat from the tree of life, which is in the paradise of God."

To Smyrna: "He who overcomes will not be hurt at all by the second death."

To Pergamum: "To him who overcomes, I'll give some of the hidden manna. I'll also give him a white stone with a new name written on it, known only to him who receives it."

To Thyatira: "To him who overcomes and does my will to the end, I'll give authority over the nations – *'he'll rule them with an iron sceptre; he'll dash them to pieces like pottery'* – just as I've received authority from my Father. I'll also give him the morning star."

To Sardis: "He who overcomes will be dressed in white. I'll never blot out his name from the book of life, but will acknowledge his name before my Father and his angels."

To Philadelphia: "Him who overcomes I'll make a pillar in the temple of my God and the name of the city of my God, the new Jerusalem, which is coming down out of heaven from my God; and I'll also write on him my new name."

To Laodicea: To him who overcomes, I'll give the right to sit with me on my throne, just as I overcame and sat down with my Father on his throne."

It is important and helpful to remember that the word Trinity is not itself a New Testament word. It is even true at least in one sense to say that the doctrine of the Trinity is not directly a New Testament doctrine. It is rather a deduction from, and an interpretation of, the thought and language of the New Testament. The most important fact of all to remember is that it was not a doctrine which anyone in the church ever sat down and, as it were, worked out from first principles by a series of logical steps; the doctrine of the Trinity has been from the beginning, and must always be seen as, an interpretation of actual Christian experience,

William Barclay: The Plain Man
Looks at the Apostles' Creed

Part 4

Jesus is not God

In support of the Trinity

One of the most influential Trinitarian theologians of the last century, Karl Barth, objected strongly to any theology of God which arose independently of the doctrine of the Trinity. Those who argue this way are right, as the doctrine of the Trinity is *the* doctrine which makes Christianity unique and priority must be given to New Testament revelation. Nonetheless, there remains a unity between the monotheistic doctrine of God as found in the Shema and the Trinitarian theology of the New Testament. Trinitarianism can be understood to be an explication of monotheism because Jewish monotheism is grounded in an understanding of the love of God. The love dimension of the Old Testament doctrine of God provides a foundation for the doctrine of the Trinity.

Brian Edgar: The Message of the Trinity. p.78

The doctrine of Trinity is not a piece of ancient dogmatic lumber; it is the fullness of God and the features of his love and the activity of his grace. We know him most fully in this truth because this is the fullest revelation of himself. We know him most fully because the Father sent the Son, because the Son is the image of the invisible God, and because the Son sent the Spirit to be the witness to Jesus in the world of men and women … while the fourth gospel is undoubtedly the main biblical source for Trinitarian doctrine, it is probably true to say that it has one rival…the Book of Revelation. It is here, more than anywhere else, that the perfect unity of the Trinity is demonstrated, it becomes almost impossible to distinguish between them…indeed we are barely aware that we are passing from one person to another…The Book of Revelation is first and foremost a revelation of the Trinity.

Peter Lewis: The Message of the Living God. p.238

… just about everything that matters in Christianity hangs on the truth of God's three-in-oneness … the entire fabric of Christian redemption and its application to human experience depend wholly on the three-in-oneness of God. The Trinity is as important as that.

Bruce Milne: Know the Truth. p.78

We should all be eager for some visible expression of Christian unity, provided always that we do not sacrifice fundamental Christian truth in order to achieve it. Christian unity arises from our having one Father, one Saviour, and one indwelling Spirit. So we cannot possibly foster a unity which pleases God either if we deny the doctrine of the Trinity or if we have not come personally to know God the Father through the reconciling work of his Son Jesus Christ and the power of the Holy Spirit.

John Stott: The Message of the
Ephesians. p.154-155

It is of the utmost importance to identify the nature and character of the God Christians worship. The uniqueness of Christianity lies in the fact that God is to be defined as Father, Son and Spirit. All gods are not the same; all spiritual roads do not lead to heaven; the uniqueness of Christ and the message of the Trinity *are* at the heart of Christian faith. The Trinity is not an 'add-on', it is not an 'extra', it is the gospel.

Brian Edgar: The Message of the Trinity. p.152

"I cannot think of the one without quickly being encircled by the splendour of the Three; nor can

I discern the Three without being straight way carried back to the one."

Words which Calvin quotes from Gregory of Nazianzus and which "vastly delighted" him, they capture the heart and soul of his theological approach, which is Trinitarian through and through…Calvin finds the doctrine of the Trinity in the very first chapter of the Bible – in the Spirit hovering over the waters and in the words "Let us make…" (Genesis 1:26). In the Old Testament, overall the doctrine is faintly, but definitely, revealed; in the New, it shines as bright as the noonday sun.

Oliver Rice: Calvin's theology of the Holy Spirit. Evangelicals Now. July 2009

We believe – would that we really believed it as we should – that God is really big. (We hold with all Christians that there is one God and that he has revealed himself as triune, that is, that the Father, the Son, and the Holy Spirit is each fully and eternally God).

Dale Ralph Davis: The House That Jesus Built. p.13

An alternative view

A survey of mainstream Christianity (carried out for Christianity Today Oct 2014) found that while most evangelicals say they affirm the Trinity, more than half (51%) actually said that the Holy Spirit is a force, not a personal being. Seven percent weren't sure. This means that half of all evangelicals are by definition not Trinitarians. Such confusion or disagreement represents a theological crisis of epic proportions.

Kegan A. Chandler: The God of Jesus
in light of Christian dogma. p.495

The main debate and argument in the early part of the 4th century (which was to continue for centuries later) was not about the Trinity, rather it was concerning what words would correctly define the relationship between God and Jesus. The famous Nicene Creed of 325 begins with:

'We believe in one God, the Father, Almighty, maker of all things visible and invisible; And in one Lord Jesus Christ, the Son of God, begotten of the Father, only begotten, that is, from the substance of the Father, God from God, Light from Light. Very God from Very God, begotten not made, of one substance with the Father...' and ends with the words 'And in the Holy Spirit.'

After these clauses, the following statements were added:

'And those who say, "There was a time when he was not," and "Before he was begotten he was not," and "He came into being from nothing," or those who pretend that the Son of God is, "Of another substance, or essence [than the Father] or "created" or "alterable" or "mutable" the catholic and apostolic church places under a curse.'

The Lion Handbook of the History of Christianity says:

'The fourth, fifth and sixth centuries were marked by prolonged controversies, chiefly in the Eastern church. These were about how Christ, the Son of God, was himself God (the doctrine of the Trinity) and how he was both man and God (the doctrine of the person of Christ, or Christology) ... it was an age of interference and even domination by the emperors, of colourful and abrasive personalities, and of bitter antagonism between leading bishoprics. Technical terms without biblical origins were made keywords in authoritative statements of belief. Their use contributed to the

Latin-speaking West and the Greek-speaking East misunderstanding and misrepresenting one another.

'Even between different segments of the Greek church misunderstandings arose; these disputes contributed to major division in the Christian world. In theory the first appeal was to Scripture, but the Bible was used in curious or questionable ways. People frequently appealed to Scripture to confirm their theology rather than to decide it. Above all, the disputes were shot through with the feeling that unless God and Christ were truly what Christian devotion and worship claimed, then salvation itself was endangered. Passions ran high because the fundamentals of the Christian religion were felt to be at stake.'

The Protestant Reformation did not bring tolerance. There were thousands of courageous Reformation-era Christians who did challenge the doctrine of the Trinity who suffered at the hands of Reformers who were no less violent than their catholic forebears. Some of the leaders of the Protestant Reformation of the 16th century acted like despots and demonstrated the same intolerance which prompted their revolt.

Edward Gibbon writes:

'The Reformers were ambitious of succeeding

tyrants whom they had dethroned. They imposed with equal rigor their creeds and confessions; they asserted the right of the magistrate to punish heretics with death. The nature of the tiger was the same.'

Thomas Jefferson, in a letter to the theologian James Smith (Dec 8, 1822) wrote, concerning the 4th century bishop Athanasius, who used violence against those he deemed dangerous to the church:

'The Athanasian paradox that one is three, and three but one, is so incomprehensible to the human mind that no candid man can say he has any idea of it, and how can he believe what presents no idea? He who thinks he does, only deceives himself. He proves, also, that man, once surrendering his reason, has no remaining guard against absurdities ... and like a ship without a rudder, is the sport of every wind ... [such faith] takes the helm from the hand of reason, and the mind becomes a wreck.'

Sir Isaac Newton worked assiduously to demolish the scriptural arguments for the Trinity but could never publish what he had written. Stuart Clark's novel 'The Sensorium of God' relates Newton's dilemma, p.188.

'Athanasius, who was exiled several times for instigating disorder and other things, attacked in writing the emperor Constantius whom he branded a persecutor worse than Saul, Ahab, Pilate, and the Jews who crucified Jesus. The emperor was no Christian at all, Athanasius declared; he was the precursor of the Antichrist.' 'When Jesus became God' Richard E. Rubenstein, p.186.

Athanasius is considered by many as a hero who helped the church to clarify its position on the Trinity.

The emperor Constantine, who presided at the Council of Nicaea and exercised final authority over its conclusion intervened with a word that, to his mind, could settle the debate over how to describe the nature of Jesus. The word was *homoousios* which means 'of the same substance' and this controversial word became part of the creed. The unity that Constantine sought had been achieved, but it was to be short-lived. Bishops soon fell out with one another and pronounced exiles on those who would not agree with the creed.

'The story that Constantine experienced a vision of the cross in the sky prior to battle is in other versions presented as a vision of the pagan Sun-god. This deity was certainly of enduring importance to him. The coins he issued in his early years as emperor include images of *Sol Invictus*, 'the Unconquered Sun,' as well as symbols of various other pagan gods, and the still-extant triumphal arch later erected in Rome to celebrate his victory over Maxentius also depicts *Sol Invictus* as Constantine's protector and refers simply to 'the divinity' unspecified. When in 321 Constantine declared the first day of the week as a public holiday (or at least a day when nonessential labour was discouraged and public institutions such as the law-courts could be open only for the charitable purpose of freeing slaves), his stated reason was not to facilitate Christian worship or practice as such but to respect "the venerable day of the Sun"

Ivor J. Davidson. A Public Faith. p.16

One of the most famous church fathers and a prominent developer of Trinitarian doctrine, the Cappadocian Gregory of Nazianzus admitted in AD 381:

'Of the wise among us, some hold the Holy Spirit to be a power, others a creature, others a God, and still others are unwilling to decide, out of reverence (or so they say) for the Scriptures, which do not speak plainly on the matter.'

It was in the same year, at the Council of Constantinople, that the divinity of the spirit was affirmed. In January of the previous year the emperor Theodosius issued the following edict to the people of Constantinople:

'It is Our will that all peoples ruled by the administration of Our clemency shall practice that religion which the divine Peter the apostle transmitted to the Romans ... this is the religion followed by bishop Damasus of Rome and by Peter, bishop of Alexandria, a man of apostolic sanctity: that is, according to the apostolic discipline of the evangelical doctrine, we shall believe in the single deity of the Father, the Son and the Holy Ghost under the concept of equal majesty and of the Holy Trinity.

'We command that persons who follow this rule shall embrace the name of catholic Christians. The rest, however, whom we judge demented and insane, shall carry the infamy of heretical dogmas. Their meeting places shall not receive the name of churches, and they shall be smitten first by divine vengeance, and secondly by the retribution of hostility which We shall assume in accordance with Divine Judgement.'

Charles Freeman writes in his 'AD 381' p.25

'When Theodosius cleverly equated his Nicene beliefs with the promise of divine approval, he was not alone. At very much the same time, in the western empire, the bishop of Milan, the formidable Ambrose, claimed that those areas of the empire where the Nicene faith was strong were stable while those where Arianism prevailed, notably alone the Danube, were the most unsettled. He was building on the tradition that God expressed his support of the ruling emperor through bringing him victory.'

Theodosius decided for all Christians that the Holy Spirit was unquestionably a third co-equal Person. The freedom to speculate openly as an individual had no place under this system.

Evangelical arguments for the deity of Jesus often feature the claim that if Jesus was not God, his death could not have paid for the sins of the world. Only God, they say, could pay such an infinite penalty; yet God is immortal, which means that whatever dying is, God cannot die. Charles Wesley's hymn, 'And can it be,' has the words, ''Tis mystery all! Th'Immortal dies!' The historic fact is that Jesus did die, but if he was immortal he did not die. There was only one Jesus, not two – one human and mortal – the other – immortal and God. He did not have two natures – one divine – and one human, which would mean that Jesus had two wills – two minds. These were the matters that the early church fought over.

'What was God's solution to the problem of

sin and death? The only solution legally available: *another* Adam! In fact, if we had to sum up the whole Bible in five seconds, we could say: "It is the story of two men and their effect on mankind. The first man wrecked everything; the second man is fixing it."

'Like the first Adam, the last Adam would have to be, first of all, *genetically* flawless and without a sin nature. It was God's responsibility to create him that way, which He did via the virgin birth. But more than that, the last Adam had to be *behaviourally* flawless. God could not be responsible for that. He could only hope that, in contrast to the first Adam, the last Adam would be obedient throughout his life and thus accomplish the redemption of mankind.'

'One God and One Lord'. The living Truth Fellowship. p.22.

The co-eternal personhood of the Spirit presented then, and still presents today, a serious problem. If the person of the Holy Spirit was eternal God, he was, therefore uncreated. Yet he could not be considered 'begotten' by God; that unique existence belonged to the 'only begotten' Son. But if the Person of the Holy Spirit was neither created nor begotten, yet was still eternal God, this would make him a second Father, but if he was generated by the Father, then there would be two sons.

Many modern Christians, even those in the Trinitarian camp, evidently still struggle with the matter. Could grasping the biblical view of the Spirit pave the way for a more rational theology in line with the teachings of Jesus?

The 'Spirit of God' or 'the Holy Spirit' is not a deity or a person distinct from the Father or Jesus. It is, in most cases, the personal power and influence of God. The spirit is God's personal operation in the world which enables the accomplishment of his work. After the Messiah's exaltation to the right hand of God, the Holy Spirit can now also be described as the personal influence of the glorified Lord Jesus, the Christians' 'Advocate with the Father' (1 John 2:1). Both God and his Son now work together through this spiritual power on behalf of the believer.

Some modern Trinitarians have even taken to calling the Holy Spirit 'the shy member of the Trinity,' as there are so many texts where you would expect him to be mentioned but is not.

The Trinity doctrine teaches that the Holy Spirit is fully God, equal in status and glory with the Father and the Son, and worthy of worship with them. If this is the case, why do we not find specific teaching from Jesus or his apostles about any necessary devotion to this unique individual?

What we do encounter in the writings of the apostles is an absence of such a supposedly crucial personality. John writes:

'Our fellowship is with the Father and with his Son, Jesus Christ' (1John 1:3). Also, 'No one who denies the Son has the Father; whoever acknowledges the Son has the Father also....' (1 John 2:24). But what about the other co-equal person? If only real persons can have relationships, is it John's lack of understanding of the Holy Spirit as a unique person that led him to leave him out?

The greetings in almost all of the New Testament epistles furnish perhaps the best and most sweeping example of the consistent apostolic omission. While all the authors recognise 'God the Father' and 'the Lord Jesus Christ' they seem to be ever missing the essential third member of the group: 2 Cor 1:2, Gal 1:1, Eph 1:2, Phil 1:2, 2 Thes 1:1, Col 1:1, 2 Thes 1:1, 2 Tim 1:2, Philemon 1:3, Jude 1:1.

We must wonder why only the Father and the Son greet the churches. Again, could this be because only real persons send personal greetings, and the apostles had no understanding of the Holy Spirit as such? If they did not, and if the true nature of the Trinity was only being progressively revealed to the church, would this not make them poor apostles, inadequately entrusted with only half-truths? If they did not understand it, why the exclusion?

Peter Lewis, quoting Gerald Bray, in his 'The Message of the Living God' writes, 'the fourth gospel is undoubtedly the main biblical source for trinitarian doctrine', it is 'probably true to say that it has one rival...the book of Revelation'. It is here, more than anywhere else, that... 'the perfect unity of the Trinity is demonstrated, so that while the persons remain fully distinct, it becomes almost impossible to distinguish between them...Indeed we are barely aware that we are passing from one person to another. The sense of the presence of God is so overwhelming that we can move among the persons almost without noticing, yet we are always fully conscious of their presence...The doctrine, culled from the rest of Scripture and laboriously constructed, is here presented to us in all its profound complexity and splendid simplicity...The book of Revelation is first and foremost a revelation of the Trinity.'

Gerald Bray, The Doctrine of God, Contours of Christian Theology.pp.149-151

Kegan A. Chandler writes, 'It is not only in the epistles, however, that we encounter the stunning neglect of the hypothetical third Person; the visions of John's Apocalypse paint a similar picture. Throughout the narrative, a distinction between Jesus and God is repeatedly recognised (Rev 7:10, 5:13, 11:15, 12:10, 20:6, 21:22), and they are each awarded a throne in Revelation 22:1. But where is the throne of the co-equal Holy Spirit? As Revelation depicts the dramatic conclusion of the Age and the ultimate resting place of God and his Christ in total victory, we wonder why the third member of the Trinity is not likewise awarded his rightful honours, or even made mention of, in these glorious closing scenes.'

'The God of Jesus' p.501

Far from simply meaning 'a person', the biblical application of the word 'spirit' (both the Hebrew *'ruach'* and the Greek *'pneuma'*) is broad. It refers to: *wind* (Dan 7:2), *breath* (2 Thes 2:8), *vitality* (Gen 2:7), *rational discernment* (Job 32:8), *the mind* (Mark 2:8), *attitude* (Deut 2:30), *disposition* (Luke 24:39, *a demon* (Matt 8:16), *power* (Ps 33:6-9), *divine knowledge* (Num 11:29), *instruction* (Neh 9:20), supernatural impulse (Acts 16:6), and more.

From this section we may see several categories

of application: a) wind or breath, b) life or intelligence, c) attitude or mind, and d) power or influence. Professor James Dunn concludes that the Jews never viewed 'the Spirit of God' or 'the Holy Spirit' as a unique person apart from God the Father:

'There can be little doubt that from the earliest stages of pre-Christian Judaism 'spirit' (*ruach*) denoted power – the awful, mysterious force of the wind (*ruach*), of the breath (*ruach*), of life, of ecstatic inspiration (*induced by divine ruach*) ... In other words, on this understanding, Spirit of God is in no sense distinct from God, but is simply the power of God, God himself acting powerfully in nature and upon men.'

Dunn, 'Christology in the Making' p.133

The imparted spirit is the intellect or understanding of a being: 'But there is a spirit in man, the inspiration of the Almighty gives them understanding' (Job 32:8). In this way spirit denotes the mind or reason of a particular person, not *another* person distinct from him.

'For who among men knows the thoughts of a man except the spirit of the man which is in him? Even the thoughts of God no one knows except the spirit of God (1 Cor 2:11).

The spirit of man is similar to the spirit of God. These were not distinct intelligences in their own right, but simply the mind of both the man and God – it is something that belongs to them – not to another person.

Though God's living place is in another realm he is able to be elsewhere via his spirit, or his presence, 'God is Spirit,' which fills the universe and also is within his servants.

In the gospels we read that Jesus himself was empowered to perform incredible wonders 'by the Spirit of God.' It should be obvious that the spirit is a personal attribute of God. The spirit is the power of God; it is God's own energy that lives in his people.

The angel told Mary that the Holy Spirit would overshadow her and produce Jesus in her womb, and it was later confirmed with Joseph: "the child who has been begotten in her is of the Holy Spirit."

If we look through Trinitarian eyes perhaps, we may wonder who Jesus' real father is? Again, the Father and the Holy Spirit are two completely different Persons. If the third Person is the one who came upon Mary, why do we call another, who did not come upon Mary, his Father? Of course, for the non-Trinitarian who understands that the Holy

Spirit is primarily the spirit (power and influence) of God, the Father of Jesus, the matter is easily settled.

In the New Testament, because the Holy Spirit is a personal influence, the literary technique of personification is sometimes employed in its description. The Spirit speaks (John 16:13), teaches (John 14:26), can be outraged (Heb 10:29), can be blasphemed against (Matt 12:32), can be lied to (Acts 5:4), and intercedes (Rom 8:26).

The 'helper' is, in effect, Jesus present with them; the spirit influences his disciples and guides them exactly as Jesus would if he were physically present (John 14:18). F.F. Bruce writes of this other version of Jesus as 'his alter ego.'

Popular theologian Charles Stanley writes that the Father, the Son and the Holy Spirit are:

'all equally omniscient, omnipotent, omnipresent, eternal and unchanging, but each one has unique functions. Scripture shows how each member of the Trinity fulfils His specific role ... each relate to mankind in a different way because He has a specific role. It's very important to understand this distinction' (In Touch Ministries. 16 Feb 2010).

But the Bible ignores a distinction between the

roles and functions of the Spirit and the risen Jesus. The Holy Spirit is called 'The Advocate'[*parakleton*] in John 14:26, and is described as the go-between, interceding on our behalf with God (Rom 8:26-27). But John writes that 'we have an Advocate [*parakleton*] with the father, Jesus Christ the righteous' (1 John 2:1). So which Person is the one Advocate between us and the Father, the third Person or the second Person? Is it both? No, there is only one go-between mediating between mankind and God, and it is specifically the man Jesus, not a non-human third who is distinctively not Jesus: 'For there is one God, and one mediator between God and men, the man Christ Jesus (1Tim 2:5).

In post-ascension Christian thought, the spirit is obviously used interchangeably with Jesus (Rom 8:9-11) but this is often bypassed by orthodox interpreters. In order to maintain the distinction of the Persons of the Trinity, Augustine needed to write: 'The Son is not the Holy Spirit.' But the apostle Paul wrote that 'the Lord [Jesus] is the Spirit' (2 Cor 3:7). Paul does not speculate about the metaphysical distinction of Persons; he does not believe that the spirit is a different Person than Jesus – to him the spirit is the Lord Jesus working through God's power.

There is a serious discrepancy between the

Bible and orthodox interpretation. Orthodoxy teaches a true distinction between three completely different Persons with different roles who share a divine essence. The Athanasian Creed threatens certain damnation for anyone who would confound or confuse the Persons.

A Protestant professor of church history, Cyril Richardson, writes:

'My conclusion, then, about the doctrine of the Trinity is that it is an artificial construct … it produces confusion rather than clarification; and while the problems with which it deals are real ones, the solutions it offers are not illuminating. It has posed for many Christians dark and mysterious statements, which are ultimately meaningless.'

Cyril C. Richardson. *The Doctrine of the Trinity* pp.148-149

Does the Bible really compel us to acknowledge Christ and the Spirit as co-equal God with the Father, as if there were no other sound alternative? No, in the teachings of Christ there is nothing but an undivided and unquestionable monotheism; the Trinity is not the God of Jesus.

The earliest followers of Jesus present him as the one true God's human Son; a uniquely, supernaturally begotten man who was anointed and empowered by God to complete the saving work as God's agent, a man whom God raised from the dead and made the source of salvation for all who would obey him. The God of the Hebrew scriptures is not a peculiar tri-personal being of post-apostolic Trinitarian theology, but the monotheistic personal identity described by the faiths of Unitarian Christians and Jews, the entity whom Jesus exclusively identified as his own God and Father (John 20:17).

Christopher B. Kaiser, in 'The Doctrine of God,' writes, 'The Church's doctrine of the Trinity would seem to be the farthest thing from [Jesus' and the writers of the New Testament] their minds.' And he went on to say, 'if it is even helpful to refer to such a dogma in order to grasp the theology of the New Testament.' We do have a choice – we are not compelled to accept the Trinity dogma.

Trinitarians maintain that Jesus pre-existed as the eternally begotten second Person of the Trinity. Other fellowships who do not accept the Trinity teaching do believe that Jesus did exist before his birth. Some teach he was a high spiritual being as the Jehovah's Witnesses do, while Mormons say that he was the first and greatest of the spirit-sons of God, with Lucifer as his brother. Followers of Herbert W. Armstrong believe that Jesus was the God of the Old Testament – the one who led Israel out of Egypt. I belonged to that group for many years totally convinced that while rejecting the Trinity doctrine of God in three persons I had found the true gospel but I little realised that I had accepted a Binitarian view of God so instead of worshiping the Three eternal beings, I worshipped the Two eternal beings.

Did Jesus literally exist as a person before the world began or in God's foreknowledge, in the mind of God? Both the Messiah and the church existed in God's foreknowledge before they physically existed. Jesus was the 'logos', the 'plan' of God from the beginning and he became flesh when he was conceived. When 2 Tim 1:9 says that each Christian was given grace … before time began, no one tries to prove that we were actually alive with God back then. Everyone acknowledges that we were 'in the mind of God'. The same is true of Jesus. His glory was 'with the Father' before the world began and in John 17:5 he prayed that he would have the glory the Old Testament foretold, which had been in the mind of God before the world began. Jesus was a man; his genesis was at his conception. He was 'made like his brothers in every way …' (Heb 2:17). Jesus 'grew in knowledge and wisdom. Scripture says that Jesus can 'sympathize with our weakness' because he was 'tempted in every way, just as we are ...' (Heb 4:15).

Those who believe that Jesus pre-existed (as I did) often turn to Genesis 1:1, 'In the beginning God created the heaven and the earth,' and point out that the word 'God' is *Elohim*, which is itself a plural form and, like most other words, has more than one definition. It is used in a plural sense of 'gods' or 'men with authority,' and in a singular sense for 'God' or 'a man with authority, such as a judge.' The Hebrew lexicon by Brown, Driver and Briggs, considered to be one of the best available, has as its first usage for *Elohim*: 'rulers, judges, either as divine representatives at sacred places or as reflecting divine majesty and power, divine ones, superhuman beings including God and angels, gods.'

Some teach that the word *Elohim* implies a compound unity when it refers to the true God. That would mean that the word *Elohim* somehow changes meaning when it is applied to the true God so that God can be a compound being. There is no evidence for this. The Jews themselves never understood *Elohim* to imply a plurality in God in any way. Jewish rabbis have debated the Law to the point of tedium and have recorded volumes of notes on the Law, yet in all of their debates there is no mention of a plurality in God. Gesenius, considered a great Hebrew scholar, wrote that the plural nature of *Elohim* was for intensification, and was related to the plural of majesty and used for amplification. He wrote:

'That the language has entirely rejected the idea of numerical plurality in *Elohim* (whenever it denotes one God) is proved especially by its being almost invariably joined with a singular attribute.' God is not compound in any sense of the word. He is the 'one' God of Israel.

When God said, 'Let us make human beings in our image, in our likeness,' Gen 1:26, he was speaking of his divine council or assembly who were spirit beings. The angelic world has a hierarchy.

Throughout the New Testament Jesus is presented as the ideal human being. More than eighty times in the gospels he spoke of himself as the 'son of man.' In the book of Ezekiel, the prophet is described and addressed as 'son of man' ninety-three times, and the phrase was used as a reference to human beings in general. Many have also recognised that Jesus, by referring himself as the son of man linked him to the 'one like a son of man' figure of Daniel 7:13, who is to receive authority and a kingdom from the Ancient of Days.

Jesus also makes the connection with himself to the second lord of Psalm 110:1 and his exaltation to the right hand of God in Matt 26:64. Jesus identifies himself as a human lord who receives from God the right to rule over not only Israel, but all nations.

Psalm 110:1 is the most frequently cited Old Testament verse in the New, being either quoted or alluded to at least 23 times by both Jesus and his disciples.

In Psalm 110:1, King David has assumed the role of prophet and witnesses an interaction between God and the future Messiah:

'The LORD said to my lord: "Sit at my right hand until I make your enemies a footstool for your feet."'

David addresses the Messiah as his lord. Trinitarians claim this as proof of the Trinity saying that in this verse, we can see two 'LORDs' and thus two who are Yahweh. The Hebrew word used for the second lord is *adoni* (pronounced 'Adon nee'). This word is always used in Scripture to describe human masters and lords, but never God. The word *adoni* in all of its 195 occurrences in the Old Testament means a superior who is human (or occasionally angelic), created and not God.

The first LORD of verse 1 is *Adonai* (pronounced

'Adon eye') which is the common stand-in for God's name.

Those listening to Peter on the day of Pentecost would clearly see the correlation in Peter's teaching that Jesus was a "man approved of God" and a created being, the 'my lord' of Psalm 110:1 which Peter quotes in Acts 2:34. The use of *adoni* in that Psalm makes it very clear that the Jews were not expecting their Messiah to be God but were expecting a human 'lord'.

Anthony Buzzard writes in his 'Focus on the Kingdom', 10 Sept 2014, [Psalm 110:1 is] the Bible's supreme proof text for telling the difference between the one God and the Messiah who is not God ... if the Messiah were called Adonai this would introduce 'two Gods' into the Bible and would-be polytheism. Psalm 110:1 should guard us all against supposing that there are two who are God. In fact the Messiah is the supreme human being and agent of the one God. Psalm 110:1 is the Bible's master text for defining the Son of God in relation to the one God, his Father.'

"Behold, the virgin shall be with child, and bear a son, and they shall call his name Immanuel," which is translated, "God with us."

We know that God was with the people in Jesus

the Messiah, and Jesus himself said that if one had seen him, he had seen the Father. The significance of the name is symbolic. God was with those who lived at that time and in that place, not literally, but in his Son. '… that God was in Christ, reconciling the world to himself' (2 Cor 5:19). God was *in* Christ, not God *was* Christ. The name Jesus is from the Greek form of a common Hebrew name, Joshua, derived from *yasha*, "he saves."

Some men brought to him a paralytic, lying on a mat. When Jesus saw their faith, he said to the paralytic, "Son, your sins are forgiven you." And some of the scribes were sitting there and reasoning in their hearts, "Why does this man speak blasphemies like this? Who can forgive sins but God alone?" (Mark 2:5-7)

On several occasions Jesus told the Pharisees that their doctrine was wrong. There is no verse in Scripture that says, 'only God can forgive sins.' That idea came from their tradition. God does grant authority to forgive sins. He granted that authority to his Son and to the apostles.

A frequently cited New Testament passage in support of the Trinity is "Go therefor and make disciples of all the nations, baptizing them in the name of the Father and the Son and the Holy Spirit (Matt 28:19).

While this passage mentions the Father, the Son and the Holy Spirit, it does not, however, teach that these are divisions within God. There is no declaration in this verse that the Father is true God, the Holy Spirit is true God, and the Son is true God, and that all three exist as co-eternal, co-equal members of the same being. If Matthew 28:19 is left as it is, what we have is the instruction of Jesus to baptize in the authority of God, Jesus, and the Holy Spirit.

If the present version of Matthew 28:19 is correct, Jesus' specific instruction seems to have been ignored in favour of baptism only 'in the name of Jesus' Acts 2:38, 8:16,10:48,19:5, Gal 3:27, Rom 6:3 – all was done in the name of Jesus. Does the triune formula's absence evidence an apostolic failure to follow Jesus' instructions or have we encountered what may actually be a textual corruption in Matthew? Eusebius (d.340AD), may provide a glimpse at an earlier version of Matthew 28:19 when he quotes it in his 'Oration of Emperor Constantine' as "Go, and make disciples of all nations <u>in my name</u>." Again, in his 'Church history,' he quotes his manuscript as reading "in my name." This does seem more in alignment with the historical practice of the figures of the New Testament Church. This discrepancy has been noted by many scholars who point to the possibility of later ecclesiastical interpolation; (Tyndale New Testament Commentaries, 1, p.275, Schaff-Herzog Encyclopaedia of Religious Knowledge, p.435, The Anchor Bible Dictionary, vol.1, p.585, F.J. Foakes Jackson & Kirsopp Lake, The Jewish Gentile and Christian Backgrounds, pp.335-337). See 'The God of Jesus' p.344.

Anthony Tyrell Hanson who was Professor of Theology in the University of Hull wrote: 'No responsible New Testament scholar would claim that the doctrine of the Trinity was taught by Jesus, or preached by the earliest Christians, or consciously held by any writer in the New Testament' (The image of the invisible God.p.87).

During an argument with his enemies Jesus says to them, "I assure you. Before Abraham was born, I am" (John 8:58). Trinitarians often explain that Jesus being 'before' Abraham proves that he literally preceded Abraham's birth. Jesus had just said to these critics, "Your father Abraham rejoiced to see my day, and he saw it and was glad." They understood this to mean that Jesus was personally older than Abraham and they said, "You are not yet fifty years old and have you seen Abraham?"

Jesus did not say that he himself had seen Abraham, rather that Abraham had seen his day.

What was this day of the Messiah that Abraham saw? Was Jesus literally alive before their mutual ancestor?

Paul wrote in Gal 3:8 the 'the gospel was preached beforehand to Abraham,' and through faith Abraham 'looked forward' (Heb 11:10). The context in John 8 is God's plan (*logos*) regarding the gospel, and in this sense the Messiah was certainly preeminent.

David and Isaiah both wrote of the sufferings of the Messiah as though they had personally seen them. Peter wrote that the Messiah was foreknown and foreordained before the foundation of the world (1Peter 1:17-21), and even spoke of themselves as each having received grace through Christ's sacrifice before the world began (2 Tim1:9). It is reasonable to see the Messiah's existence before Abraham in John 8 as the future intentions of God. Even the Trinitarian theologian Hugo Grotius viewed that passage as meaning, 'that Jesus was before Abraham in the divine decree.' The reformer and Trinitarian Theodore Beza agrees with that interpretation, saying, 'I do not think that Christ here simply speaks of himself as God, but as he was seen by Abraham with the eye of faith ... otherwise he would not have spoken to the purpose.'

After saying that Abraham looked forward

to him, Jesus added, "Before Abraham was I am." Hearing these words they picked up stones intending to kill him but somehow, he was able to walk away. Was Jesus claiming to be God by saying "I am"? We can sometimes forget that Jesus repeatedly leaves his audience, especially his most antagonistic critics, to founder in their ignorance. For example, when Jesus said to the Jews that they must eat his flesh and drink his blood, his hearers were outraged and perplexed. They took what he said as literal and he did not correct them – even his own disciples were left to wonder at his sayings. His frequent refusal to directly and immediately counter that misunderstanding must be considered here. We are left with his enemies' response – not what he actually said.

Jesus' use of the phrase "I am" (Greek: *ego eimi*) is used by Trinitarians to claim that Jesus was the God of the Old Testament – the One who spoke to Moses from the burning bush. From this verse, it does look plausible, yet we need to take a closer look at Jesus' use of "I am." This Greek phrase is, in reality, the usual way people identify themselves throughout the New Testament.

The traditional translation of the Hebrew in Exodus 3:4 as "I am who I am" is not really the best rendering. The Hebrew literally means "to become" or "to be," therefore the precise wording does not match Jesus' "I am" language in the gospel of John.

The claim is that those listening to what Jesus said would make the link to the burning bush episode and see that Jesus was openly claiming to be the God of Exodus. But if this is true, we have a serious theological problem in the New Testament as many others use the same phrase to describe themselves:

- Judas Iscariot: *"ego eimi"* (Matt 26:25)

- The blind man: *"ego eimi"* (John 9:9)

- Paul of Tarsus: *"ego eimi"* (1 Tim 1:15)

- John the Baptist: *"ego eimi"* (John 1:27)

No one argues that these men were quoting Exodus, much less claiming to be God. The truth is that "ego eimi" is not any sort of divine name; it is simply the Greek for "I am he," or "I am the man," or "I am the one you are speaking about/in question." For example, in John 9:9, the people were looking for the blind man whom Jesus healed, and when they found him some said, "This is he," others said, "He is like him," but he said, "I am he," or "I am the man." Neither the words, 'he' or 'the man' are actually in the text, but the translators understand that they are implied by his use of the simple phrase "ego eimi" (I am). Trinitarian translators have even followed this model with Jesus' other sayings such as John 8:24, "Therefore I said to you that you will die in your sins; for if you do not believe that <u>I am he</u>, you will die in your sins." But when the same phrase appears in John 8:58 their practice shifts to: "I am," in capital letters! Creating the connection with the inadequate, traditional translation of Ex 3:14.

John, early in his gospel, actually demonstrates what Jesus' use of "ego eimi" means. In John 4:25, the Samaritan woman says to Jesus: "I know that the Messiah is coming (who is called Christ). When he comes, he will tell us all things." Jesus said to her, "I who speak to you am he." The Greek in Jesus' answer is "ego eimi" – he means "I am the Messiah you are speaking about." Jesus identifies himself as the Messiah, not as the one God. This is John's stated purpose in writing his gospel (John 20:31).

C.K. Barrett, in his Essays on John, writes, 'It is intolerable that Jesus should be made to say, "I am God, the supreme God of the OT, and being God I do as I am told." Jesus said, "I do nothing on my own initiative, but I speak these things as the Father taught me" (John 8:28).

James Dunn writes, 'There is no thought in any of the passages we have studied of Jesus existing prior to his birth whether as an angel or archangel, a spirit or the Spirit. There is no thought whatsoever of Jesus on earth as the incarnation of an angel or archangel, spirit or Spirit.' *Christology in the Making, p.159.*

John 1:1-3 is, without doubt, the one text that has served as the single greatest source of dispute in the history of the church.

In the beginning was the Word, and the Word was with God, and the Word was God. He was in the beginning with God. All things were made through Him, and without Him nothing was made that was made (NKJV).

In the King James version, the translators have translated the Greek term 'logos' as 'Word'. This is not an incorrect translation but notice that the translators have chosen to capitalize the *W.* Obviously the capitalization of 'Word' is a not-so-subtle attempt at presenting the word/logos as the proper name of a person. The term 'logos' occurs over 300 times in the New Testament, but in translations like the NIV and KJV it is only capitalized 7 times. Not only that, but they disagree with one another on exactly when it should be capitalized – much of it comes down to the translators' personal interpretation.

The 'word' (logos) should not be thought of as a unique Person. The term has a broad scope that has to do with logic or reason and speech or word. Logos is translated 37 different ways by the NASB, including, account, answer, exhortation, message, news, matter, report ... the list goes on. One guide effectively sums up the meaning of 'logos' as 'reasoning expressed by words.' Strong defines it as 'a word (as embodying an idea).'

No lexicon defines 'logos' as 'a person' yet this is what Trinitarians demand the word means in John. One Catholic scholar wondered: 'Why do we instinctively read: 'In the beginning was the Son and the Son was with God'? Dr Brown of Fuller Seminary reminds us that 'to read John 1:1 as if it said, 'In the beginning was the Son' is patently wrong.'

C.J. Wright, in his book 'The Mission and Message of Jesus'p.677 says, 'What we do know is that John was steeped in the Old Testament Scriptures. If we wish to understand the historical ancestry of John's Logos concept as he himself understood it, we have to go back to those Scriptures.'

John, like Jesus, was a committed Jew. John himself wrote passionately to protect the faith from encroaching Hellenistic influences which threatened to destroy the legacy of the human Messiah. In the Hebrew Scriptures, all of creation came into being through God's spoken word. God 'said' and the universe was made. All things came to be by his speech. The Hebrew 'word' (davar) and the Greek 'logos' are synonymous for the Jew – they indicate God's expressed ideas. Dunn writes, 'nowhere either in the Bible or in the extra-canonical literature of the Jews is the word of God a personal agent or on the way to become such.'

Everything had first existed in God's mind or plan. When God finally spoke, his word made all these things manifest. God's wisdom and creative word is personified as a woman in the book of Proverbs. But no worship is offered to wisdom and wisdom had no priests in Israel. Wisdom never became more than a personification of God's own activity. Not one of the 1,400 uses of 'davar' (word) in the Hebrew Bible means a person. But Trinitarians and modern-day Arians contend that John was indeed a great innovator on this point who suddenly and dramatically deviated from the historical, Jewish usage of the word.

John is simply speaking out of his Old Testament

worldview while recruiting a common place term from the culture of his day.

But John did write that the word 'became flesh and dwelt among us' or literally: 'pitched his tent among us.' It is the man Jesus who became God's wisdom. He was a living personification of that principle. John says in his prologue that God's word (or wisdom) 'became flesh' – was embodied or personifies – in the living man Jesus.

The common Trinitarian translation of John 1:3 is: 'All things came into being through Him, and apart from Him nothing came into being that had not come into being.'

Notice the use of the capitalized 'Him' for the logos. The pronoun in John 1:2-3 could (and arguably should) be translated 'it' since no lexicon defines logos as a person. In fact, before the King James Version of 1611, The Tyndale Bible (1535), Matthew (1535), Taverner (1539), Cranmer's (1539), Whittingham (1557), Geneva (1560) and the Bishop's Bible (1568) used the word 'it' instead of 'Him'. God is many things: love, light, spirit, but they are not entities of themselves – they are to do with God's character and his word is part of him – not a separate being.

'He was in the world, and the world was made through Him, and the world did not know Him.'

John 1:10

This verse is a reference to the Father, not to Christ. The context is the section beginning at verse 6, 'There was a man sent from God whose name was John. He came bearing witness of the light, and God's light was shown through Jesus who was 'the light of the world'. Though God was in the world in many ways (Paul wrote to the Romans: 'For since the creation of the world His invisible attributes are clearly seen, being understood by the things that are made, even His power and deity, so that they are without excuse.') including through his Son, the world did not recognise Him. He came to His own by sending his exact image, Jesus the Messiah, to them, but even then, they did not receive God, in that they rejected His emissary.

The 'word' is the wisdom, plan or purpose of God and the word 'became flesh' as Jesus. Thus Jesus was the word in the flesh – human. Scripture is also the word, but it is the word in writing and as the word in writing had a beginning so the word as a human being had a beginning.

Paul writes: 'Yet for us there is but one God, the Father, from whom all things came and for whom we live, and there is but one Lord (*kurios eis*), Jesus Christ, through whom all things came and through whom we live.' This is a long way from the developed Christian creeds of the fourth and fifth centuries.

Trinitarians use Hebrews 1:2 as a proof text that Jesus was active in the creation of the world: 'but in these last days he has spoken to us by his Son, whom he appointed heir of all things, through whom also he made the worlds.' The Greek word translated 'worlds' is the plural of the word *aion*, and actually means 'ages.' There are other Greek words that mean 'world' such as *kosmos* and *oikoumene*, and when the devil tempted Jesus by showing him all the kingdoms of the world, these words are used. This verse is referring to the ages not the world.

Since most translators are Trinitarian and think that Jesus was the one who made the original heavens and earth, they translate ages as world in this verse. It was not Jesus who spoke the creation into being because before Jesus was born God spoke at various times by prophets but only in what the writer of Hebrews calls 'these last days' has God spoken to us through his Son. This, and other verses, show that the Son is subordinate to God. If Christ was God, then he could not be appointed heir of all things. God is the original owner and will give all things to his heir, Jesus.

It is fair to ask in what sense God has made the ages through Jesus. The Greek word *poieo*, translated as made is translated more than 100 different ways in the NIV, and so has a wide range of meanings. Although most people read *poieo* in Hebrews 1:2 as referring to the original creation, yet the context dictates that the 'ages' being referred to are the ages after Christ's resurrection. In verse 2, Christ became heir after his resurrection. In verse 3, he then sat at God's right hand having become so much better than the angels, as he has by inheritance obtained a more excellent name than they (verse 4). The God of Jesus, the Father, established a new power structure when exalted Jesus, a new organization that continues into 'the age to come.' And so the author of Hebrews writes that 'the ages' have been established by God through Jesus; that is, the rearrangement of the heavens and the earth was initiated through the Father's elevation of Jesus to his right hand.

Some Trinitarian theologians portray the Jewish idea of God as underdeveloped or unrealized, treating the Jews like theological children unable to master the concept of the Trinity. The monotheism of Israel, and those who affirmed it (like Jesus), must not be underestimated. Since he was a faithful Jew, even the ultimate Jew, we should not expect to find in Jesus' sayings about his identity a less than clear meaning.

Neither Jesus nor his earliest followers present him as identical to the one true God of Israel, but instead as God's human son; a uniquely, supernaturally begotten man who was anointed and empowered by God to complete the saving work as God's agent, a man whom God raised from the dead and made the source of salvation for all who would obey him. The God of the Hebrew Scriptures is not therefore the tri-personal being of post-apostolic Trinitarian theology, but the monotheistic identity described by the faiths of Unitarian Christians and Jews, the entity who Jesus exclusively identified as his own God and Father.

'For in him (Jesus) God in all in all his fullness chose to dwell.'

Col 1:19.
REB

The Holy Spirit is likewise not a distinct third Person within God, but the power and personal influence of the Father, and in the post New Testament era, also of the glorified Jesus.

'No historical fact is better established, than that the doctrine of one God, pure and uncompounded, was that of the early ages of Christianity; and was among the efficacious doctrines which gave it triumph over the polytheism of the ancients ... Nor was the unity of the Supreme Being ousted from the Christian creed by the force of reason, but by the sword of civil government.'

Thomas Jefferson, 1822

The doctrine of Christ's reign upon earth was at first treated as a profound allegory, was considered by degrees as a doubtful and useless opinion and was at length rejected as the absurd invention of heresy and fanaticism.

Edward Gibbon
The Decline and Fall of the Roman Empire

As the early history of both Donatism and Arianism showed, the decisions of church leaders on matters of the faith were now bound up as never before with the whims and stratagems of secular authority, and the process of framing statements of Christian belief was capable of being powerfully influenced by political interests, often regardless of biblical or spiritual considerations.

Ivor J. Davidson
A Public faith

Part 5

The Judgement and Grace of God

As the train left Barry Dock station on its way to Cardiff Central I looked out of the window and saw painted in large white letters on the slate roof of a house GOD IS LOVE. I saw this message most mornings and evenings until it just became part of the scenery.

In Cardiff I saw a man covered front and back with a sandwich board proclaiming the coming WRATH OF GOD. One message about the love of God and the other his anger. Both were biblical but in one the deity was kind and gentle while the other was extremely violent.

For me this raised the question of could a loving and kind God possibly allow all the wars, disasters and grief to have gone on throughout history and not to have stopped them. An all powerful and loving God surely would have put everything right long ago. It didn't make sense. To my mind it made more sense not to believe in God.

Suffering is perhaps the major question why so

many people understandably reject the belief in a just and loving God.

One lady I knew was advised by her minister to read the book of Job to help her understand suffering. If you can get through all forty-two chapters of Job you might well be disappointed to find that there's no answer within that book to the problem of suffering. When Job lost everything and was covered with painful boils his wife was ready with some helpful advice,

'Are you still holding on to your integrity? Curse God and die!'

'You're talking like a foolish woman,' Job responded, 'shall we accept good from God and not trouble?'

At the end of the story Job's life dramatically improves and the reader (but not Job) knows that an enemy's cruel attempt to get Job to curse God had failed. What the book of Job does show is that to blame Job (as his friends did) was wrong.

His friends took the position that the sooner he 'fessed up' the better it would be for him because if you're suffering, they said, it must be down to your sins.

Yes, we all sin, but suffering can come to us for many reasons apart from our sins.

Sin is falling short of God's standard of living.

Sin causes suffering but much of the suffering people experience isn't their fault. Suffering comes in many ways: crime, abuse, neglect, violence, oppression, loss of freedom, diseases, disabilities, famines, floods, earthquakes, storms, wars, poverty, civil strife, terrorism, mental illness …

On March 24, 2015, Flight 9525, an Airbus A320, took off from Barcelona at 10:01a.m. bound for Dusseldorf. The co-pilot, Andreas Lubitz locked the cabin door when the pilot went to the toilet. The plane then descended rapidly and crashed at 10:31a.m. There were one hundred and forty-four passengers and six crew members on board. Those men, women and children were innocent victims of one man's sin.

Suffering isn't going to end by the efforts of any human government or the work of a church or any combination of churches. The promise made by many pastors, priests and ministers that we'll find everlasting peace and bliss in heaven is a deeply unsatisfactory answer to the problem of suffering and is also an unbiblical teaching that has deceived millions of people.

The earliest biblical record may surprise some as it's not where you would expect the story to begin.

Most Christians hold the belief that when you die you either go to a wonderful loving existence that will last forever or you'll go to a dark place where fire and torture will be your lot for eternity. So if the good people are having a great time in heaven – doing what we may ask – why should they be interested in what's going on with those still on earth? Surprisingly, what's happening on earth after those fortunate ones arrive at their heavenly hotel is of little interest or concern to those whose sights are focused on the wonder and beauty of heaven while avoiding that other place where no one wants to go.

Ask a Christian what's going to happen to earth when all the good people get to heaven and they're likely to say something like this …

'The earth is going to be burnt up and be the home of demons,' or 'We'll be in heaven, so I don't really care what's going to happen to this world,' or, 'After the Rapture (Christians air-lifted to heaven – don't be left behind!) the unselected people will remain on earth to suffer the Great Tribulation.' There've been many innocent people who have not escaped severe persecution in our dark history so why would this latter group escape? Yet, a few Christians have candidly admitted with a shrug of their shoulders that 'It's not clear what will happen.'

We'll come back to the question of what will happen to the earth later, and ask another interesting question; do we really go to heaven? And if we all have an immortal soul, as many believe, where did that teaching come from?

The first 'Star Wars' film began with part four and later three more films arrived to tell us how we got to part four and how the annoying Anakin Skywalker became the lovely (just ask my wife) Darth Vader. Then came 'Rogue One' which dramatically explained how the plans of the Death Star got into the hands of the rebel alliance and from them to Luke Skywalker.

The beginning of a film or a book isn't always the beginning of the story, that's why we get so many prequels. The first two verses of the book of Genesis contain enough space for several prequels but it's not before verse one; it comes between verse one and verse two. Perhaps there should be a wide space there. Here are the two verses:

In the beginning God created the heavens and the earth.

Now the earth was formless and empty, darkness was over the surface of the deep, and the spirit of God was hovering over the waters.

Although many Christians believe that the world is only 6,000 years old a closer reading could and does allow millions, if not billions of years to run their course between verse one and two.

Here's the backstory: The original creation happened at an unknown time long before we get to verse two and the world then was very different from what it is now. There were no humans like us on earth. At some unrecorded time, there was war between spiritual beings (the reason for this war will come shortly) which resulted in destruction for own solar system.

All physical life was destroyed, and the world lay dormant and in darkness for, again, an unknown length of time until God spoke the words, 'Let there be light' and the work of re-creation began.

A footnote in the NIV (New International Version) says the word *was* in verse two (the earth was) can also be read as *became* which would indicate that the earth wasn't originally created as verse two describes it.

The Hebrew words translated as '*without form and void*' or '*formless and empty*' can be translated as *'chaotic and desolate'* or in a state of *'ruin and confusion.'*

The prophet Isaiah wrote, 'For thus says the Lord, who created the heavens, who is the God who formed the earth and made it, who has established it, who did not create it in *vain*, who made it to be inhabited.' The Hebrew word translated as vain is the same word found in Genesis 1:2 as void or chaotic.

We should ask if God created the world in a state of ruin and waste or did something happen to earth to bring all life to an end?

Both Isaiah and Ezekiel wrote about boastful and proud kings. Isaiah wrote of the king of Babylon (chapter 14) and Ezekiel wrote of the king of Tyre (chapter 28). They describe these corrupt kings but within each passage the language turns from a human leader to speak of a person greater than a man – a powerful non-human. Reading from both sections we learn that this entity had been in Eden and was the seal of perfection, full of wisdom and perfect in beauty; this is no human. He is called 'the Day Star' or 'Shinning One' (Isa 14:12). Named 'Lucifer' in the King James Version, who has fallen from heaven and was the son of the morning [star]. This spiritual being said in his heart, 'I'll ascend into heaven, I'll exalt my throne above the stars (angels) of God … I'll be like the Most High.' He was a created being who was a mighty angel – a cherub – these were multiform and awesome creatures (not chubby babbies) who had walked back and forth in the midst of fiery stones. He was perfect in his ways from the day he was created until iniquity was found in him. Both accounts then revert to the human kings and their downfall.

This cosmic war, initiated by a created angel of God who originally was like the bright morning star, resulted in the destruction of much of our solar system and the crater covered planets like Mars and our moon are silent witnesses to the devastation caused by that angelic rebellion.

The 1611 Authorised Version of the Bible has God instructing Adam and Eve to 'replenish' the earth in just the same way he instructed Noah and the other seven survivors of the great flood (Gen 9:1, 1:28). This word, replenish, is not in later translations.

'You send forth your spirit, they are created;
and you renew the face of the earth.'

Psalm 104:30

In chapter three of Genesis we find Adam and Eve in a literal paradise – the word means a beautiful garden or parkland, but they were not alone.

The malignant being that had once been the devoted servant of God had now become his adversary bent on destroying what God had made and now he would pursue his aim of misrepresenting whatever God says. Adam was there listening to what this serpent-like character said to Eve. Derek Kidner's commentary on that passage is helpful.

'The tempter begins with suggestion rather than argument. The incredulous tone – 'So God has actually said …?' is both disturbing and flattering: it smuggles in the assumption that God's word is subject to our judgement. The exaggeration, 'you shall not eat of any tree' is a further and favourite device: dangled before Eve it will draw her into debate on her opponent's terms.

'Eve is duly drawn, and by adding 'neither shall you touch it' she overcorrects the error, magnifying God's strictness (she was to have many successors). After the query, the flat contradiction: 'You shall not die.' It is the serpent's word against God's, and the first doctrine to be denied is judgement. If modern denials of it are very differently motivated, they are equally at odds with revelation: Jesus fully reaffirmed the doctrine.'

'Enter by the narrow gate; for wide is the gate and broad is the way that leads to destruction, and there are many who go in by it.'

Matt. 7:13

Eve thought it over, looked at the fruit again, and reconsidered – she wanted that knowledge and didn't, as she saw it, want to be kept in the dark and in ignorance, so she took it and ate, and it tasted good, so she shared it with Adam who hadn't been misled by the serpent's reasoning: he was deliberately and knowingly disobeying what God had said.

When their maker confronted them with their action the man blamed the woman that God had given him, and the woman blamed the serpent for deceiving her. That didn't help them.

All that was ahead of Adam – rule of the world – a close relationship with his creator, was predicated on obedience to what he was commanded. This glorious future was now lost. Their ideal environment was shut off to them and life now was going to be very difficult and different from what it could have been.

Adam and Eve went on to have two sons, and the elder son, the grandson of God, murdered his brother and brought down on himself a curse. God had earlier warned him: 'Why are you angry and why has your countenance fallen? If you do well, will you not be accepted? And if you do not do well, sin is lurking at the door; its desire is for you, but you must master it.' This warning of the inclination to do wrong, which we can and must control, was lost on Cain. He chose to ignore the warning and humanity has been following in Cain's footsteps ever since.

The apostle Paul, also known as Saul, wrote, 'just as through one man (Adam) sin entered the world, and death through sin, and thus death spread to all men, because all sinned ... therefore, as through one man's offence judgement came to all men, resulting in condemnation ...' Humans, in our natural state, are alienated from God and are his enemies, as well as being spiritually dead because of our sins without ever realising it, which is the outcome of our rejection of him (Rom 5:10,18, Isa 59:2, Eph 2:1, Col 1:21). This is as true today for us as it was for Adam. We're incapable of being reconciled to God by our own efforts and what's worse, we don't even want to.

The apostle John identifies who that serpent is

in the 12th chapter of that highly symbolic book, Revelation:

'And war broke out in heaven: Michael and his angels fought with the dragon; and the dragon and his angels fought, but they did not prevail, nor was a place found for them in heaven any longer. So the great dragon was cast out, that serpent of old, called the devil and Satan, who deceives the whole world; he was cast to the earth, and his angels were cast out with him.'

Revelation 12:7-9

('Slanderer' is the meaning of the Greek word *diabolos*, usually transliterated as 'Devil,' and Satan means 'Adversary' from the Greek Satanas).

There is a thought that many hold that we're all children of God, yet Jesus said to his critics:

'You're of your father the devil, and the desires of your father you want to do. He was a murderer from the beginning, and doesn't stand in the truth, because there's no truth in him. When he speaks a lie, he speaks from his own resources, for he is a liar and the father of lies' (John 8:44).

The Christadelphians, who rightly look forward to the return of [the] Christ don't, however, believe in a literal devil – 'he doesn't exist' they say, while the Jehovah Witnesses, who also look forward to an earthly kingdom of God, believe that Jesus was the brother of Lucifer. 'Jesus,' they say, 'was Michael the archangel in his pre-existent life.'

Most Christians believe that Jesus is God – which is a unity of three co-eternal Persons (a doctrine that became state law in the late 4th century) but a minority do not believe that Jesus existed before his birth.

The Council of Chalcedon declared in November 451:

'*Therefor, following the holy fathers, we confess and all with one voice teach our Lord Jesus Christ to be one and the same Son, the same perfect in Godhead, the same perfect in manhood, truly God and truly man ...born of the Virgin Mary, the Theotokos* (mother of God), *acknowledged in two natures, without confusion, without change, without division, without separation; the distinction of the natures being in no way abolished because of the union but rather the characteristic property of each nature being preserved and concurring into one person and one substance, not as if Christ was parted or divided into two persons but one and the same Son and only begotten God, Word, Jesus Christ ...*'

Couldn't be clearer! Yes, it could: Jesus had one nature, not two. He was one person with one mind and one will, and was not God, but a descendent of King David. His birth was by a miracle, as was Adam but Adam lost everything through disobedience while Jesus regained everything through obedience. 'Adam was a type of him who was to come' (Rom 5:14b), 'The first man Adam became a living being. 'The last Adam became a life-giving spirit' (1Cor 15:45). On the day of Pentecost Peter said that 'Jesus was a man accredited by God to you by miracles, wonders and signs, which God did among you through him … (Acts 2:22).

Cain allowed his misplaced emotions to harden him for the act of killing his brother. John wrote, 'Whoever hates his brother is a murderer, and you know that no murderer has eternal life residing in him' (1John 3:15). James wrote that 'each one of us is tempted when we're drawn away by our own desires and enticed. Then when desire has conceived it gives birth to sin, and sin, when it's full-grown, gives birth to death' (James 1:14-15).

The early history of man, much like today, is summed up as God seeing 'that every intent of the thoughts of men's hearts was only evil all the time … the earth was corrupt in God's sight and was full of violence' (Gen 6:5,11. Unlike the wars of today which we see in graphic and horrific detail, we know nothing of those prehistoric conflicts.

Right now, we can see and read, in photographic detail, the terrible sufferings of people around the world, but even though we can't comprehend the enormity of each person's grief and pain, this is the tragic world we live in. There are no detailed records in existence of what humanity experienced in those earliest of times, but their suffering and cruelty was as real then as it is today.

Winston S. Churchill wrote an article in 1925 called 'Shall we all commit suicide?' The first line is: 'The story of the human race is war. Except for brief and precarious interludes, there has never been peace in the world; and before history began, murderous strife was universal and unending.'

Mankind was made to be like God, but they became the children of the serpent because they listened to his lie that God didn't really mean what he said. God responded to the corruption and violence as a parent whose heart was broken by the behaviour of his children to the extent that he regretted making humans and he decided all life on earth except for one family who listened and acted on what he said.

The regret and grief of God will be encountered later in this account. The creator God isn't without strong feelings. Judgement on evil is a consistent teaching in both testaments. Paul, in writing to the Galatians says, 'Don't be deceived, God isn't mocked; for whatever a man sows, that will he also reap'.

The history of the Israelites clearly demonstrates that God deals impartially with all people, no matter who they are. Moses experienced at first hand the rebellious nature of those who were called 'God's people'. Amongst the last things Moses wrote was an accurate evaluation of what the future prospects for Israel were:

'For I know that after my death you'll become utterly corrupt and turn aside from the way which I've commanded you. And evil will befall you in the latter days, because you'll do evil in the sight of the Lord, to provoke him to anger through the work of your hands.'

Deuteronomy 31:29

God never forced anyone to obey him; it was, and still is, a matter of choice. For most of church history that choice has been absent. All the groups and individuals who didn't agree with the church authorities, whether Catholic or Protestant, were persecuted, along with the Jews.

A good example, and there are many, is the Anabaptist movement which began in 1523 and what they courageously taught was closer to New Testament teaching than what the orthodox churches taught. Here's an extract from Nick Page's book 'A nearly Infallible History of the Reformation':

'As they (a number of reformers) made their way through the book of Acts they worked out what conversion looked like. First you had preaching, then preaching led to repentance, repentance led to faith, and faith led to baptism, Boom. Tick all the boxes and you were in. But then they looked at the church and saw that it wasn't doing things in that order at all. In their four-step programme to How to Become a Proper Christian, baptism came last, after you heard and believed the message. But in the Church, infants were baptised, and they hadn't even done step one – which involved staying awake and listening to a sermon – let alone all the repenting stuff …While these (Anabaptist leaders) were in prison, the government of Zürich clamped down even further. The Council decreed that anyone who continued to perform unauthorised baptisms would be executed.'

Page 204-205

Meic Pearse's book 'The Great Restoration' is an in-depth study of the Anabaptist movement. Martin Luther said on them in his introduction to his commentary on the letter to the Galatians:

'Who cannot see here in the Anabaptists, not men possessed by demons, but demons themselves possessed by worse demons?'

Antisemitism was present from the beginning of the church and throughout its history. Kegan Chandler writes in his book 'The God of Jesus' 'It was at this time (early 4th century) that conditions rapidly began to deteriorate for Jews living in the Roman Empire because of Christian theological dogmas that fuelled an antipathy towards Judaism and things Jewish. The eventual passage of Church and State codified ordinances such as the Justinian Code would not only prohibit Jewish worship like the recitation of Jesus' own *Shema* confession (see Mark 12:29) but would strip away even the most basic of civil rights ...There was an active push to separate Christians from the unique God of the Jews.'

pp. 264-266

Getting back to Moses – in his last message to the people he said:

'I call heaven and earth as witnesses today against you, that I've set before you, life and death, blessing and cursing; therefore choose life, that both you and your descendants may live; that you may love the Lord your God, that you may obey his voice, and that you may cling to him, for he is your life and the length of your days; and that you may live in the land which God swore to your fathers, to Abraham, Isaac and Jacob, to give them' (Deut 30:19-20).

The emphasis and encouragement of these words is to listen and obey – God isn't passive or indifferent – he desires our wellbeing yet, at the same time, it's our choice, and the stark reality of what's at stake was clearly laid out – to live or die. 'Do I take any pleasure in the death of the wicked?' God says, 'Rather, am I not pleased when they turn from their ways and live?' (Ezek 18:23)

In the second letter from Peter he writes about what seems like a very long time in waiting for God to intervene, 'The Lord isn't slow in keeping his promise, as some understand slowness. He's patient with you, not wanting anyone to perish, but everyone to come to repentance.' Jesus said, 'unless you repent you too will perish' (Luke 13:3,5). We'll perish if we don't repent (change our heart and mind) but God doesn't want anyone to choose the wrong way.

The biblical record continues to follow, in detail, everything they did after the death of Moses. After the next generation died it all fell apart. They lived as though they knew nothing of what had happened before them. Their history was either ignored or forgotten by a leaderless nation.

They served the gods known as Baal and Ashtoreth.

Then, when they experienced the oppression of being ruled over by other nations they begged God to rescue them and because God had pity on them he did send individuals – leaders – who restored order to them. But once the people felt safe again they reverted to the same gods that got them into the oppression that they had begged God to get them out of.

These individuals were called Judges but they were nothing like the judges we have today. One whole book covers the period when they lived – it could be subtitled 'It gets worse'.

The tragic downward spiral of rebellion, repentance, rescue, peace for a number of years and a return to rebellion continued for a long time until God said to them, 'When the Egyptians, the Amorites, the Ammonites, the Philistines, the Sidonians, the Amalekites and the Midianites oppressed you and you cried to me for help, did I not save you from their hands? But you've forsaken me and served other gods so I'll no longer save you. Go and cry out to the gods you've chosen – let them save you when you're in trouble!' (Judges 10:11-16)

Then they got rid of the foreign gods among them and served the Lord as he (God) could no longer bear to see Israel suffer.

But they had repented before, or had gone through the physical motions of removing idols, but still went back to them when conditions improved. God's compassion rises not from their repentance but the misery and suffering they were going through. Repentance is important, 'Repent' Jesus said, for the Kingdom of God is near.' The same words John the Baptist used.

The prophet Joel wrote, 'Even now, return to me with all your heart, with fasting and weeping and mourning. Rend your heart and not your garments. Return to the Lord your God, for he is gracious and compassionate, slow to anger and abounding in love, and he relents from sending calamity. Who knows? He may turn and have pity and leave behind a blessing – grain offerings and drink offerings for the Lord your God.' (Joel 2:12-14)

Isaiah wrote, 'In all their distress he too was distressed.' (Isa 63:9)

Dale Ralph Davis writes in his commentary on Judges, 'That is why we have this seeming tension between judgement and grace in Scripture, a tension not merely in the texts of Scripture but in the character of Yahweh himself, for he is the God whose holiness demands he judge his people yet whose heart moves him to spare his people. If it is a tension, its origin is in the bosom of God himself. 'He could bear Israel's suffering no longer.' Many Christians, especially those who have a lively sense of God's severity but little of his kindness, should meditate on this text. You must see Yahweh's heart. And don't forget where he showed it to you: in the Old Testament, the book of the grace of God'. (pp. 136-137)

There was a man named Elkanah and he had two wives. One was Peninnah, who had children, and Hannah, who didn't. Peninnah made life uncomfortable for Hannah, no doubt because Elkanah loved Hannah and gave more to her than he did for Peninnah even though she bore him no children.

Each year they travelled to Shiloh to worship and sacrifice to God. The priest at Shiloh was Eli, his two sons, Hophni and Phinehas served there but they were only interested in what they could get from their position – extra chunks of prime meat from the animals that people had sacrificed and any woman that they could seduce – you could say that it didn't put the ministry in a good favourable light as everyone knew about it. This annual visit was used by Peninnah as a good time for making Hannah even more miserable than she normally was. While they were there the provoking got worse and an increasingly sad Hannah went off her food.

'Hannah,' asked her husband, 'you're not eating and you're crying – what's wrong – aren't I better than ten sons?' He might have phrased the question better. She got up and walked out.

Hannah came to the enclosure that contained the ark of the covenant which was hidden away in a separate part of the tented area.

She stopped at the entrance near to where Eli was sitting and began praying. Her lips were moving although she couldn't be heard, and tears were running down her cheeks. Eli looked at her and thought that she had too much to drink.

'O Lord of Hosts,' she said, 'look at what I'm going through and give me, your servant, a boy, then I'll give him to you for all of his life ... no razor will cut his hair ...'

'How long have you been drunk?' Eli interrupted her. 'Get rid of your drink!'

'No, my lord, I'm sorrowful – I've not been drinking – I've been pouring out my trouble to God.'

'Go in peace,' Eli said, 'and the God of Israel grant your petition.'

Hannah felt a weight lift from her and went back and had some food.

The next morning, they packed up and returned to Ramah.

Shortly after she conceived and had a son. They named him Samuel which means 'Heard by God.' How Peninnah reacted isn't recorded.

The same time the following year the family went to Shiloh, but Hannah stayed at home deciding to wait until the boy was on to solid food and then take him to Eli. Elkanah agreed with her.

When the time came she took the boy and a bull, some flour and a skin of wine and brought him to the house of God at Shiloh. The bull was slaughtered, and the boy brought to Eli. She had to remind Eli who she was and when he remembered she said that now she's here she would hand over the boy to his care for as long as he lives.

Hannah then prayed:

'My heart rejoices in the Lord; in the Lord my strength is increased.

I'll boast over my enemies because I delight in your rescue.

There's no-one holy like the Lord; there's no-one beside you;

There's no rock like our God.

Stop talking proudly and arrogantly because God knows and he weighs what we do,

The bows of the warriors are broken but those who stumbled are armed with strength.

Those who are full hire themselves out for food but those who were hungry hunger no more.

She who was barren has borne seven children but she who has had many sons pines away.

The Lord brings death and makes alive; he brings down to the grave and raises up.

The Lord sends poverty and wealth; he humbles and he exalts.

He raises the poor from the dust and lifts the needy from the ash

Heap; he seats them with princes and has them inherit a throne of Honour.

For the foundations of the earth are the Lord's; upon them has he set

The world.

He will guard the feet of his saints, but the wicked will be silenced in darkness.

It is not by strength that one prevails; those who oppose the Lord will be shattered.

He will thunder against them from heaven; the Lord will judge the ends of the earth.

He will give strength to his king and exalt the horn of his anointed.'

1 Samuel 2:1-10

Both judgement and grace, kindness and severity.

Samuel grew and served God at Shiloh. Each year Hannah made him a little robe and took it to him when she went up with her husband to offer the annual sacrifice. Eli would bless Elkanah and his wife saying, 'May the Lord give you children by this woman to take the place of the one she prayed for and gave to the Lord.' Then they would go home to Ramah.

Hannah conceived and eventually she had three sons and two daughters (after Mary, known as Miriam, had Jesus, known as Joshua, she went on to have James, Joseph, Judas and Simon, and at least two daughters).

An unnamed man of God came to Eli and said, 'Why do you and your sons scorn my sacrifice and offering that I prescribed for this place where the ark of the covenant is? Why do you honour your sons more than me by fattening yourselves on the choice parts of every offering made by my people Israel? I promised that your house and your father's house would serve me forever – not anymore – those who honour me I will honour but those who despise me will be rejected … and what happens to your two sons, Hophni and Phinehas, will be a sign to you – they'll both die on the same day and I'll raise up for myself a faithful priest who will do according to what's in my heart.'

(Eli had talked to his sons about their abuse of the people by their greed and immorality but they didn't listen to him and he didn't remove them from their positions of authority)

There was a battle between Israel and the Philistines and Israel lost 4,000 men. They couldn't understand why that had happened – after all, they were God's people – weren't they? Desperate times deserve desperate measures so they decided that they would remove the ark of the covenant from its enclosure and take it to where the army was encamped. That seemed a good idea; God is on our side – we have his furniture! What could go wrong? There the sons of Eli took care of the ark. Success was assured.

When the ark arrived there was such a loud shout from the soldiers that the Philistines heard it and when they learned what the reason was for the noise they said, 'A god has come into the camp! They've got the mighty gods with them that rescued from the Egyptians – what chance do we have?'

'Be strong Philistines,' one of their leaders spoke up, 'conduct yourselves like men, unless you want to become slaves of the Hebrews! Be men and fight!'

The Philistines fought and Israel lost. 30,000 men of Israel were killed including Hophni and Phinehas. And the ark of the covenant was captured.

A survivor from the battle arrived back in Shiloh and went to Eli, who was then 98 years old and blind. The whole town was in an uproar at the news. 'What happened?' asked Eli, 'Israel ran from the Philistines and the army has suffered terrible loses ... and your two sons are dead ... and the ark of God has been captured.

When Eli heard this, he fell backwards off his chair and broke his neck. He had led Israel for forty years.

Eli's daughter in law, the wife of Phinehas, was pregnant and when she heard all that had happened, she went into labour and gave birth, but was overcome by her labour pains and as she was dying the women attending her said, 'Don't despair – you've given birth to a son,' but she didn't respond yet was able to name the boy Ichabod, which means *no glory*. Her last words were, 'the glory has left Israel ... because the ark of God is captured.'

The ark of God was to remain with the Philistines for seven months before being sent back into Israel – but that's another story – back to Samuel.

Samuel continued as judge over Israel for all of his life. When he was old he appointed his two sons as judges but they didn't follow his example. They were dishonest, accepted bribes and perverted justice. Again, the people knew all too well what they were up to and demanded an end to the system of judges. 'We want a king to lead us just like all the other nations have.'

Long before this moment God had foreseen this eventuality and had told Moses to write:

'When you're settled in the land God has given you and you decide to have a king just like the nations around you be sure to appoint a king that God chooses. He must be an Israelite and shouldn't multiply war horses or make the people return to Egypt to get more of them. He mustn't accumulate wealth for himself, neither must he take many wives, or his heart will be led astray. When he becomes king, he is to write for himself a copy of this law and it's to be with him and he's to read it every day of his life so that he'll learn to highly respect and honour his God and follow carefully this law and these decrees and not consider himself better than his fellow Israelites. And if he does this, he and his descendants will reign a long time.'

And so, every king over Israel obeyed these wise instructions and peace and prosperity followed Israel throughout their history ... hold up! This isn't a happy ending story – that's not what happened.

Samuel was hurt to hear what the people wanted but God said to him, 'Listen to what they're saying, it's not you they're rejecting, but me. They've always been this way – forsaking me and serving other gods – warn them and let them know what the king who will reign over them will do.' Samuel told them in detail that their king will oppress them, and they'll regret ever asking for one.

But the people didn't listen.

'No, we want a king over us – then we'll be like all the other nations – with a king to lead us and take us into battle.'

'Give them a king,' God told Samuel.

Easily said, but how was Samuel to do it?

A Benjamite named Kish losing his donkeys was the first step.

Kish sent his son (a good-looking man taller than most people) and a servant to go and find those donkeys. They travelled for some distance but couldn't find them so Kish's son said, 'Right, let's get back, or my father will start worrying more about us than the donkeys.'

The servant remembered that a man of God lived in the town they were close to and suggested that they ask him which way to go. 'That's fine, but what can we give him – the food's run out and we don't have a gift to give him,'

'I've got some money,' the servant said, 'I'll give it to the man of God.'

'Good, let's go.'

On their way into town they met some girls coming out to draw water, so they asked them, 'Is the prophet here?'

'He is, he's ahead of you,' they answered, 'be quick because he's going up to the high place where the people will make a sacrifice and then they'll be eating there. The prophet is going to bless the sacrifice first.'

As they entered the town, they saw a man walking towards them, 'Can you tell me where the prophets house is?'

'That's me,' Samuel answered.

'Go ahead to the high place – you're going to eat with me today and in the morning I'll tell you all you need to know, and by the way, those donkeys you lost three days ago, don't worry about them, they've been found. All that Israel desires is now focused on you and your family.'

Open mouthed and a shiver running up his back the young man gulped and said, 'But I belong to the smallest tribe in Israel … and my clan is the least of all the clans of Benjamin … why do you say such a thing to me?'

(The day before, Samuel received a message from God, 'About this time tomorrow I'll send you a man from the tribe of Benjamin. Anoint him leader of my people Israel – he'll deliver my people from the Philistines. I have looked on my people, for their cry has reached me.')

Donkeys lost, and a leader found.

Samuel seated the young man whose name was Saul, and his servant, at the top table in the hall and said to the cook, 'Bring the piece of meat I gave you – the one I told you to lay aside.' The cook brought the cooked leg with what was on it and placed it in front of Saul.

'This has been saved for you,' Samuel said, 'eat up.'

Later that evening, under a starry sky, Saul and Samuel talked on the roof of his home, and at daybreak Samuel called to Saul, 'Get ready, I'll send you on your way.' When they had packed, the three of them went out together and Samuel asked

Saul to send his servant on ahead as he wanted to pass on a message for Saul from God.

To Saul's surprise Samuel took a flask of oil and poured the lot over Saul's head and as he stood there dripping oil Samuel said, 'Hasn't the Lord anointed you leader over his inheritance?' He then outlined various people and circumstances that Saul would encounter that day as signs that the anointing was valid. 'Once these signs are fulfilled do whatever you need to do because God is with you.'

Everything that Samuel said would happen did happen – Saul became a changed man that day. People began to say, 'What's happened to the son of Kish? Is Saul among the prophets?' When Saul got back home his uncle asked him, 'Where have you been?'

'Looking for the donkeys … when we couldn't find them we went to Samuel.'

'And what did Samuel say?'

'He told us the donkeys have been found – that's all.'

Samuel summoned the people to gather at Mizpah (a short distance from Samuel's home town of Ramah) to publicly select the new king. But first

Samuel needed to tell them some hard truths that they probably didn't want to hear:

'This is what the Lord, the God of Israel says, 'I brought Israel out of Egypt and saved you from all those who oppressed you.' 'But now you've rejected your God – who saves you from all your calamities and distresses and you've said, 'No! Set a king over us.' Now present yourselves before the Lord by your tribes and clans.'

Eliminating the other tribes, Benjamin was chosen by lot, next, the clan of Matri was chosen, finally it came down to the son of Kish – but where was he? They looked for him but couldn't find him. Had he decided that the position of king wasn't for him or was he just delayed in getting to Mizpah? They asked Samuel and God told him that Saul was hiding among the baggage. They ran and brought him out and there he was; standing a head taller than all the others and Samuel said, 'Do you see the man God has chosen? There's no-one like him among the people.'

'Long live the King!' the people shouted.

Samuel explained the regulations of the kingship and that those laws should eliminate tyranny and the abuse of power because the king would be in submission to the law of God (without obedience it all falls apart. Over a thousand years later Jesus was to say, 'Therefore everyone who hears these words of mine and puts them into practice is like a wise man who built his house on a rock …'). Then the people were dismissed.

A short time later Saul was confirmed as king in Gilgal (very near Jericho) and Samuel uses that occasion to give a speech – a farewell speech in which he replays their history, which doesn't sound too good and in it he says, '… but when you saw that Nahash king of the Ammonites was moving against you and you said, 'We want a king to rule over us,' even though the Lord your God was your king. Now here is the king you've chosen, the one you asked for. If you fear the Lord and serve and obey him and don't rebel against his commands and if both you and the king who reigns over you follow the Lord your God – good! But if you don't obey the Lord and if you rebel against his commands, his hand will be against you, as it was against your fathers … As for me, far be it from me that I should sin against the Lord by failing to pray for you – and I'll teach you the way that's good and right. But be sure to fear the Lord and serve him faithfully with all your heart; consider what great things he's done for you. Yet if you persist in doing evil, both you and your king will be swept away.'

Saul didn't follow what God told him through Samuel and it came to the point that God said to Samuel, 'I'm grieved that I made Saul king, because he's turned away from me and hasn't carried out my instructions.'

Samuel was troubled, and he cried out to the Lord all that night. The next morning, after learning where Saul was, he confronted him with his rebellion and arrogance and that as he had rejected what God told him that God had rejected him as king.

'I've sinned,' Saul said, 'I violated the Lord's command and your instructions ... I was afraid of the people, so I gave into them. Now I beg you, forgive my sin and come back with me so that I may worship the Lord.'

'I'll not go back with you,' Samuel replied, 'You've rejected the word of the Lord, and the Lord has rejected you as king over Israel.' As Samuel turned to leave Saul caught hold of the hem of his robe and tore it. Samuel said, 'The Lord has torn the kingdom of Israel from you today and has given it to one of your neighbours – to one better than you. He who is the glory of Israel doesn't lie or change his mind – he's not a man, that he should change his mind.'

I've sinned,' Saul repeated, 'but please honour me before the elders of my people and before Israel; come back with me so that I may worship the Lord your God.' Samuel went back with Saul, and Saul worshipped the Lord. (for all the details see 1 Samuel 15)

Samuel then left for Ramah, but Saul went up to his hometown in Gibeah. Mary J. Evans gives a helpful insight to that situation in her commentary on Samuel:

'God is never portrayed as separate from his creation or his people, dispassionately observing what is going on. Saul's failure brought God great pain. For Samuel, apparently learning of Saul's disobedience directly from God, the news brought a troubled and sleepless night. His extended, broken-hearted praying only confirmed what he already knew, that Saul was going to come under the judgement of God. He probably remembered another sleepless night when as a young child he had to bring the message of judgement to Israel's leader.' (see 1 Samuel 3)

Samuel never saw Saul again, though he did mourn for him. And the Lord was grieved that he had made Saul king over Israel.

God had grieved and regretted making mankind

in the Genesis account of their nonstop corrupt and violent behaviour. So he destroyed them all except for eight people. Between the time Israel left Egypt and entered Canaan they had almost continually rebelled and complained about God and it grieved him to the point where he came close to destroying them all except for the few that did trust him. In fact, that's what he did do – of all the Israelites who left Egypt who were twenty years old or over only two of them (Joshua and Caleb) finally entered the promised land. (see Numbers 14 and Psalm 78)

For those who think that when Jesus came all that anger and grieving was over, they need to realise that Jesus felt exactly the same way towards those who were critical and resistant to what he was doing.

In one of his frequent visits to the synagogue some of those present were watching him closely to see if he would dare, as they saw it, break the Sabbath by healing a man with a shrivelled hand. Jesus asked the man to stand up in front of them, so this wasn't going to be handled discreetly after the service in perhaps in a private place – this action of Jesus was confrontational.

'Which is lawful on the Sabbath; to do good or to do evil, to save life or to kill?' Their unspoken answer was to kill anyone who would defy their historic tradition. They didn't say a word.

Jesus looked round at them in anger and deeply distressed at their stubborn hearts said to the man, 'Stretch out your hand,' and when he did it his hand was completely healed. Did that soften their hearts and bring joy to them that such a great miracle had happened before their very eyes? These religious leaders then left the building and plotted with others how they could kill Jesus.

The next king, after Saul, was the most famous of all Israel's kings, David. He was promised that his son, Solomon, would build a house for God – which turned out to be an incredibly costly one and that meant high taxes for the people.

When Solomon's son decided, against the advice of the elders, to raise taxes even higher the House of Israel (the northern tribes) split from the southern tribes (Judah). It was no longer a united nation but a divided one and very often they were at war against each other – Jews against Israel and Israel against the Jews.

The majority of the succeeding kings, of both north and south, re-established the pagan deities as the gods to be worshipped. Eventually the northern kingdom was taken into captivity by the Assyrians and about 130 years later the southern kingdom of Judah were also taken into captivity by the Babylonians.

70 years later, as Jeremiah foretold, many of the Jews returned to the difficult work of rebuilding the temple. When it was finished some who had seen the first temple cried because they remembered its splendour.

Throughout the history of those kings, prophets were sent from God to warn the leadership to turn their lives around and do what was right, but they didn't listen. The prophets also spoke of a greater David whose rule would never end (Isa 9:7), and that he would sit on the throne of David (Jer 23:5, 33:15). This shepherd king David will feed them (Ezek 34:23-24,37:24-25).

The apostle Paul, while speaking in the synagogue at Antioch said:

'... After that he (God) gave them judges until Samuel the prophet, and afterwards they asked for a king, so God gave them Saul, a man of the tribe of Benjamin, for forty years. After removing Saul, he made David their king, of whom he said, 'I've found David, son of Jesse, a man after my own heart, who will do my will.' From this man's descendants God has brought to Israel the Saviour Jesus, as he promised.' (Acts 13:20-23)

When young Mary was calm enough to hear what the angel said. (it's not every day a supernatural alien being stands in your living room and says 'hello') She heard the words:

'You'll conceive and have a son and his name will be Jesus (Joshua), He'll be great and will be called the son of the Highest and the Lord God will give him the throne of his father David and he will reign over the House of Jacob for ever and his Kingdom will never end.'

That '*His Kingdom will never end*' has a connection with what God told David through Nathan; speaking of Solomon when he said, 'I'll be his father and he shall be my son and I'll not take my mercy away from him, as I took it from Saul. And I'll establish him in my house and in my kingdom forever, and his throne shall be established for ever.' Which also ties in with what Daniel saw in vision:

'In my vision at night I looked, and there before me was one like a son of man, coming with the clouds of heaven. He approached the Ancient of Days and was led into his presence. He was given authority, glory and sovereign power; all nations and peoples of every language worshipped him. His dominion is an everlasting dominion that will not pass away and his Kingdom is one that will never be destroyed.' (Daniel 7:13-14)

However, what Jesus did wasn't what the people expected. Nick Page in his book 'The Wrong Messiah' writes:

'Views differed about what, exactly, a messianic kingship might be like – some saw it as a restoration of the House of David, others as a return to political independence as had been enjoyed under the Maccabees. To the peasant masses it must have symbolised a rule of justice and equality. But all these differing views assumed that it meant kicking out the Romans'. Nick Page goes on to say, 'Whatever Judaism you espoused, Jesus failed his messianic exam in every module he took. The Messiah was expected to purge the pagans from the land, but he had been killed by them. The Messiah was supposed to renew the temple, but the temple party had caused his downfall. The Messiah was supposed to bring in the new age, but life was much the same as it had ever been.

'He had been beaten and humiliated, spat upon, scourged, bloodied, mocked and finally killed. He had been a great teacher. A miracle worker. A prophet, certainly. But not the Messiah.

That was simple delusion. And yet, consistently, determinedly, in the face of ostracism, ridicule and persecution, Jesus' followers claimed that they were right, that Jesus was the Messiah.

'Why? Because he had come back from the dead.'

To the two men on the road to Emmaus, Jesus said, 'How foolish you are, and how slow to believe all that the prophets have spoken. Did not the Messiah have to suffer these things and then enter his glory? And beginning with Moses and all the prophets, he explained to them what was said in all the scriptures concerning himself.'

As well as the general public, even his closest disciples didn't realise that Jesus was going to suffer and be killed. That's why when that horrendous event happened his followers couldn't understand why God had allowed Jesus to die. They were broken hearted and afraid of what would happen next.

And just as he had explained to the two on the road, without them realising who he was, it was time for the rest of the disciples to understand as well. The one thing they didn't expect was to see Jesus again. They'd locked themselves in and there he was standing in the middle of the room saying,

'Shalom!' The shock was too much for them and they were terrified. It took a little time for them to settle, after all, he hadn't disappeared, he was still there – the man that was dead a few days before!

After eating some food most were convinced that it was a real person and they were ready to listen to him, 'This is what I told you while I was still with you. Everything must be fulfilled that is written about me in the law of Moses, the prophets and the psalms.' Then he opened their minds so that they could understand the scriptures, 'This is what is written: The Messiah will suffer and rise from the dead on the third day, and repentance and forgiveness of sins will be preached in his name to all nations, beginning at Jerusalem ...'

At their last meeting with the resurrected Jesus the disciples were understandable keen to know when the promised Kingdom of God would arrive, 'Lord, are you at this time going to restore the Kingdom to Israel?'

'It's not for you to know the times or dates the Father has set by his own authority, but you'll receive power when the Holy Spirit comes on you and you'll be my witnesses in Jerusalem and in all Judea and Samaria, and to the ends of the earth.'

After he had said those words they saw him

leave the ground and ascend into the sky until he was hid from their view by the clouds. As they were looking up two men in white stood by them, 'Men of Galilee, why are you standing here looking into the sky? This same Jesus, who's been taken from you into heaven will return in the same way you've seen him leave.'

Liberation for the whole world is coming – it's just a lot longer coming than anyone thought. The world continues in wars, famines, earthquakes, murders and grief of all kinds while many Christians celebrate as though God's Kingdom were already here, but it's not. We need to remember that Jesus said, 'Blessed are those who mourn …' because this world is still in the grip of the enemy of mankind (1John 5:19) and it's seen in the horrors and extreme difficulties that many are experiencing right now. People are called into that future Kingdom now, and have been since the beginning, but that Kingdom, or Empire, isn't here yet – there is worse to come, so it's premature to jump up and down in celebration now.

When Jesus was here he released many people from suffering no matter what the causes were. But that was for a limited time in one small area of the earth. In the age to come all the causes of suffering will be removed – until that time Christians are to urgently and repeatedly ask for that Kingdom to come so that God's perfect will for all people can be done.

As the Messiah will return and end all wars and conflict what reason would there be in going to heaven? Jesus will be here, on earth. The dead 'sleep' in death until they're resurrected, 'Multitudes who sleep in the dust of the earth will awake …' (Dan 12:2). '[the] Christ has indeed been raised from the dead, the firstfruits of those who have fallen asleep. For since death came through a man (Adam) the resurrection of the dead comes also through a man. For as in Adam all die, so in [the] Christ all will be made alive, but each in his own turn: [the] Christ, the firstfruits, then, when he comes, those who belong to him …' (1Cor 15: 20-23).

Resurrection is the dominate theme in the New Testament – not going to heaven. First, the resurrection of Jesus, next, the resurrection of those who belong to God, after that, the resurrection of all humanity. Unfortunately, the ancient Greek philosophical teaching of the immortality of the soul has been, from the early church fathers on, grafted into mainstream Christian thinking. This belief in an immortal soul has greatly muddied the water and almost air-brushed the resurrection out of the picture. If, as is traditionally taught, you're experiencing eternal bliss in heaven what need, or reason is there for a resurrection? How will you be awakened from death (John 5:28, John 11:11) if you're already awake?

Death is presented, in both Testaments, as sleeping and importantly having no consciousness or awareness of the passage of time – until they're woken at the resurrection – either the first or the second. Heaven does hold the Christian's reward, but It'll only be received on that day, when the Messiah returns to earth (2 Tim 4:8, 1 John 2:28, 3:2, Isa 40:10, 62:11, 1 Peter 1:4-5, Rev 22:12).

Just as the traditional teaching of going to heaven is a distortion of what the Bible teaches so is the teaching on hell a serious misrepresentation of the character of God – it's Satan who would torture humans for an eternity. When God 'condemned the cities of Sodom and Gomorrah by burning them to ashes, [he] made them an example of what is going to happen to the ungodly (2 Peter 2:6).

In the last book of the old Testament Malachi writes, 'Surely the day is coming; it will burn like a furnace. All the arrogant and every evildoer will be stubble, and that day that is coming will set them on fire.' Anything that's thrown into a furnace is reduced to ashes.

If you find yourself in heaven and are surprised not to see anyone else there, please remember that they're on earth working under the Messiah in restoring the earth to what it should be. And if you find yourself in a very dark and hot place being prodded with something sharp, wake up! You're having a bad dream.

A short time after Jesus left for heaven Peter spoke to a large crowd, many of those there were the same people who had yelled, mocked and cursed as Jesus hung on that cross and Peter said to them:

'Now brothers, I know that you acted in ignorance, as did your leaders, but this is how God fulfilled what he had foretold through all the prophets, saying that his Messiah would suffer. Repent then, and turn to God, so that your sins may be wiped out, that times of refreshing may come from the Lord, and that he may send the Messiah, who has been appointed for you – even Jesus. Heaven must receive him until the time comes for God to restore everything, as he promised long ago through his holy prophets. For Moses said, 'The Lord your God will raise up for you a prophet like me from among your own people; you must listen to everything he tells you. Anyone who doesn't listen to him will be completely cut off from their people.

'Indeed, beginning with Samuel, all the prophets who have spoken have foretold these days. And you're heirs of the prophets and of the covenant God made with your fathers. He said to Abraham, 'through your offspring all people on earth will be blessed. When God raised up his servant, he sent him first to you to bless you by turning each of you from your wicked ways.'

While Peter and John were speaking the religious authorities and the temple police arrived and arrested them and put them in jail yet many of those who heard that message believed it and the church grew.

It's the same message today although there are many counterfeits, as the writers of the New Testament warned about (I Peter 2:1, Matt 24:4, 2 Tim 4:4, and consider what Jeremiah wrote concerning false prophets, 23:25-26).

The psalmist wrote, 'Today, if you'll hear his voice, don't harden your hearts as you did at Meribah (see Exodus 17:1-7 and Numbers 20:1-13), as you did at Massah in the wilderness, where your ancestors tested me; they tried me, though they had seen what I did. For forty years I was angry at that generation; I said, 'They're a people whose hearts go astray, and they've not known my ways.' So I declared an oath in my anger, 'They'll never enter my rest' (Psalm 95:8-11).

For those who may think this was for an Old Testament readership – that's true – yet the very same words are used for the New Testament readership who were warned that the same forgetful and complaining attitude exhibited by the ancient Israelites is just as real today. The entire third chapter of the letter to the Hebrews and most of chapter four are an exposition of those words: 'Today, if you hear his voice ...'

Today: that's not yesterday or tomorrow – it's now. If we want to enter that promised land, the city with foundations, the Empire of God, we must 'make every effort to enter that rest, so that no one will fall by following their example of disobedience, for the word of God is living and active. Sharper than any double-edged sword, it penetrates even to dividing soul and spirit, joints and marrow; it judges the thoughts and attitudes of the heart. Nothing in all creation is hidden from God's sight. Everything is uncovered and laid bare before the eyes of him to whom we must give account' (Heb 4:11-13).

If we hear his voice we're challenged to respond to that message. That's our choice. That decision is critical for our future – it was true for those in the

Old Testament period and it's true for us today. Our life depends on the choices we make. 'If' is a very big word in the Bible. If we reject what God offers it will end in disaster but if we accept what God offers and remain faithful, eternal life and an effective productive life in the age to come will be ours.

See to it that you do not refuse him who speaks. If they did not escape when they refused him who warned them on earth (Moses), how much less will we, if we turn away from him who warns us from heaven? At that time his voice shook the earth (at Mount Sinai) but now he has promised, 'Once more I will shake not only the earth but also the heavens.'

The story of the crusades was a hideous chronicle of human suffering, fanaticism and cruelty. I read of massacres in which the blood flowed up to the knees of the crusader's horses; of Jews herded into their synagogues and burned alive; and of women and children raped and slaughtered. An Anglican bishop recently rebuked me during a radio discussion for my condemnation of crusading. It was simply Europe 'flexing its muscles' and 'getting a little bit carried away'. I was unable to reply, because I found this one of the most shocking remarks I have ever heard. These crimes were committed deliberately and in cold blood. The crusaders enjoyed hating their victims. When an eyewitness described the conquest of Jerusalem in July 1099, in which some forty thousand Jews and Muslims were massacred in two days, he crowed in delight that this was a 'glorious' day and the most important historical event since the crucifixion of Jesus

Karen Armstrong
The Spiral Staircase

Part 6

Death or Life

Bethel, 930 BC

His arm outstretched, he pointed at the man who had the audacity to interrupt his carefully prepared religious performance.

King Jeroboam was standing next to the newly made altar when this unnamed man addressed the altar itself, "O altar, altar, God says that a descendant of David named Josiah will sacrifice your priests on these altars and human bones will be burnt on them and the sign that this will happen is that this altar will crack open and the ashes on it will spill out of it."

Jeroboam, who had served as an official of Solomon, was recently made king of Israel after he led a rebellion against king Rehoboam, son of Solomon, who planned, on the advice of his young advisors, to raise the taxes even higher than they were under Solomon. Now there were two kingdoms: The Southern kingdom of Judah, called the house of David, the second and greatest king in

Israel's history, and the Northern kingdom of Israel with its first king. There would be constant hostility between these two independent nations from then on. At one time Israel itself was allied with Syria in attacking Judah.

Out of Jeroboam's need that the people of Israel did not return to Jerusalem to sacrifice and worship on the annual feast days Jeroboam made two golden calves and under the cover of what would be more convenient for them, and to protect his position, he announced, "It's too much for you to go up to Jerusalem – here are your gods who brought you up out of Egypt." One of the idols was set up in Bethel, just north of Jerusalem and the other in Dan, in the north of Israel.

Jeroboam also built worship sites called high places and appointed priests from any tribe, as long as they brought a young bull and seven rams, they got the job that the law only permitted the sons of Aaron to have.

The Levites, who lived in Israel abandoned their pasturelands and property and came south to Judah and Jerusalem because Jeroboam and his sons had rejected them as priests and those who set their hearts on seeking God also followed the Levites to Judah so that they could worship at the temple in Jerusalem. Jeroboam also changed the dates of the annual feast days as another way to keep the people in Israel from moving down to Jerusalem on those special days.

That unnamed prophet who turned up at the bull worship service at Bethel was unmoved when the king, pointing directly at him, ordered his arrest and just as he gave that order his hand knotted together and his arm froze so that he was unable to draw it back to his body, at that moment the altar he stood next to split in half and its ashes poured out.

Shocked, the king asked the man of God, "Intercede with the Lord your God and pray for me that my hand be restored." The prophet interceded with God and the king's hand was restored. "Come home with me," the king said, "and have something to eat, and I'll give you a gift."

"Even if you were to give me half your possessions, I would not go with you, nor would I eat or drink here, because I was commanded by God not to eat or drink or return the way I came." So, the prophet took another road and did not return by the way he had come to Bethel.

Jeroboam did not let this incident change his policy of counterfeiting the revealed way of worship given to Moses. Eighteen years later, after a battle against Judah, that was then ruled by Rehoboam's son, Abijah, involving hundreds of thousands of fighting men, Bethel and other towns were returned to Judah and Jeroboam was severely wounded and died shortly after.

*

Three hundred years later the fifty-five-year reign of Manasseh ended. Under him the nation of Judah sunk lower than it had ever been. The chronicler of the kings wrote, 'He followed the detestable practices of the nations the Lord had driven out before the Israelites. He rebuilt the high places his father Hezekiah had demolished, he also erected altars to the Baals and made Asherah poles (dedicated to the goddess Asherah – the Canaanite mother goddess of love and fertility – her Mesopotamian equivalent was Ishtar). He bowed down to all the starry host and worshipped them. Altars were dedicated to them inside of the temple of God. He even sacrificed one of his sons in the fire in the Valley of Ben Hinnom (that area later became known as Gehenna, translated as hell in our Bibles), practised sorcery, divination and witchcraft, and consulted mediums and spiritists. He took the carved image he had made and put it in God's temple'.

God said, through his prophets, "Manasseh king of Judah has done more evil than the Amorites who preceded him has led Judah into sin with idols – this is what I am going to do – I will wipe out Jerusalem as one wipes out a dish, wiping it and turning it upside down. I will forsake the remnant of my inheritance and hand them over to their enemies. They will be looted and plundered by all their foes, because they have done evil in my eyes and have provoked me to anger from the day their forefathers came out of Egypt until this day."

Manasseh shed so much innocent blood that he had filled Jerusalem from one end to the other end.

After Manasseh died his twenty-two-year-old son Amon took over. He did exactly the same, and after two years he was assassinated in his palace. His son Josiah, aged eight, then became king. When he was sixteen he began to seek the God of his father David (he was of the lineage of David). Four years later he began to purge Judah and Jerusalem of high places, Asherah poles and carved idols. Under his direction, the altars of the Baals were torn down and he cut to pieces the incense altars that were above them.

At the age of twenty-six Josiah set in motion the repair work that was needed to restore the temple.

Timber and dressed stone were required and skilled masons and carpenters were hired.

In the process of clearing the temple after fifty-seven years of misuse the high priest came across the book of the law written by Moses. He gave it to Shaphan, the king's secretary, and he read it in the presence of the king. Such was the effect of hearing the words being read that Josiah tore his robes and gave orders to the high priest and four others to find out what is going to happen to him and the nation because of God's anger due to their fathers not obeying the words written in the book.

These five men met with the prophetess Huldah, who held an important position in Jerusalem. She told them, "This is what the God of Israel says; tell the man who sent you to me that I am going to bring disaster on this place and on this people, according to everything written in the book the king of Judah has read. Because they have forsaken me and burned incense to other gods and provoked me to anger by all the idols they have made my anger will burn against this place and will not be quenched. Tell the king of Judah, who sent you to enquire of the Lord, this is what the God of Israel says concerning what you heard read to you. Because your heart was responsive and you humbled yourself before the Lord when you heard the message, and you tore your robes and wept in my presence, I heard you and because of that I will gather you to your fathers and you will be buried in peace. Your eyes will not see all the disaster I am going to bring on this place."

They took her answer back to the king and he called all the elders of Judah and Jerusalem together at the temple and he read all the words of the book of the covenant which had been found. He renewed that covenant – to follow the Lord and keep his commands with all his heart and all his soul and the people pledged themselves to the covenant.

Josiah continued his reforms. All the pagan objects found in the temple were removed and burned outside Jerusalem. He also torn down the quarters of the male shrine-prostitutes which were in the temple of God and where women did weaving for Asherah. He desecrated Topheth, which was in the Valley of Ben (son) Hinnom, so no-one could use it to sacrifice his son or daughter in the fire to Molech (the word Molech means 'sacrifice' it was part of Baal worship and done in service to other gods as well).

Everything that was dedicated to sun worship was burned to ashes. Solomon had built high places for Ashtoreth the goddess of the Sidonians on the Mount of Olives and for Chemosh the god of Moab and for Milcom the god of the people of Ammon. They were all destroyed, and he covered the sites with human bones.

The altar made by Jeroboam at Bethel was demolished. He burnt the high place and ground it to powder. As Josiah looked around and saw the tombs that were there on the hillside, he had the bones removed from them and burned on the altar to defile it just as the prophet three hundred years before had said would happen.

"What is that tombstone there?" the king asked.

"It marks the tomb of the man of God who came from Judah and pronounced against the altar of Bethel the very things you have done to it," the local men told him.

"Leave it alone," the king said, "Do not let anyone disturb his bones."

Just as he had done at Bethel, Josiah removed and defiled all the shrines at the high places that the kings of Israel had built in the towns of Samaria that had provoked the Lord to anger. Josiah slaughtered all the priests of those high places on the altars and burned human bones on them. Then he went back to Jerusalem.

The order went out to all the people: 'Celebrate the Passover to the Lord your God, as it is written in the book of the covenant. Not since the days of the judges who led Israel, nor throughout the days of the kings of Israel and the kings of Judah, had any such Passover been observed. Neither before or after Josiah was there a king like him who turned to God as he did – with all his heart and with all his soul and with all his strength, in accordance with the law of Moses.

'Nevertheless, God did not turn away from the heat of his fierce anger, which burned against Judah because of all Manasseh had done'. The northern kingdom of Israel by this time had already ceased to exist and its people deported.

*

There were four more kings yet to reign over Judah. Twenty-two years and Judah would be finished.

The last king, Zedekiah, was twenty-one when he began his reign and it lasted for eleven years. He did evil in the eyes of God and did not humble himself before Jeremiah the prophet, who pleaded with him to submit to Nebuchadnezzar, but this weak leader was stiff-necked and would not turn to God. Jeremiah passed on to him a message from God, "If you surrender to the officers of the king of Babylon, your life will be spared and this city will not be burned down; you and your family will live, but if you will not surrender this city will be handed over to the Babylonians and they will burn it down and you will not escape."

"I am afraid of the Jews," the king answered, "who have gone over to the Babylonians, because I might be handed over to them and they will ill-treat me."

"They will not hand you over," Jeremiah replied, "Obey God by doing what I tell you. Then it will go well for you, and your life will be spared, but if you refuse to surrender, this is what God has revealed to me; all the women left in your palace will be brought out to the officials of the king of Babylon. Those women will say to you, 'those trusted friends of yours have misled you and overcome you – your feet are sunk in the mud, your friends have deserted you.'

"All your wives and children will be brought out to the Babylonians. You will not escape from their hands. You will be captured and this city will be burned down."

"Do not let anyone know about this conversation," Zedekiah answered, "or you may die. If my officials hear that I talked with you and they ask you to tell them what you said to me and what I said to you, then tell them that you were pleading with me not to send you back into that cistern where you almost died."

When Jeremiah was confronted by court officials he said as the king advised him to say and they allowed him to remain in the courtyard of the guard until the day Jerusalem was captured.

When the Babylonians breached the city wall Zedekiah and his family plus high-ranking officials and the palace guard left the city at night and headed for the Jordan Valley. The Babylonians saw them leave and overtook them in the plains of Jericho; then the royal party were taken to Nebuchadnezzar, who had made Zedekiah king in the first place when he deported the former king, Jehoiachin, Zedekiah's nephew, to Babylon.

Nebuchadnezzar was at Riblah in the land of Hamath, north of Israel. There, Zedekiah's sons were put to death in front of him and then his eyes were taken out. He was bound with bronze shackles and taken to Babylon.

The prophet who in 930 BC spoke to Rehoboam in Bethel saying that a descendent of David named Josiah would sacrifice the priests of Baal on their altars did not know that it would be three hundred years before it happened; but it still happened.

In 662 the prophetess Huldah spoke of Judah ending in disaster which it did in 587 BC. God was faithful to what he had said – to build up or to tear down. Our response, whether it is stubbornness, or repentance, does have a bearing on our future. The apostle Paul, a former Pharisee, gave both a positive and a negative statement about being faithful to Jesus in a letter he wrote to Timothy; 'If we died with him, we will also live with him; if we endue, we will also reign with him'. (now the negative part) 'If we disown him, he will also disown us; if we are faithless, he will remain faithful, for he cannot disown himself.' Endurance and patience is part of what Christians are called to. Paul, in writing to the Philippians said, 'for it has been granted to you on behalf of [the] Christ not only to believe on him, but also to suffer for him'.

Jesus said that "whoever denies me before men, I also will deny before my Father who is in heaven." If we are faithless he will be faithful to his warnings.

The many Christian teachers who say, "Once saved always saved," are not being consistent with the many warnings against faithlessness. This is a consistent theme in both testaments.

*

Josiah was deeply moved by the words that were read to him from the book of the law, as many others have been. David wrote with great feeling about the law and in one of the Psalms he said;

'The law of the Lord is perfect, reviving the soul. The statutes of the Lord are trustworthy, making wise the simple. The precepts of the Lord are right, giving joy to the heart. The commands of the Lord are radiant, giving light to the eyes. The fear of the Lord is pure, enduring for ever. The ordinances of the Lord are sure and altogether righteous. They are more precious than gold, than much pure gold; they are sweeter than honey, than honey from the comb. By them is your servant warned; in keeping them there is great reward.'

The very first psalm reads,

'Blessed is the man who does not walk in the counsel of the wicked or stand in the way of sinners or sit in the seat of mockers. But his delight is in the law of the Lord, and on his law he meditates day and night'.

David believed what he wrote yet he was human; his faithfulness was less than complete and what he did was, at times, more controlled by his sinful nature rather than by God's law. We should not hero worship individuals who were servants of God and at the same time sinful, as we all are. Paul, who said of himself, 'I do not even deserve to be called an apostle because I persecuted the church of God. But by the grace of God I am what I am.' He also wrote, 'For it is by grace you have been saved, through faith – and this not of yourselves, it is the gift of God – not by works, so that no-one can boast.'

David's descendant Jesus was the only one who could honestly say, in regard to his Father, "I always do what pleases him."

It was important that whoever ruled Israel should know and understand the law and so to equip the leader to rule wisely Moses wrote instructions specifically for the king who 'must not acquire great numbers of horses for himself or make the people return to Egypt to get more of them. He must not take many wives, or his heart will be led astray. He must not accumulate large amounts of silver and gold. When he takes the throne of his kingdom, he is to write for himself on a scroll a copy of this law, taken from that of the priests, who are Levites. It is to be with him and he is to read it all the days of his life so that he may learn to revere the Lord his God and follow carefully all the words of this law and these decrees and not consider himself better than his brothers and turn from the law to the right or to the left. Then he and his descendants will reign a long time over his kingdom in Israel.'

There is no indication that this instruction was followed by any of the kings of Israel.

The law was not only divinely inspired, but it was also practical and down to earth in what it taught:

Justice for all without partiality was demanded.

Provision for the poor was to be done.

Lists of what was safe to eat and what was not were given.

Sanitation rules were to be followed.

Infectious diseases dealt with.

Safety in buildings regulated.

Unlawful sexual relations listed.

Respect for parents.

Man-made idols forbidden.

Respect for neighbour and hired workers.

Care for the deaf and blind.

Intelligent care of the land.

Respect for the elderly.

Not to mark your bodies either by scaring or tattoos.

Not to oppress or misuse aliens living among you.

Use only honest weights and scales.

Care for domestic animals and wildlife.

Seven meaningful holy festivals in the year to be kept.

Every 50 years, liberty is to be made. All are to return to their own

property. Rules were to govern how this was done.

The land was to rest every seventh year.

Protection of property and rules concerning personal injury and

liability for accidents required.

Perjury condemned.

A tenth of produce for income tax.

A second tenth for financing your observing the annual feasts.

A third tenth every third year for the Levites (who had no land), the aliens, the fatherless and widows so that they could have enough to eat.

At the end of every seven years all debts are

cancelled. Rules were given to control misuse of this regulation.

Moses wrote, 'There will always be poor people in the land. Therefore, I command you to be open-handed towards your brothers and towards the poor and needy in your land.'

But as well as blessings through obedience there would be the reverse for disobedience. Both blessings and curses were set before the people and Moses summed up the good things that would happen due to diligently following all that was commanded and what rejection of God's commands would lead to.

"Now what I am commanding you today," Moses said, "is not too difficult for you or beyond your reach …no, the word is very near you; it is in your mouth and in your heart so that you may obey it.

"See, I set before you today life and prosperity, death and destruction. I command you today to love the Lord your God, to walk in his ways, and to keep his commands, decrees and laws; then you will live and increase, and the Lord your God will bless you in the land you are entering to possess. But if your heart turns away and you are not obedient, and if you are drawn away to bow down to other gods and worship them, I declare to you this day that you will certainly be destroyed. You will not live long in the land.

"This day I call heaven and earth as witnesses against you that I have set before you, life and death, blessings and curses. Now choose life, so that you and your children may live and that you may love the Lord your God, listen to his voice, and hold fast to him. For the Lord is your life, and he will give you many years in the land he swore to give your fathers, Abraham, Isaac and Jacob."

Not only would these blessings be good for all who lived there; it would also provoke the nations on their borders and those further away who hear of what is happening in Israel to say, "Surely this great nation is a wise and understanding people." Moses goes on to say, "What other nation has a god close at hand as the Lord our God is close to us whenever we call to him? What great nation is there whose statutes and laws are so just, as is all this code of laws which I am setting before you today?"

The people served the Lord throughout the lifetime of Joshua, who took over when Moses died, and the elders who outlived him and who had seen all the great things the Lord had done for Israel. After that whole generation had died the next generation grew up who neither knew God or what he had done for Israel. They followed and worshipped various gods of the people around them including the Baals – he was their new Lord.

The problem was not the law.

The fault was with the people; and God said through Jeremiah, 'The time is coming when I will make a new covenant with the house of Israel and the house of Judah. It will not be like the covenant I made with their forefathers when I took them by the hand to lead them out of Egypt, because they did not remain faithful to my covenant and I turned away from them. This is the covenant I will make with the house of Israel after that time – I will put my laws in their minds and write them on their hearts. I will be their God and they will be my people. No longer will a man teach his neighbour, or a man his brother, saying, 'Know the Lord,' because they will all know me, from the least of them to the greatest.

As part of those who made up the first deportation from Judah to Babylon the priest Ezekiel gave a similar message to the captives he lived among. He wrote of a return to their own land (the exile would last seventy years) and a condemnation of their pagan traditions in which their leaders, back in Jerusalem as well as among the exiles, maintained. They had not fulfilled their positions as faithful shepherds. "I am against the shepherds," God said, "and will hold them accountable for my flock." And he gave the promise that sometime in the future he would place over them one shepherd, my servant David, and he would tend them, "I the Lord will be their God, and my servant David will be prince among them … I will give you a new heart and put a new spirit in you; I will remove from you your heart of stone and give you a heart of flesh and I will put my spirit in you and move you to follow my decrees and be careful to keep my laws."

The sacrificial system, the Levitical priesthood and the central importance of the temple at Jerusalem are now obsolete.

"I will put my laws in their minds and write them on their hearts."

But what has become obsolete has taken on a greater reality – there are still sacrifices, there still is a priesthood and there still is a temple.

This is what Peter wrote, 'As you come to him, the living stone – rejected by men but chosen by God and precious to him – you also, like living stones, are being built into a spiritual house to be a holy priesthood, offering spiritual sacrifices acceptable to God through Jesus Christ (Hebrew-*Messiah* which means *the anointed one* Greek-*Christos*) … you are a chosen people, a royal priesthood, a holy nation, a people belonging to God, that you may declare the praises of him who called you out of darkness into his wonderful light. Once you were not a people, but now you are the people of God; once you had not received mercy, but now you have received mercy. Dear friends, I urge you, as aliens and strangers in the world, to abstain from sinful desires, which war against your soul. Live such good lives among the pagans that, though they accuse you of doing wrong, they may see your good deeds and glorify God on the day he visits us.' The Greek word for church is *ekklēsia*; the same word used for the people of Israel – the church is the Israel of God with all of its failings and shortcomings that are seen in ancient Israel.

Having God's law in our minds and in our hearts, does not remove our human nature, as Peter wrote about these sinful desires waring within us, so did Paul, in writing to the Galatians, 'So I say, live by the spirit, and you will not gratify the desires of the sinful nature. For the sinful nature desires what is contrary to the spirit, and the spirit what is contrary to the sinful nature. They are in conflict with each other, so that you do not do what you want. But if you are led by the spirit, you are not under the law.'

What does 'under the law' mean?

The law, as Paul wrote, 'is holy, and the

commandment is holy, righteous and good,' but the law is powerless to change a person or make them righteous, and we, as sinful by nature, are condemned as lawbreakers – guilty before God and under sentence of death ('the wages of sin is death', not living in eternal suffering; that dreadful teaching is not biblical and has been a heavy burden placed on Christians and a strong reason why many have rejected Christianity). Paul had concluded that both Jews and Gentiles – all humanity – are under sin. There is no-one who can make themselves righteous through their obedience to the law because it is through the law that we become conscious of sin – in that we are by nature lawbreakers.

James wrote that 'If you really keep the royal law found in Scripture, "Love your neighbour as yourself," you are doing right, but if you show favouritism you sin and are convicted as law-breakers because whoever keeps the whole law and yet stumbles at just one point is guilty of breaking all of it.' To the Galatians Paul said, 'All who rely on observing the law are under a curse, because it is written, "cursed is everyone who does not continue to do everything written in the book of the law." Clearly no-one is justified before God by the law.'

He also wrote of his fellow Jews who were zealous over the law, just as he had been, 'I can testify about them that they are zealous for God, but their zeal is not based on knowledge. Since they did not know the righteousness that comes from God and sought to establish their own, they did not submit to God's righteousness. Christ is the end of the law so that there may be righteousness for everyone who believes.'

In John Stott's commentary on Romans he writes, 'When Paul wrote that we have 'died' to the law, and been 'released' from it, so that we are no longer 'under' it, he was referring to the law as the way of getting right with God ... if righteousness is by the law, it is not by Christ, and if it is by Christ through faith, it is not by the law. Christ and the law are both objective realities, both revelations and gifts from God. But now Christ has accomplished our salvation by his death and resurrection, he has terminated the law in that role. 'Once we grasp the decisive nature of Christ's saving work', writes Dr Leon Morris, 'we see the irrelevance of all legalism.'

Legalism is the man-made means of controlling what people think and how they behave. Jon Krakauer, in his book '*Under the banner of Heaven*,' describes in detail the history of the Church of Jesus Christ of Latter-Day Saints, the Mormons. Joseph Smith, who founded Mormonism in 1830 taught as a divinely inspired revelation that polygamy is the 'the most holy and important doctrine ever revealed to man on earth,' section 132 of *The Doctrine and Covenants.* As Joseph Smith is believed to be a true prophet of God then faithful Mormons obey this and other doctrines, such as the supremacy of the white race which must be obeyed.

Karen Armstrong writes eloquently about her training to become a nun in her book, '*Through the Narrow Gate, a nun's story,*' in which we see 'the painful and stupid application of blind obedience where free thinking is considered worldly and close friendships and relations are to be sacrificed to the goal of totally giving your heart to God'.

Legalism spreads its dark net over more than Mormonism and Catholicism. It is a frame of mind that can and does exist in every denomination and within other faiths. They may call it inspired tradition rather than legalism, but it was one of obstacles that Jesus faced throughout his ministry. The power of traditionally held beliefs can blind our minds unless our minds are open.

Jesus was frequently criticised for breaking the rules on how the Sabbath was to be observed, even though there were many added rules that covered the Sabbath that were not part of the covenant given to Moses. Jesus said to those religious leaders at one time, "You study diligently the scriptures because you think that by them you possess eternal life. These are the scriptures that testify about me, yet you refuse to come to me to have life. I do not accept praise from men, but I know you. I know that you do not have the love of God in your hearts ... but do not think I will accuse you before the Father. Your accuser is Moses, on whom your hopes are set. If you believed Moses, you would believe me, for he wrote about me. But since you do not believe what he wrote, how are you going to believe what I say?"

"The love of God in your hearts ..."

When God promises to put his laws in minds and hearts, he is placing his love within his people who will daily seek to please him and although sins so easily entangles them, they are encouraged to persevere through all hardships. If sins are acknowledged God promises to forgive and purify them from all unrighteousness. "Blessed are those mourn for they will be comforted" – this saying of Jesus was given to show that mourning was appropriate in considering our own sins and the sins of those around us. Paul wrote to the Corinthians, 'Even if I caused you sorrow by my letter, I do not regret it – I see that my letter hurt you, but I am happy, not because you were made sorry, but because your sorrow led you to repentance. For you became sorrowful as God intended and so were not harmed in any way by us. Godly sorrow brings repentance that leads to salvation and leaves no regret, but worldly sorrow brings death. See what this godly sorrow has produced in you: what earnestness, what eagerness to clear yourselves, what indignation, what alarm, what longing, what concern, what readiness to see justice done.'

In writing to the Romans, Paul said, 'We rejoice in the hope of the glory of God. Not only so, but we also rejoice in our sufferings, because we know that suffering produces perseverance; character; and hope. And hope does not disappoint us, because God has poured out his love into our hearts through the holy spirit that has been given to us.' The New International Version has in this verse, 'by the Holy Spirit, whom he has given us.' The *whom* points to the holy spirit as a person and we find that some Greek words in the text have been changed to give a Trinitarian bias that is not there in many other translations, such as when the NIV has Jesus saying twice to Mary after his resurrection that "I have not yet *returned* to the Father," and, "I am *returning* to the Father," in other words, 'I'm going back to where I was before.' The Greek in both cases uses the word *ascend* or *ascending*. The *word* of 'In the beginning was the word and the word was with God and the word was God. He was with God in the beginning,' is the Greek word logos, which, according to the notes in the Harpers Collins Study Bible, New Revised Standard Version, has, 'the *logos*, in Greek thought the divine principle of reason that gives order to the universe and links the human mind to the mind of God. Jewish traditions about divine wisdom (Prov 8:22) lie behind this image.' 'Word' is not necessarily an incorrect translation, but when the translators choose to capitalize the *W*, it is an attempt to present the word/logos as a person, but the word is not a person. In 1526, the pronoun associated with *logos* was translated 'it' and not 'he' by William Tyndale. The Wycliffe translation of 1380, the Cranmer Bible of 1539 and the Geneva Bible of 1557 also translated the pronoun associated with *logos* as 'it'. The word *logos* is used many times throughout the New Testament'.

Logos is variously translated as 'statement' (Luke 20:20), 'question' (Matt 21:24), 'preaching' (1Tim 5:17), 'said' (Rom 15:18), 'command' (Gal 5:14), 'message' (Luke 4:32), 'matter' (Acts 15:6), 'reason' (Acts 10:29). In all cases logos is an 'it'. The word logos should not be thought of as a unique person as the term has a broad scope but is essentially represented by two general meanings in the Bible: 'logic' (or reason), and 'speech' (or word).

No lexicon defines 'logos' as a 'person,' yet this is what Trinitarians demand the word means in John. Colin Brown of Fuller Seminary writes, 'to read John 1:1 as if it said, 'In the beginning was the Son' is patently wrong.'

What has been poured out into the believer's heart is the divine nature of God, so that, as Paul wrote to the Corinthians, 'we may understand what God has freely given us … the man without the spirit does not accept the things that come from the spirit of God, for they are foolishness to him, and he cannot understand them because they are spiritually discerned. The mind of [the] Christ is the same as the spirit of God. All humans have a spirit which enables us to reason and make choices – it is our mind and attitude and our nature. Obviously, our spirit is not a separate entity any more than God's spirit is separate to him. "God is spirit", Jesus told the Samaritan woman, "and his worshipers must worship in spirit (with their innermost being) and in truth (knowing the only true God)".

*

Out of the two and a half million men, women and children who were liberated from Egypt and began their prolonged journey to Canaan, only two of that original number (plus those who were under twenty when they left Egypt) crossed the Jordan into the land – one was Joshua and the other was Caleb. When Moses prayed to God that he would forgive the Israelites their rebellious actions God replied, "I have forgiven them, as you asked, nevertheless, as surely as I live and as surely as the glory of the Lord fills the whole earth, not one of the men who saw my glory and the miraculous signs I performed in Egypt and in the desert but who disobeyed me and tested me ten times – not one of them will ever see the land I promised on oath to their forefathers. No-one who has treated me with contempt will ever see it. But because my servant Caleb has a different spirit and follows me wholeheartedly, I will bring him into the land he went to and his descendants will inherit it."

Twelve men who were selected from the tribes of Israel were chosen to investigate the land of Canaan; Joshua and Caleb were a part of that group, and when they returned the ten others gave a negative report because, in spite of the excellent fruit of the land, they were afraid of the people who lived there who were all very tall and had fortified cities. Caleb spoke up and said, "We should go up and take possession of the land because we can certainly do it," yet the majority were against moving into the land and the grumbling against Moses and Aaron began and spread throughout the vast camp. "If only we had died in Egypt or in this desert. Why is the Lord bringing us to this land only to let us fall by the sword? Our wives and children will be taken as plunder. Wouldn't it be better for us to go back to Egypt?" And they said to each other, "We should choose a leader and go back to Egypt." The whole assembly talked about stoning Moses and Aaron, who were at that time, along with Joshua and Caleb, praying for the people to change their minds and trying to persuade them not to rebel or be afraid because with God going before them these giants of men will have no protection and they will be swallowed up by the Israelites, but they would not listen.

God said to Moses and Aaron, "How long will this wicked community grumble against me? I have heard their complaints so tell them that I will do to you the very things I heard you say. In the desert your bodies will fall – every one of you twenty years old or more who was counted in the census and all who grumbled against me. Not one of you will enter the land, except Caleb and Joshua. As for your children that you said would be taken as plunder, I will bring them into in to enjoy the land you have rejected, but you – your bodies will fall in this desert. Your children will be shepherds here for forty years, suffering for your unfaithfulness, until the last of your bodies lies in the desert. For forty years – one year for each of the forty days you explored the land – you will suffer for your sins and know what it is like to have me against you."

The ten others in the party that had explored the land and had led the people to grumble against Moses were struck down with a plague and died. The people then regretted their rebellion and in a change of mind decided that they would enter the land, but Moses warned them not to go up because God would not be with them and they would be defeated but determined to do it they moved into the hill country and attacked the enemy positions, but it ended in military disaster for the rebellious Israelites.

*

Hundreds of years as slaves, a miraculous liberation, rebellion in the desert and finally entry into a land of hills, rivers, trees and good soil had etched its history into the hearts of those living in Israel even though many questioned whether it was all true or not – those sorts of things were not happening anymore. Life was good, for some; What God had done was in the realm of myth and legend.

The people needed to be reminded.

'Today, if you hear his voice,' the psalmist wrote, 'do not harden your hearts as you did at Meribah (*quarrelling*), as you did that day at Massah (*testing*) in the desert, where your fathers tested and tried me, though they had seen what I did. For forty years I was angry with that generation; I said, "They are a people whose hearts go astray, and they have not known my ways." So I declared an oath in my anger, "They shall never enter my rest."'

Each generation needed reminding although very few listened. Jesus likened the religious leaders to tenants who had rented a well-made vineyard and each time the owner sent a servant to collect the rent some were beaten up and others killed, this happened many times. In the end, he sent his son who he loved thinking that he would be respected but when the tenants saw that it was the heir to the property, they decided to kill him which they did, and they threw the body outside of the vineyard. Jesus asked those listening what they thought the owner of the vineyard would do, and Jesus answered his own question, "He will come and kill those tenants and give the vineyard to others, have you not read this scripture: 'The stone the builders rejected has become the keystone – this is the Lord's doing; it is marvellous in our eyes'".

The religious leaders looked for a way to arrest him because they knew he had spoken the parable against them, but they were afraid of the crowd, so they went away.

Isaiah had written seven centuries earlier, 'The vineyard of the Lord Almighty is the house of Israel, and the men of Judah are the garden of his delight. And he looked for justice, but saw bloodshed; for righteousness, but heard cries of distress.'

*

So important is the principle of both listening and implementing what is heard that the author of the book called Hebrews took what the psalmist said and repeated it with extra emphasis. The emphasis was on the words 'Today' and 'Rest'. Today is important because delay can lead to a hardening of our heart due to our natural sinful nature which ultimately will end in disaster just as it did for those Israelites who rebelled against God's instruction because their fear was greater than their trust. "They shall never enter my rest," this was true for those who died in the wilderness and never made it to the land that was promised to them. But when those words were written by the psalmist the people were settled in the land and enjoyed a reasonable degree of peace, and as those same words are used to first-century Christians who had or were going through a period of persecution. What rest applied to them, and significantly, to those reading the same words today?

Rest is commonly seen as stopping work in order to relax or to recover your strength. It is written that 'by the seventh day God had finished the work he had been doing, so on the seventh day he rested from all his work.' God does not sleep or becomes faint through overwork – Jesus said, "My Father is always at his work to this very day and I too am working," this was said on the Sabbath when he had healed a man who had been an invalid for thirty-eight years.

The rest is to be spiritually rooted and settled knowing the only true God and Jesus the Messiah whom God sent. Paul had written that he had been imprisoned, lashed, beaten, shipwrecked, lived in danger and gone without food and sleep. Physically he was not resting.

In one of his last letters that we have, Paul wrote, 'For I am already being poured like a drink offering and the time has come for my departure. I have fought the good fight, I have finished the race, I have kept the faith. Now there is in store for me the crown of righteousness, which the Lord, the righteous judge, will award me on that day – and not only to me, but also to all who have longed for his appearing.'

"Come to me," Jesus said, "all you who are weary and over-burdened and I will give you rest. Put on my yoke and learn from me. For I am gentle and humble in heart and you will find rest for your souls. For my yoke is easy and my burden is light." The words of finding rest are an echo of what God inspired Jeremiah to write, "Stand at the crossroads and look; ask for the ancient paths, ask where the good way is, and walk in it, and you will find rest for your souls. But you said, 'We will not walk in it.'"

Ellen MacArthur relates in her book, '*Taking on the world*', how, after covering 26,000 miles she crossed the finish line on 11 February 2001, 'Adrenalin surged through me. The RIB (a Rigid Inflatable Boat) pulled alongside us. Its passengers jumping aboard like a raiding party, and as the horns blow and the voices screamed, I was embraced and wrapped up in loving arms – my first human contact for over three months. Strangely, there were no tears, just the most incredible feeling of relief. As if a plug had been pulled, my concentration ebbed away in the time it takes for a gun to fire. No longer did I need to sleep for just ten minutes to recover, no longer did I need to look at the instruments each time I blinked. It was over, the race was over, and if it weren't for the adrenalin I'm sure I would have collapsed. We had made it. Together, *Kingfisher* and I had made it.'

In the accomplishment of something great there is celebration. What God had done, was doing and is yet to do can be rightly celebrated.

Jesus had compared the rules and regulations demanded by the religious leaders, who were ultra-legalistic, as heavy loads placed on the shoulders of those who were taught that the way to please God was through strict observance to all the details of law-keeping that they learned from childhood and any deviation or change from that rule was a punishable offence. The term *yoke*, which was sometimes in the Old Testament used as a symbol of oppression and also used in a good sense of the service to God, was later to be used commonly in Jewish writings for obedience to the law – the 'yoke of the law' is one every Jew should be proud to carry (*Mishnah Aboth 3:5*). The yoke of Jesus is better because it represents entering into a disciple-relationship with the one who is gentle and humble. Paul wrote of the 'gentleness and meekness of [the]

Christ' and it is the character Jesus expects and creates in his disciples, "blessed are the meek for they will inherit the earth." A humility that was lacking in the legalists.

What made the rule of the Pharisees worse was that these teachers of the law were hypocrites. What they did, they did to be seen. Their prayers and offerings and fasting were always public, always with an eye to maintaining the respect and honour due to a representative of God.

Dr A. Nyland writes in her translation of the New Testament:

'*hupokrites*, meant "hypercritical", "overcritical", not meaning critical of people, but critical in overly examining matters. It refers to a nit-picking, pedantic sort of person, someone who splits hairs and is legalistic.'

An even greater wrong was that what they taught was the traditions of men, and not what was from God. It was a counterfeit religion just as much as the changes made by King Jeroboam when the northern tribes of Israel split from the southern tribes of Judah nine-hundred years before Jesus condemned the religious leadership of his time. But why should this ancient history be of any concern to us today?

The distortion and counterfeiting of the original message of the Kingdom of God (which has to do with the restoration by God of everything) has been and remains a continuing reality that points to our human inability to solve the sharp divisions and disagreements among those who claim the name Christian. Tragically, in attempting to comfort those who have experienced evil, Christian leaders fail in speaking of the reality of our present age as Paul did at the beginning of his letter to the Galatians, 'Grace and peace to you from God our Father and the Lord Jesus [the] Christ, who gave himself for our sins to rescue us from *the present evil age.*' They also fail in speaking of the age to come – when the Kingdom (or Empire) of God is here on earth with a righteous and perfect government that brings, by divine force, peace. We are concerned with being able to pay our bills, our health and all the concerns of life and those real needs can become our priority but Jesus said that our heavenly Father knows that we need those things, but the better priority is seeking, waiting for, preparing for and longing for His Kingdom and the righteousness from God, the righteousness that come through faith in the Messiah Jesus to all who believe.

People who are suffering are not given that hope, and they are misled by ministers and pastors who focus only on God's love when the anger and justice of God against all evil is ignored or not understood. They do not speak of the evil of today and the better world to come because many do not believe it will come. Who would acknowledge and worship a supreme being who could not or would not stop evil? That failure would be a great injustice. Everyone will have to give an account for what they have done in this life.

*

The earliest division among those who believed that Jesus was the promised Messiah came from those who insisted that all non-Jews who came to the faith must be circumcised and obey the law of Moses (this would have included all the additional teaching that was piled on top of what Moses received at Sinai). This issue occurred repeatedly to those who took the message to the Gentiles. Peter addressed a meeting of the leadership in Jerusalem saying, "Brothers, you know that some time ago God made a choice among you that the Gentiles might hear from me the message of the gospel and believe. God, who knows the heart, showed that he accepted them by giving the holy spirit to them, just as he did to us. He made no distinction between us and them, because he purified their hearts by faith. Why do you test God now by putting on the necks of the disciples a yoke that neither we nor our fathers have been able to bear? No. We believe it is through the grace of our Lord Jesus that we are saved, just as they are."

The law, which Paul called holy, righteous and good, could not impart life, if it could, then righteousness would definitely be achieved through the law. But the scripture shows us that the whole world is a prisoner of sin – the psalmist had written, 'There is no-one righteous, not even one; there is no-one who understands, no-one who seeks God. All have turned away, they have together become worthless; there is no-one who does good, not even one' – the function of the law was to convince us of our need for forgiveness as law-breakers and to be reconciled to God. The law is holy, and we have not obeyed it and so are guilty before God. The legalisers would say, 'keep the law and you will gain life,' but because we break it the law cannot justify us. We are helpless to save ourselves from the judgement of God. Paul, in writing to the Christians at Ephesus says, 'As for you, you were dead in your transgressions and sins in which you once lived, following the course of this world, following the ruler of the power of the air, the spirit that is now at work among those who are disobedient ... but

God, who is rich in mercy, out of the great love with which he loved us even when we were dead through our trespasses, made us alive together with [the] Christ …'

Dietrich Bonhoeffer wrote, 'It is only when one submits to the law that one can speak of grace … I don't think it is Christian to want to get to the New Testament too soon and too directly.' John Stott writes in his commentary on Galatians, 'Is this not why the gospel is unappreciated today? Some ignore it, others ridicule it. So in our modern evangelism we cast our pearls (the costliest peal being the gospel) before swine. People cannot see the beauty of the pearl, because they have no conception of the filth of the pigsty. No man has ever appreciated the gospel until the law has first revealed him to himself. It is only against the inky blackness of the night sky that the stars begin to appear, and it is only against the dark background of sin and judgement that the gospel shines forth … The apostle has painted a vivid contrast between those who are 'under the law' and those who are 'in [the] Christ', and everybody belongs to one or the other category. If we are 'under the law', our religion is a bondage. Having no knowledge of forgiveness, we are still, as it were, in custody, like prisoners in goal or children under tutors. It is sad to be in prison and in the nursery when we could be grown up and free. But if we are 'in Christ', we have been set free. Our religion is characterised by 'promise' rather than by 'law'. We know ourselves to be related to God, and to all God's other children in space, time and eternity.

'We cannot come to Christ to be justified until we have first been to Moses to be condemned. But once we have gone to Moses, acknowledged our sin, guilt and condemnation, we must not stay there. We must let Moses send us to Christ.'

*

Paul used to speak in the synagogues about the kingdom of God, but they stubbornly refused to believe. He had told them that through Jesus the forgiveness of sins is granted and that through him everyone who believes is justified from everything that they could not be justified from the law of Moses. But they accused him of being against the law so Paul, and Barnabas said to them, "We had to speak the word of God to you first. Since you reject it and do not consider yourselves worthy of eternal life, we now turn to the Gentiles because this is what the Lord has commanded us: 'I have made you a light for the Gentiles, that you may bring salvation to the ends of the earth.' The Gentiles were glad to hear this, but the Jews instigated persecution against Paul and Barnabas and had them expelled from the region.

These types of incidents where this ongoing conflict and hostility between Jews and Gentiles due to cultural differences created a dividing wall between both that was only broken down by the understanding that both the circumcised and the uncircumcised had the same access to God through Jesus because he was their peace and through him they became fellow citizens with God's people and members of God's household.

Paul knew that he was to leave the area that he had spent so much time in so he called a meeting with the elders of Ephesus and they met at Miletus, which was a large seaport just south of Ephesus. Paul said to them, "Now I know that none of you among whom I have gone about preaching the kingdom will ever see me again. Because of this I say to you that I am innocent of the blood of all men (Ezekiel had written, '… if anyone hears the trumpet to warn the people but does not take warning and the sword comes and takes his life, his blood will be on his own head). For I have not hesitated to proclaim to you the whole will of God. Keep watch over yourselves and the flock of which the holy spirit has made you overseers. Be shepherds of the church of God, which he bought with his own blood. I know that after I leave, savage wolves will come in among you and will not spare the flock. Even from your own number men will arise and distort the truth in order to draw away disciples after them. So be on your guard – remember that for three years I never stopped warning each of you night and day with tears'.

That distortion of the truth began with Satan misrepresenting what God told the first humans and undermining God's command to them. Satan has been doing the same throughout history. People have invented their own ideas about God and harshly treated those who did not conform to it. The history of the church is full of coercion and the dreadful edicts that sent many to their deaths.

Paul warned Timothy that 'the time will come when men will not put up with sound doctrine. Instead, to suit their own desires, they will gather around them a great number of teachers to say what their itching ears want to hear. They will turn their ears away from the truth and turn aside to myths.' Jesus too, warned of false prophets who would convince the many that they are the one to lead them. He said that the many would be deceived. To this day this worldwide deception is still with us.

Millions from one branch of Christianity deeply disagree with millions from another; and smaller groups, teaching virtually the same thing do not speak to each other; each group thinking they are the true representatives of God. But God looks on the heart – not which denomination they are from.

One of the teachers of the law saw how well Jesus answered the Sadducees and he took his chance to ask him, "Of all the commandments, which is the most important?"

"The most important one is this: 'Hear O Israel, the Lord our God, the Lord is one. Love the Lord your God with all your heart and with all your soul and with all your mind and with all your strength.' The second commandment is this: 'Love your neighbour as yourself.' There is no commandment greater than these."

One command from Deuteronomy and one from Leviticus. The monotheistic understanding of God was not changed by Jesus. But today that has been distorted into God in three persons which became church law for all in the fourth century.

"I will put my law in their minds and write it on their hearts."

Paul was later to write, '... he who loves his fellow man has fulfilled the law. The commandments,

"Do not murder," Do not steal," "Do not commit adultery," "Do not covet," and whatever other commandments there may be, are summed up in this one rule: "Love your neighbour as yourself." Love does no harm to its neighbour. Therefore love is the fulfilment of the Law.'

All the injustices, cruelty, lies and tyrannical misuse of authority comes from the breaking of God's law – whether from ecclesiastic powers or secular, God's law has been broken and humans in their millions have suffered.

*

Is this misuse of power and distortion of the good news going to continue? All the divisions and sectarian hostility that are still with us remain deeply held and seemingly unstoppable even though many urge the warring parties to resolve their differences through peaceful means. No church or combination of churches have brought peace to the world, neither have they been able to stop disasters, torture, atrocities, social unrest and crime even though songs are sung and prayers are said the world continues to go from one horror to another with grief, pain and futility as constant companions.

The well-known and highly respected leaders in church history, such as, Athanasius of Alexandria, (d. 373) Augustine of Hippo, (d. 430) Luther (d. 1546) and Calvin, (d. 1564) and many bishops before, during and after, have advocated violence to destroy dissenting voices.

Athanasius' personal history is sordid at best. He was charged with forcing his way into his bishopric after the death of his predecessor, defiling a sacred altar, stealing church grain away from the poor and selling it for personal gain, and even suppressing dissent through murder. While the truth behind these accusations may never be known, there is no doubt that Athanasius was well-known by all as an aggressive firebrand who would succeed by whatever means necessary (See Timothy D. Barnes, *Athanasius and Constantius: Theology and Politics in the Constantinian Empire*). He had said that "one is not supposed to kill, but killing the enemy in battle is both lawful and praiseworthy" (Meic Pearse, *The Gods of War*).

Augustine's disagreement with the Donatists lead him to ask for and justify the use of force in dealing with them. Coercion could even be presented as obedience to the Lord's command to "compel them to come in." He did not scruple to exploit state authority to justify his strategy. He depicted the fate inflicted upon the Donatists as a matter of spiritual discipline. Sometimes, he argued, punishment and fear might move people to repentance in ways that love and patience do not. Whatever the complexities of his case against the Donatists, his stance served ever after as an example to which some of the European churches' darker tacticians might appeal, and in the medieval, Reformation, and Counter-Reformation periods legitimacy would be sought for more than a few programs of brutal repression by citing Augustine's moves against the Donatists (Read Ivor J. Davidson, *A Public Faith: From Constantine to the Medieval World*). This most influential theologian recognized that Christianity was now a program for running society, and so he began to formulate a definite theory of warfare and to discuss how, in certain circumstances, it might be considered just. All of this stood the body of Christian teaching that had been accepted for the first three centuries on its head. 'Nations cannot be Christian,' Meic Pearse writes, 'only individuals can. If Christians can fight, then it cannot be for Christianity, for that is a contradiction of Christ himself.'

In Martin Luther's own commentary on the letter to the Galatians, he writes in his introduction in regard to the Anabaptists, who did not agree with infant baptism, 'Who cannot see here in the Anabaptists, not men possessed by demons, but demons themselves possessed by worse demons?' He also advocated the burning of the houses and synagogues, prayer books and Talmuds of what he called "this insufferable devilish burden – the Jews" who refused to convert to Christianity (Martin Luther, *On the Jews and Their Lies*).

John Calvin personally hunted and finally authorized the torturing to death by slow burning of Michael Servetus who wrote against the Trinity. He defended the burning of Servetus as perfectly lawful in his 1554 treatise on the doctrine of the Trinity, and in the final edition of the *Institutes* continued to assail this executed heretic as a "foul dog" (Andrew Atherstone, *The Reformation: Faith & Flames*).

Kegan A. Chandler writes in his '*The God of Jesus – In light of Christian Dogma*,' 'Herein lies the justification for Calvin's wanton murder of Michael Servetus for denying the doctrine of the Trinity, and the foundations for all similar persecutions. *Heresy*, that most dreaded of words defined by the imperial synods of ages past, still condemns such devoted persons to this day and precludes many scripturally grounded theological submissions from the marketplace of Christian ideas. Today, the fire beneath the feet of the martyrs in the Roman and Reformation eras continues to burn in a social and spiritual sense.'

*

Christian orthodoxy, which originates from the creeds of the fourth and fifth centuries, has not produced peace, freedom and security, but what is not realised is that the church was never intended to be a powerful force in the world. Jesus said to Pilate, "My kingdom is not of this world, if it were, my servants would fight to prevent my arrest by the Jews. But as it is, my kingdom is not from here." He had earlier spoke of his disciples as, "not of the world, even as I am not of it," but they were to be the "light of the world." His life and message was not peace for the world but a call to repentance because the kingdom of God was near. "If the world hates you, keep in mind that it hated me first. If you belonged to the world, it would love you as its own. As it is, you do not belong to the world but I have chosen you out of the world, that is why the world hates you." "Do not suppose that I have come to bring peace to the earth," Those words of Jesus would not be considered fitting for Christmas cards as the world wants messages of peace and does not want to listen to what Jesus actually said, or for that matter, what the prophets and apostles said.

Isaiah had written, 'They say to the seers, "See no more visions," and to the prophets, "Give us no more visions of what is right. Tell us pleasant things, prophecy illusions. Leave this way, get off the path, and stop confronting us with the Holy One of Israel."

Paul's speech before King Agrippa encapsulates the result of believing the good news of the Kingdom of God. He repeats what Jesus, in vision, had told him, "I will rescue you from your own people and from the Gentiles. I am sending you to them to open their eyes and turn them from darkness to light and from the power of Satan to God, so that they may receive forgiveness of sins and a place among those who are sanctified by faith in me."

The reason why there is so much evil and corruption in the world is that the Kingdom of God has not arrived yet, even though many Christians say it has and that through evangelism the world will get better and better – this is the opposite of what the scriptures teach and what has happened in the world, even after two-thousand years of Christianity – that is because the church has been that small, faithful and persecuted people who see themselves as 'aliens and strangers on earth,' who are looking for a country and a city that is to come – not the state sanctioned enforcer of faith that held 'a bow and was given a crown and rode out as a conqueror bent on conquest.' The false religions and ideologies that have deceived the whole world are depicted in vivid imagery as the first of the four horsemen of Revelation.

*

Paul said of the Thessalonian Christians, '… how you turned to God from idols to serve the living and true God, and to wait for his Son from heaven, whom he raised from the dead – Jesus, who rescues us from the coming wrath.'

The body of Christians are to wait. Luke records Jesus as saying, "Be dressed ready for service and keep your lamps burning, like men waiting for their master to return … so that when he comes and knocks they can immediately open the door for him." Christians wait for the liberation of the creation, 'we groan inwardly,' Paul told the Roman Christians, 'as we wait eagerly for our adoption as sons, the redemption of our bodies. For in this hope we are saved. But hope that is seen is no hope at all. Who hopes for what he already has? But if we hope for what we do not yet have, we wait for it patiently.'

Near the beginning of this letter Paul wrote of God's kindness which had led the Roman Christians towards repentance and then goes on to speak of those who deliberately rejected that kindness, 'But because of your stubbornness and your unrepentant heart, you are storing up wrath against yourself for the day of God's wrath when his righteous judgement will be revealed. 'God will give to each person according to what he has done' (a quote from the Psalms and Proverbs). To those who by persistence in doing good seek glory, honour and immortality (humans are mortal – we do not have an immortal soul), he will give eternal life. But for those who are self-seeking and who reject the truth and follow evil, there will be wrath and anger. There will be trouble and distress for every human being who does evil; first for the Jew, then for the Gentile; but glory, honour and peace for everyone who does good: first for the Jew, then for the Gentile, for God does not show favouritism. All who sin apart from the law will also perish apart from the law, and all who sin under the law will be judged by the law. Because it is not those who hear the law who are righteous in God's sight, but it is those who obey the law who will be declared righteous. When Gentiles, who do not have the law, do by nature things the law requires, these, though not having the law, are a law to themselves. They show that what the law requires is written on their hearts, to which their own conscience also bears witness; and their conflicting thoughts will accuse or perhaps excuse them on the day when, according to my gospel, God through Jesus the Messiah, will judge the secret thoughts of all.'

A few notes from John Stott may be helpful here: '*it is those who obey the law who will be declared righteous*'. 'This is a theoretical or hypothetical statement, of course, since no human being has ever fully obeyed the law (Paul also wrote that, 'no-one will be declared righteous in his sight by observing the law; rather, through the law we become conscious of sin'). So there is no possibility of salvation by that road. But Paul is writing about judgement, not about salvation. He is emphasizing that the law itself did not guarantee the Jews immunity to judgement, as they thought. For what mattered was not possession but obedience.'

'*Gentiles, who do not have the law, do by nature things required by the law*'. 'Not all human beings are crooks, blackguards, thieves, adulterers and murderers. On the contrary, some honour their parents, recognise the sanctity of human life, are loyal to their spouses, practice honesty, speak the truth and cultivate contentment, just as the last six of the ten commandments require.'

'In addition, *their consciences* are *bearing witness*, especially by a negative, disapproving voice when they have done wrong, and so are *their thoughts* in a kind of interior dialogue, *now accusing, now even defending them*, as if in a lawcourt in which the prosecution and the defence develop their respective cases. It seems that Paul is envisaging a debate in which three parties are involved: our *hearts* (on which the requirements of the law have been written), our *consciences* (prodding and reproving us), and our *thoughts* (usually accusing us, but sometimes even excusing us).' We know what we do and we know what is right and what is wrong – our own heart condemns us. Isaiah reveals God's heart concerning our sins, "Come now, let us reason together," says the Lord. "Though your sins are like scarlet, they shall be as white as snow; though they are red as crimson, they shall be like wool. If you are willing and obedient, you will eat the best from the land; but if you resist and rebel, you will be devoured by the sword."

We can be in touching reach of the law; we can hear it, read it and copy it out yet we can still be far from the spirit of the law. The history of the exodus and the later story of Israel clearly demonstrates that being given the law does not guarantee the faith to live by it, rather, we learn that lawlessness has been the overall record from those who had been given so much.

One of the great themes of the Bible is that God will put his laws in their minds and write it on their hearts – no longer an outside legalistic code that in human hands can become a burden but a new covenant – not of the letter but of the spirit; because the letter kills but the spirit gives life.

Paul, in talking of the law, wrote 'that the commandments are summed up in this one rule; "Love your neighbour as yourself." Love does no harm to its neighbour. Therefore love is the fulfilment of the law.'

*

In teaching his disciples to keep their prayers short and simple Jesus gave an example of how to pray which includes the words, "Your Kingdom come – your will be done on earth as it is in heaven." The sobering reason why there are continual wars and unsolvable problems on earth (as Isaiah wrote, 'We look for light but all is darkness, for brightness, but we all walk in deep shadows … see, darkness covers the earth and thick darkness is over the peoples') is that God's kingdom is a future event. The prayer for God's will to be done on earth just as it is in heaven is that there is spiritual opposition here that is against that will being done so that God's will (what God wants) in so many cases, is not done. John wrote that 'we know that we are children of God, and that the whole world is under the control of the evil one'. Satan has led the whole world astray and until this enemy and his demons are nullified the control of this age remains in his deadly grip. The end of that satanic influence will come when Jesus returns.

In all the beauty and wonder of life there has been too much loss, too much suffering, too many lies for this world to be allowed to continue indefinitely. Tragically, according to scripture, world conditions will become much worse. The words, "Today, if you hear his voice, do not harden your hearts," speaks to each of us as individuals not to reject these words. As Peter wrote, 'The Lord is not slow in keeping his promise, as some understand slowness. He is patient with you, not wanting anyone to perish but everyone to come to repentance.' The 'door' is still open but at some time in the future that 'door' will close and then it will be too late. It is literally a question of death or life.

Let us glimpse a preview of the new age – the age that will hopefully come soon, "In the last days the mountain of the Lord's temple will be established as chief among the mountains; it will be raised above the hills. And nations will stream to it. Many people will come and say, "Come, let us go up to the mountain of the Lord, to the house of the God of Jacob. He will teach us his ways, so that we may walk in his paths." The law will go out from Zion, the word of the Lord from Jerusalem. He will judge between the nations and will settle disputes for many peoples. They will beat their swords into ploughshares and their spears into pruning hooks. Nation will not take up sword against nation, nor will they train for war anymore. Come, O house of Jacob, let us walk in the light of the Lord.'

That is worth getting excited about.

Postscript

The unnamed prophet from Judah, who appeared at the beginning of this chapter, who boldly confronted king Jeroboam at the altar in Bethel had been commanded by God to give that message and then come back to Judah by another route and for the duration of the mission neither eat or drink anything. Bethel was six miles from the border of Judah so it would be a twelve-mile round trip.

Sons of an old prophet who lived in Bethel told

him what had happened and he asked them which way the prophet had gone home. Knowing which way to head he ordered his donkey saddled and rode after the servant of God. He found the man sitting under an oak tree and asked, "Are you the man of God who came from Judah?"

"I am," he replied.

"Come home with me and eat," the old prophet said.

"I cannot turn back or go with you, nor can I eat bread or drink water with you in this place, that is the command I have."

"I too am a prophet, as you are." The old man said. "And an angel of the Lord said to me, 'bring him back with you to your house so that he may eat and drink.'" (He lied.) So the man of God returned with him and ate and drank in his house. While they were eating the word of the Lord came to the old man who blurted out the message to the prophet from Judah, "You have defied the word of the Lord and have not kept his command. You came back and ate and drank in the place where I told you not to eat and drink; because of this your body will not be buried in the tomb of your fathers."

When they had finished eating and drinking the old man saddled his donkey for the prophet who then set off for home. As he travelled back a lion attacked and killed him. People who passed that way saw both the donkey and the lion standing by the corpse. This was no normal lion attack. The old prophet in Bethel got to hear what happened and he saddled another donkey and went out and found the body still with the lion and donkey standing beside it. He lifted the body on to the donkey and took it back to Bethel. The body was laid in the old man's tomb, and he told his sons, "When I die, bury me in the grave where the man of God is buried. What he said about against the altar in Bethel and against all the sacred places here and in Samaria will certainly come true,"

Many questions arise from such an account: Why not accept the hospitality offered to him? Why did he have to go home by a different route? Why was this man of God sitting under a tree instead of getting back as quickly as possible? Why did the old prophet lie to the man of God? Why did the man of God go back with the old prophet without questioning what he said or showing any suspicion? Why is there no protest when the man of God hears about what will happen to him?

The questions remain unanswered as the text gives us no clues.

If the answers do not really matter then what does matter?

King Jeroboam heard, saw and experienced the word of God but he did not change his policies.

The man of God did not reject the counter-revelation claim even though it contradicted the clear command of God.

The old man spoke with authority, as a fellow prophet of God, but he was not speaking the truth.

Faithfulness matters. The apostle John's words of warning are for us today: "Dear friends, do not believe every spirit (teaching that claimed to be inspired) but test the spirits to see whether they are from God because many false prophets have gone out into the world."

"Watch out for false prophets," Jesus warned, and went on to say, "Not everyone who says to me, 'Lord, Lord, will enter the kingdom of heaven, but only he who does the will of my Father who is in heaven. Many will say to me on that day, 'Lord, Lord, did we not prophecy in your name, and in your name drive out demons and perform many miracles?' Then I will tell them plainly, 'I never knew you; depart from me, you who practice lawlessness!'"

Sadly, many have made sections of the New

Testament church doctrine when those texts, such as Mark 16:9-20 and 1Cor 14:34-35, 1Tim 2:11-12, are of dubious authenticity.

I am indebted to Dale Ralph Davis for his helpful and insightful commentary on the 'Book of First Kings', as well as his other books.

Eusebius of Caesarea went on to develop a theology of the Christian empire and emperor. He claimed that both empire and church were images of the kingdom of heaven. Through both God was saving humanity.

A Lion Handbook: *The History of Christianity p.169*

In an authoritarian State it is considered permissible to alter the truth, to rewrite history retrospectively; to distort the news, supress the true, add the false. Propaganda is substituted for information. In fact, in such a country you are not a citizen possessor of rights but a subject, and as such you owe to the state (and to the dictator who represents it) fanatical loyalty and supine obedience.

Primo Levi: *Postscript*: IF THIS IS A MAN / THE TRUCE

Pope Gregory the Great (590-604) was prepared to acknowledge that the councils of Nicaea (325), Constantinople (381), Ephesus (431) and Chalcedon (451) were the foundations of orthodoxy.

Charles Freeman: A New History of Early Christianity p.317

Part 7

The Empire of God

From that time Jesus began to proclaim, "Repent, for the kingdom of heaven has become near."

Matthew 4:17

> *Kingdom* (Greek *basileia*), perhaps
> "rule," "reign," but also "empire."
> The contrast of God's empire with
> the Roman Empire would have had
> serious political implications. The
> *Kingdom* is Jesus' central teaching.

New Revised Standard Version. The
Harper Collins Study Bible. p.1673

Recently a leading Christian gave their definition of what the gospel is, which was: "The Lord Jesus Christ gave his life for us to take away our sin that would have taken us to hell so that we might rejoice and know that we will be his in heaven. This is the great and glorious gospel."

This statement is based on assumptions that are not consistent with what Jesus himself expressed. We assume, whether we believe in the biblical account or not, that when we die, we either go to a lovely place called heaven or a terrible place called hell. We assume that the good news is Jesus dying on the cross so that our sins can be forgiven.

As profound and deeply significant as that death was, and is, it is not the good news that Jesus taught. "God loves you" is not the gospel.

When Jesus sent his disciples to proclaim the kingdom of God what were they to say? It obviously was not the death and resurrection of Jesus as that was definitely not in their thinking at that time, so what was their message?

Tom Wright, who was formally Bishop of Durham and is now Research Professor of New Testament and Early Christianity at the University of St Andrews, writes in his introduction to 'Paul A Biography', 'I assumed without question, until at least my thirties, that the whole point of Christianity was for people to "go to heaven when they died." Hymns, prayers, and sermons (including the first few hundred of my own sermons) all pointed this way. So, it seemed, did Paul: "We are citizens of heaven," he wrote. The language of "salvation" and "glorification," central to Romans, Paul's greatest letter, was assumed to mean the same thing: being "saved" or being "glorified" meant "going to heaven," neither more nor less ... Looking back now, I believe that in our diligent searching of the scriptures we were looking for correct biblical answers *to medieval questions.*

'These were not, it turns out, the questions asked by the first Christians. It never occurred to my friends and me that, if we were to scour the first century for people who were hoping that their "souls" would leave the present material world behind and "go to heaven," we would discover Platonists like Plutarch, not Christians like Paul. It never dawned on us that the "heaven and hell" framework we took for granted was a construct of the High Middle Ages, to which the sixteenth-century Reformers were providing important new twists, but which was at best a distortion of the first-century perspective. For Paul and all the other early Christians, what mattered was not "saved souls" being rescued *from* the world and taken to a distant "heaven," but the *coming together* of heaven and earth themselves in a great act of cosmic renewal in which human bodies were likewise being renewed to take their place within that new world. (When Paul says, "We are citizens of heaven," he goes on at once to say that Jesus will come *from* heaven not to take us back there, but *to transform the present world* and us with it.) And this hope for "resurrection," for new bodies within a newly reconstructed creation, doesn't just mean rethinking the ultimate "destination," the eventual future hope. It changes everything on the way as well.'

"My Kingdom is not of this world," Jesus said to Pilate, "if it were, my servants would fight to prevent my arrest by the Jews. But now my Kingdom is from another place."

"You are a king, then!" replied Pilate.

"You are right in saying I am a king. In fact, for this reason I was born, and for this I came into the world, to testify to the truth. Everyone on the side of truth listens to me."

Then Pilate said, "What is truth?" At that he left the room.

Not knowing what that kingdom, or empire, is, has left many without an answer to the question of evil and suffering in this world. The darkness in the human heart also needs to be recognised. False assumptions have led millions into doctrines that are the opposite of what Jesus and the apostles taught. The purpose of the life, death and resurrection of Jesus is distorted by myth and orthodox tradition. The future liberation of the world has been replaced with the lie of going to heaven; a teaching which sprang from the misguided and unbiblical belief that we all have an immortal soul. A further false assumption is that eternal *life* in hell is biblical when the Bible teaches that death will be the fate of the wicked.

The scale of religious deception has been worldwide, and every culture has been affected.[45]

The central message of Jesus was the Empire of God. A real empire but different and superior to all other empires. The beginning of his message was a call for a radical change of thinking because that empire was close.[46] After his resurrection he appeared to his disciples and spoke about the empire of God. The last words in the book of Acts describe the apostle Paul discussing the empire of God and the Messiah Jesus.[47]

Over a comparatively short span of time that core message dealing with God's empire and the man Jesus, who was the Messiah, was gradually changed to the teaching of going to heaven. No longer was there to be a thousand-year reign on earth of God's government although writers such as

---

[45] Rev 12:9.

[46] 46 Matt 4:17; Acts 1:3b.

[47] Acts 28:30-31.

Justin Martyr and Irenaeus believed in an earthly millennial reign of God as part of the eschatological vision for creation.[48]

The parables of Jesus point to the character of those who will ultimately serve under Jesus in that empire, and those characteristics are the same qualities that the Old Testament prophets declared that God's people need to have:

"For I desire steadfast love," God speaks through Hosea, "and not sacrifice, the knowledge of God rather than burnt offerings."[49]

"Hate evil and love good," Amos writes, "and establish justice in the gate ... let justice roll down like waters, and righteousness like an ever-flowing stream."[50]

"Do not my words do good to the one who walks uprightly?" Later he writes, "He has told you, O mortal, what is good; and what does the Lord require of you but to do justice, and to love kindness, and to walk humbly with your God." At the end of his message he writes, "Who is a God like you, pardoning iniquity and passing over the transgression of your possession? He does not retain

---

[48] Ivor J. Davidson. 'The Birth of the Church' p.227, 383n3.

[49] Hos 6:6

[50] Amos 5:15, 24.

his anger forever, because he delights in showing clemency."[51]

Habakkuk wrote, "Write this vision; make it plain on tablets, so that a runner may read it. For there is still a vision for the appointed time; it speaks of the end and does not lie. If it seems to tarry, wait for it; it will surely come, it will not delay … the earth will be filled with the knowledge of the glory of the Lord, as the waters cover the sea."[52]

Jesus taught his disciples to "preach the message: 'The Kingdom of God is near' … I'm sending you out like sheep among wolves, so be as shrewd as snakes and as innocent as doves."[53] They were going into a hostile environment – a dark enemy held territory. Much later Peter was to write, 'That they were to rid themselves of all malice and all deceit, hypocrisy, envy and slander of every kind.' To see themselves 'as aliens and strangers in the world, who had been called out of darkness into God's wonderful light'.

'They were to submit to every authority, whether to Caesar or to governors because it was God's will that by doing good they should silence the ignorant talk of foolish men … live as free men,

---

[51] Micah 2:7b; 6:8; 7:18-19.

[52] Hab 2:2-3, 14.

[53] Matt 10:7, 16.

but do not use your freedom as a cover-up for evil; live as servants of God. Show proper respect for everyone. Love the brotherhood of believers, fear God, honour the king ... but if you suffer for doing good and you endure it, this is commendable before God. To this you were called, because the Messiah suffered for you, leaving you an example, that you should follow in his steps. *He committed no sin, and no deceit was found in his mouth.*' Peter was recalling what Isaiah had written seven-hundred years before in chapter 53.

'When they hurled their insults at him, he did not retaliate,' Peter had personally witnessed that event. 'When he suffered, he made no threats. Instead, he entrusted himself to Him who judges justly. He himself bore our sins in his body on the tree, so that we might die to sins and live for righteousness; by his wounds you have been healed, because you were like sheep going astray, but now you have returned to the Shepherd and Overseer of your lives.'[54]

At the end of Jesus' last Passover supper, he prayed to his Father, "I have given them your word and the world has hated them (he saw what was to

---

[54] 1 Peter, chapter 2.

come) for they are not of the world any more than I am of the world …"[55]

Jesus had called them a 'little flock.'[56]

But the flock grew and changed; the lambs were becoming lions.

The apostles who recorded the early years of the church warned that both distortions to their message and an aggressive attitude from the church leadership was underway.

The apostle John writes of Diotrephes 'who loves to be first and will have nothing to do with us … not satisfied with gossiping maliciously about us he refuses to welcome the brothers. He also stops those who want to do so and puts them out of the church.'[57]

Diotrephes belonged to this world while those who belonged to God were not part of this world; and behind those who opposed the disciples of the Messiah was the one that is in control of this world.[58]

Peter wrote that 'there will be false teachers

---

[55] John 17:14.

[56] Luke 12:32.

[57] 3 John 9-10

[58] 1 John 5:19; John 8:42-44; 14:30; 16:11; 2 Cor 4:4; 11:14; Eph 2:2; 1 Peter 5:8-9.

among you. They will secretly introduce destructive heresies …'[59]

When Paul (a former Pharisee) spoke to the Ephesian leadership, he said, "I know that after I leave, savage wolves will come in among you and will not spare the flock. Even from your own number men will arise and distort the truth in order to draw away disciples after them."[60]

Later, he wrote to Timothy, 'In the presence of God and of the Messiah Jesus, who is to judge the living and the dead, and in view of his appearing and his Empire, I solemnly urge you: proclaim the message … For the time will come when men will not put up with sound doctrine. Instead, to suit their own desires, they will gather around them a great number of teachers to say what their itching ears want to hear. They will turn their ears away from the truth and turn aside to myths.'[61]

The unseen enemy of the young church needed to alter, change and distort the original message that Jesus and his disciples were given. They knew this would happen and that the flock of God's people would remain small and persecuted. The enemy

---

[59] 2 Peter 2:1
[60] Acts 21:29-30.
[61] 2 Tim 4:1-4.

is 'filled with fury because he knows his time is short.'[62]

The enemy's method was two-fold: antisemitism and the very strong influence of Platonism over Christian thinking.

Both have been poisonous companions since the beginning.

A statement of the obvious: Jesus was a Jew. His lineage was traceable back to king David[63] of whom the prophets said that he would have a descendant who would sit on his throne and rule over Israel.[64]

Jesus had been raised on the Hebrew scriptures. In those historic and prophetic books, he read of the great themes of light and darkness, the guilty and the innocent and punishments and rewards which lay at the heart of his teaching. For their special times of worship, they needed only to read the book of Leviticus, chapter 23 (they didn't have chapters and verses in those days).

Those days of worship looked back to being liberated from slavery and celebrating their new life in the promised land. What they did not know

---

[62] Rev 12: 12b.

[63] See Mark Rutland's 2018 'David the Great,' for an honest and helpful assessment of the king's life.

[64] Isa 9:7; 16:5; Jer 23:5-6; Luke 1:30-33.

was that those special days also pointed forward to future events. There had been many times when God had judged the Israelites for the hypocritical way they observed those days. The outward performance of a ritual often covered a heart that was far from wanting to please God. They had a condition that was described as stiff-necked and hard-hearted. They did not even believe in what they were doing and often turned to worship Baal, the fertility god and Astarte who was the goddess of fertility and war, she was also known as Ishtar and the Queen of heaven.[65]

Today, we can be just as stiff-necked and hard-hearted. That is why the writer of the letter to the Hebrews says, 'Let us make every effort to enter that rest, so that no-one will fall by following their example of disobedience.'[66] Just as the shepherds (leaders) in the Old Testament scattered and terrified the flock the same havoc happened in the early church and continued, with the same results, for many centuries.

When Jesus and his disciples kept that last supper together they were not observing Easter and would be shocked that such a pagan name now covers what was the Passover. That appointed

---

[65] Jer 7:18; 44: 18,25.
[66] Heb 4:11.

feast is the first festival mentioned in Leviticus and the day following, beginning at sunset, is the first of seven sacred assemblies where no work was permitted. It was called the Feast of Unleavened Bread. It was kept for seven days and the first day and the last day were observed as a Sabbath.

The first day of unleavened bread has been erased, in books and films, from the chronology of that last week of Jesus' life. John, in his account, calls it 'a special Sabbath.'[67]

Paul wrote to the Corinthians, 'For the Messiah, our Passover lamb, has been sacrificed. Therefore, let us keep the Festival, not with the old yeast (hypocrisy), the yeast of malice and wickedness, but with bread without yeast, the bread of sincerity and truth.'[68]

In the *Didache*, a book of church order from the late first or early second century, we find an explicit concern to differentiate Christian and Jewish behaviour. Fasting, for example, was to be observed on different days from Jewish fast days of Monday and Thursday (this was a post exile Jewish tradition; only one day of fasting was commanded in the Law and that was on the Day of Atonement; this was the fifth annual holy day)

---

[67] John 19:31

[68] 1 Cor 5:7b-8.

so, in their teaching, 'Do not let your fasts coincide with those of the hypocrites, believers should fast on Wednesday and Fridays instead.'

The historian Catherine Nixey writes in her book 'The Darkening Age,' 'There was little interest in Hebrew writings by now. According to the hectoring sermons being preached by a new generation of intolerant Christians clerics, the Jews were not a people with an ancient wisdom to be learned from; they were instead, like the pagans, the hated enemies of the church. A few years earlier, the preacher John Chrysostom had said that, 'The synagogue is not only a brothel ... it is also a den of robbers and a lodging for wild beasts ... a dwelling of demons ... a place of idolatry.'[69] Chrysostom's writings would later be reprinted with enthusiasm in Nazi Germany.'

Antisemitism meant a dislocation with the Hebrew culture, its history and traditions. Yet these were what Jesus grew up with, the books he read and quoted from and the laws and traditions he endorsed.

When asked, by an expert in the law, "which commandment is the first of all?" Jesus answered, "The first is: 'Hear (*Shema*, the Hebrew for 'hear'

---

[69] John Chrysostom, 'Discourses Against Judaizing Christians' 1.3.1. Quoted in 'The Darkening Age' p.133

or 'listen') O Israel: The Lord our God, the Lord is one; you shall love the Lord your God with all your heart, and with all your soul, and with all your mind, and with all your strength.' The second is this: 'You shall love your neighbour as yourself.' There is no other commandment greater than these."[70]

In AD 529, the emperor Justinian banned this core Jewish prayer and statement of faith known as the *Shema*.

Jesus did not take that opportunity to reveal some new understanding on his nature or his origins with his Father; yet the early church fathers were to spend an inordinate period of time wrestling with the question of who Jesus really was and that long bitter debate was the cause of many bishops losing their position, and, in some cases, regaining them as the theological winds would change. There are texts enough within the Bible that could be used as a creed without having to invent a series of creeds which did much to divide Christians. Consider what Paul wrote:

> *There is one God*
>
> *There is also one mediator*
>
> *between God and humans,*

---

[70] Deut 6:4-5; Lev 19:18; Mark 12:28-31.

the Messiah Jesus, himself human,

who gave himself a ransom for all[71]

As well as distancing themselves from the Hebrew scriptures church leaders turned instead to the works of Greek philosophy. 'Eusebius of Caesarea calls Plato "the only Greek who has attained the hight of truth," and Augustine describes, "the utterance of Plato, the most pure and bright in all philosophy, scattering the clouds of error." 'There had occurred within the Alexandrian schools a re-examination of Platonism in light of the Bible, and an active process of reconciliation took place. They came to believe that he [Plato] was inspired by the Holy Spirit or had received his wisdom from Moses and were somehow able to find in his writings the Christian Trinity, the Word, the Church and the immortality of the soul. The church fathers did not consider their Platonic worldview compromised by the advent of Christianity.'[72]

It is thought by many that Constantine became a Christian after seeing a vision of Christ just before facing Maxentius close to a crossing over the Tiber known as the Milvian Bridge. His victory there was seen as a divine blessing from the Christian God.

---

[71] 1 Tim 2:5-6.

[72] See Kegan A. Chandler's 'The God of Jesus' pp66-67.

This was 28 October 312. The coins Constantine issued in his early years as emperor included images of *Sol Invictus*, "the Unconquered Sun" (as well as symbols of various other pagan gods), and the still extant triumphal arch later erected in Rome to celebrate his victory over Maxentius also depicts *Sol Invictus* as Constantine's protector, referring simply to "the divinity," unspecified. When in 321 he declared the first day of the week a public holiday (or at least a day when nonessential labour was discouraged and public institutions such as the law-courts could be open only for the purpose of freeing slaves), his stated reason was to respect "the venerable day of the Sun."

Not everyone saw Constantine in a positive light. 'Many treated his sudden conversion to Christianity with profound suspicion and more than a little distaste. This man of 'evil disposition' and 'vicious inclinations' had converted, wrote one non-Christian historian, not because of any heavenly burning crosses but because, having recently murdered his wife (he had – allegedly – boiled her in a bath because of a suspected affair with his son), he had been overcome with guilt … at this moment of personal crisis Constantine happened to fall into conversation with a man who assured him that 'the Christian doctrine would teach him how to cleanse himself from all his offences, and that they who received it were immediately absolved from all their sins'. Constantine, it was said, instantly believed.'[73]

In Deuteronomy, God had commanded that His chosen people should overthrow altars, burn sacred groves and hew down the graven images of the gods.[74] If Constantine attacked the temples then he was not being a vandal. He was doing God's good work. The great Roman and Greek temples were broken open and their statues brought out and mutilated. Constantine's attack on paganism emboldened many Christians who spontaneously, without any command of the emperor, destroyed the adjacent temples and statues, and erected houses of prayer.

The desecration continued for centuries. In the fifth century the colossal statue of Athena, the centrepiece of the Acropolis in Athens, and one of the most famous works of art in the empire, was torn down from where she had stood guard for almost a thousand years and shipped off to Constantinople.

Martin of Tours, still one of the most popular

---

[73] Nixey. 'The Darkening Age' pp 91-92. For more details on this event see A New History of Early Christianity by Charles Freeman. pp.229-230.
[74] Deut 12: 2-3.

French saints of the fourth-century, 'set fire to a most ancient and famous shrine and went on to completely demolish a temple belonging to the false religion and reduced all the altars and statues to dust.'[75] In Egypt, Theophilus razed one of the most beautiful buildings in the ancient world – the temple of Serapis in Alexandria, which contained thousands of books. In Italy, Benedict overturned a shine to Apollo. In Syria, ruthless bands of monks terrorized the countryside, smashing down statues and tearing the roofs from temples.

Augustine himself declared to a congregation in Carthage that 'all superstition of pagans and heathens should be annihilated is what God wants, God commands, God proclaims!'[76] When you enter Room 18 in the British Museum you will see there the Parthenon Marbles; heads are missing, limbs broken off, great damage has been done to these great works, some of it is down to wars but much was the work of zealots, calling themselves Christian, who saw themselves as attacking the 'demonic' gods.

John Chrysostom encouraged his congregations to spy on each other. Enter each other's homes, he

---

[75] Sulpicius Severus, *Life of St Martin,* 14.1-7. In *Early Christian Lives,* C White, quoted in 'The Darkening Age' p.109.
[76] Augustine, Sermon 279.4.

said. Pry into each other's affairs. Shun those who don't comply with the new rules on lifestyle, then report all sinners to him and he would punish them accordingly.

The men leading these campaigns of violence were not embarrassing eccentrics but men at the very heart of the church. Chrysostom also wrote that his congregation should hunt down sinners and drive them into the ways of salvation as relentlessly as a hunter pursues his prey into nets. That principle is still used today by many Christians.

Jesus was blunt in informing his disciples what to expect in the future; "*They will put you out of the synagogue; in fact, a time is coming when anyone who kills you will think he is offering a service to God. They will do such things because they have not known the Father or me.*"[77]

Church history documents that many antisemitic bishops and leaders aggressively pursued those who held a different understanding on scripture and condemned them to death. Their targets were heretics, Jews and pagans.

Jonathan Wright, in his book 'Heretics,' says, 'Many would come to lament this new Christian world: a place in which coercion was acceptable

---

[77] John 16:2-3

and which religious faith and political power were so closely intertwined. More than a thousand years later some Christians were still mumbling their dissent. In the middle of the 17th century the Massachusetts politician Henry Vane looked back affectionately on the pure time before Constantine and Augustine, the "wilderness state," as he called it. For Vane, it was regrettable that Christianity has become the religion of the Roman Empire and began to deploy "the carnal weapons of worldly power" like a persecutory beast.'[78]

Jonathan Wright, later in his book, examines in detail the trial and execution by slow burning of Michael Servetus. His Spanish name was Miguel Serveto. He was a scientist and a freethinking theologian and is credited with the discovery of the pulmonary circulation in the human body. He had written a book against the Trinity doctrine and was against infant baptism. Servetus was arrested in Geneva where John Calvin headed the reform movement. Calvin worked to turn that city into a Protestant paradise and ruled through the establishment of the "consistory" (a weekly meeting of clergy and laity that was responsible for doctrinal and moral discipline) which was resisted by many influential families who resented the intrusion into

---

[78] Wright, pp.77,200.

their private affairs. When Servetus proposed a visit to Geneva, Calvin told a close associate, Farel, "I am unwilling to guarantee his safety, for if he does come and my authority counts for anything, I will never let him get away alive."[79]

The attorney general for Geneva was Claude Rigot and he became the counsel for the prosecution of Servetus. During the trial he presented a revised list of thirty charges. These were aimed at showing that Servetus was a menace to society. "Had Servetus not communicated with Jews?" Rigot claimed, "Was he not a Jew himself? Had he not he read the Koran and become friendly with infidel Turks? ... Had he not come to Geneva solely to disseminate his blasphemous ideas? Had he not lived a besotted and dissolute life? Had he not attended Mass as a loyal Catholic?" And on the charges came. These allegations did not succeed so Rigot abandoned his thirty charges and substituted a new list of thirty-seven. But this time the charges were actually written by Calvin himself.

Once again Servetus fended off the attack and at the next session of the court, the attorney general was replaced by Calvin. But there was to be no face-to-face confrontation. Servetus was given paper and the list of charges and was then returned

---

[79] Andrew Atherstone, 'The Reformation, Faith & Flames' p.115.

to his cell to prepare written responses in Latin. In the meantime, Calvin wrote private letters to the reformers in Bern, Basel, Zurich and Schaffhausen stressing the enormity of Servetus's heresy and how vital it was that nothing interfere with swift and certain punishment. If Servetus escaped with his life, who knew where he would next choose to spread his filth?

By October 23, 1553, after a month's delay, replies from the other cities were in hand and translated from Latin into French. All the ministers agreed. Michael Servetus was spouting heresy of the vilest sort and must not be allowed to continue. Servetus was put under a special guard – two new wardens to watch him twenty-four hours a day. If anything happened to the prisoner, these guards would pay with their lives.

"We condemn you, Michael Servetus," the council of Two Hundred announced, "to be bound and taken to Champel and there attached to a stake and burned with your book to ashes,"

According to Calvin, Servetus received the news of his sentence with disbelief and frantic self-pity, moaning and crying out "Misericordia!" [Mercy!] He then begged for an audience with the Reformer, which Calvin granted.

During this meeting, Calvin held out the possibility that if Servetus were to publicly renounce his views, he might die more quickly and mercifully. Servetus was himself worried that in a moment of extreme pain, he would recant and lose his soul. He begged Calvin to be allowed to die by the sword. Calvin refused.

The council wasted no time. The next day, October 27, Michael Servetus was led to the stake. Even now, his enemies would not leave him alone. Every step of the way, Farel walked next to him, whispering in his ear, urging him to confess his errors and be spared the flames.

Finally, they arrived at the hill at Champel, with its stake and pile of green wood. Servetus was seated; an iron chain was wrapped around his body and a thick rope wound several times around his neck. The crown of straw and leaves and sulphur was placed on his head, and his book was lashed to his arm.

The fire was lit. Servetus shrieked. At the end of the half hour that it took him to die, he was heard to moan, "Oh Jesus, Son of the eternal God, have pity on me!" This final cry was perfectly consistent with his anti-Trinitarian views.[80] As Farel observed, even

---

[80] For much more detail see, 'Out of the Flames,' Lawrence & Nancy Goldstone, pp.184-197.

in his dying moments the heretic had obstinately refused to acknowledge Jesus as *"eternal* son of God."

One contemporary, the French theologian Sebastian Castellio (1515-1563), found the whole episode deeply shameful. For Castellio, the execution was an unforgivable act of tyranny. He began to wonder if the very notion of persecuting heretics was not a betrayal of the entire Christian cause. "Just what were heretics?" Castellio asked, "simply those with whom we disagree. And while you might detest the people with whom you quarrelled, it really was not appropriate to torture and kill them. Force and violence had no role to play in the arena of religious belief because the truth could not be hammered into people's minds. Persuasion was endlessly more efficient than coercion."[81]

Castellio looked for an emphasis upon Christian morality rather than doctrinal correctness and maintained: "It would be better to let a hundred, even a thousand heretics live than to put a decent man to death under pretence of heresy." Calvin described Castellio's teaching as, "malignant, unmanageable and pernicious." He defended the burning of Servetus as perfectly lawful in his 1554

---

[81] Wright, pp. 202-203

treatise on the doctrine of the Trinity, and in his final edition of the *Institutes* continued to assail this executed heretic as a "Foul dog."[82] Just three copies of Servetus's book, '*Christianismi Restitutio*' have survived.

Jesus said that his Kingdom is not of this world and that his servants are not called to fight or destroy the property of others or frighten people into a corruption of biblical teaching. The Christian's fight is a spiritual one involving the heart and mind. The new covenant is that God's laws would be in our hearts and minds.[83] Or as Ezekiel puts it, 'I will give you a new heart and put a new spirit in you; I will remove from you your heart of stone and give you a heart of flesh, and I will put my spirit in you and move you to follow my decrees and be careful to keep my laws.'[84] The very first psalm has, 'his delight is in the Law of the Lord and on his law he meditates day and night.'[85]

Paul wrote, '... so then, the law is holy, and the commandment is holy, righteous and good.'[86] And

---

[82] Atherstone, p.118.

[83] Jer 31:33; Heb 8:8-13; 10: 15-18.

[84] Ezek 36:26-27.

[85] Psalm 1:2; 19:7-11; speaks of the benefits of God's law and the whole of the longest psalm (119) is a devotion to the law of God.

[86] Rom 7:12, NIV.

James wrote of 'the royal law found in Scripture.'[87] God's law teaches us what God is like.

Jesus said to the Samaritan woman, "a time is coming and has now come when the true worshippers will worship the Father in spirit and truth – they are the kind of worshippers the Father seeks. God is spirit and his worshippers must worship in spirit and truth."[88] The people of God were to see themselves as strangers and aliens in the world, looking forward to the city with foundations whose architect and builder is God.[89]

That empire of God is not here, yet people can be citizens of that empire now. Paul, Peter and John saw it as moving from an empire of darkness to an empire of light.[90] We either walk in the light or walk in darkness. What has been seen since the 4th century was an attempt to establish that kingdom of God by force, the exact opposite of what Jesus taught. It was not the triumph of Christianity, as many have called it, but a tyranny that imposed and demanded complete conformity. This darkness is still with us.

---

[87] James 2:8. 'The sinful mind is hostile to God. It does not submit to God's law…' See Romans 8:7-8.
[88] John 4:23-24.
[89] I Peter 2:11; Heb 11:10.
[90] Eph 6:12; Col 1:12-13; Acts 26:18; 1 Peter 2:9; 1 John 1:5-7

Two dreams, separated by 48 years, dramatically describe that at the tail end of a fourth world empire God's Kingdom will arrive.

The first of those empires, according to the interpretation Daniel was given of a dream that Nebuchadnezzar, king of Babylon, had, was that he was the head – the first of these empires. After him would come another empire, then a third, finally, a fourth. These empires were presented as part of a giant statue and each empire as a metal. The first was gold, the second, silver, the third, bronze, the fourth, iron. But the feet and toes of that last empire were a mixture of iron and clay – a divided empire, partly strong and partly brittle. Then a rock destroyed the lot and became a huge mountain.

"It is in the time of those kings," Daniel explained to the king, "that God will set up a kingdom that will never be destroyed, nor will it be left to other people. It will crush all those kingdoms and bring them to an end, but it will itself endure for ever. This is the meaning of the vision of the rock cut out of the mountain, but not by human hands – a rock that broke the iron, the bronze, the clay, the silver and the gold to pieces."[91]

The second dream happened to Daniel and

---

[91] Dan 2:24-45.

presented the same four empires as predatory beasts. (I'll leave out much of the detail that you can read for yourself) The first was like a lion, the second, like a bear, the third, like a leopard, and the forth – terrifying, powerful and frightening – was different from the other beasts. It had iron teeth and ten horns and could speak!

Later in his vision of these tyrannical beasts and their fate he saw a heavenly vision of 'the Ancient of Days' sitting on his throne and multiple thousands attending this being. "In my vision at night I looked, and there before me was one like a son of man (this was the way Jesus spoke of himself) coming with the clouds of heaven. He approached the Ancient of Days and was led into his presence. He was given authority, glory and sovereign power; All peoples, nations and men of every language worshipped him. His dominion is an everlasting dominion that will not pass away, and his kingdom (empire) is one that will never be destroyed."[92]

Peter H. Wilson writes in his 800+pages 'The Holy Roman Empire,' 'The book of Daniel recounts how the Old Testament prophet responded to a request to interpret Nebuchadnezzar's dream about the future of his empire. Thanks to an influential reading by St Jerome in the fourth century, this

---

[92] Dan 7: 1-28.

was understood as a succession of four 'world monarchies': Babylon, Persia, Macedonia and Rome. The notion of 'empire' was singular and exclusive. Empires could not co-exist but followed each other in a strict sequence that was epochal, involving the transfer of divinely ordained power and responsibility for humanity, rather than merely changes of ruler or dynasty. The Roman Empire had to continue, since the appearance of a fifth monarchy would invalidate Daniel's prophecy and contradict God's plan.'[93]

Peter H. Wilson had previously written, 'The holy element was integral to the Empire's primary purpose in providing a stable political order for all Christians and defending them against heretics and infidels. To this end, the emperor should act as chief advocate, or guardian, of the pope, who was the head of a single universal Christian church. Since this was considered a divine mission, entrusted by God, it opened the possibility that the emperor and Empire were themselves sacred … Moreover, though no longer considered a god, the emperor retained a sacred role as mediator between heaven and earth. The *Pax Romanum* remained an imperial mission but changed from providing an earthly

---

[93] Wilson, p.38.

paradise to advancing Christianity as the soul path to salvation.[94]

'The Frankish king Charlemagne was crowned the first Holy Roman emperor on Christmas day 800 (yet the words, Holy, Roman and Empire were only combined as *Sacrum Romanum Imperium* in June 1180. Both Pope and emperor were considered essential to proper order. Neither could ignore the other without negating his own position. Both remained locked in a dance that each struggled to lead, yet neither was prepared to release his partner and go solo.'

The Empire was dissolved by Emperor Francis II on 6 August 1806 to prevent Napoleon Bonaparte from usurping it. It had lasted for a thousand years.

On page 683 of Wilson's 'The Holy Roman Empire,' he writes, 'Since the 2004 enlargement and 2008 economic crisis, opinion on the EU has divided ever more sharply into two camps, one advocates forging a closer political union, the counter-argument is provided by nationalists who believe that the EU can never match the vitality of sovereign states. Some are looking and hoping for a fully federal system where the EU would become a 'The United States of Europe.'

---

[94] Wilson, p.19,29.

It might be that a revived 'Holy Roman Empire' where a strong political leader and a religious leader can provide the leadership to bring about such a revival. If that happens, the 'stone, not made by human hands' of Nebuchadnezzar's dream in 604 BC will destroy the 'feet and toes' of that final fourth empire.

In an article for the Times, Saturday June 16, 2018, Ben Macintyre writes of the huge 'deprogramming' that would be required to free the people of North Korea. He compares that state with its religious devotion to its leader with the rule of medieval kings ruling by divine right, and goes on to say, 'Survival depends on orthodoxy; heresy is death. In a population of evangelical devotees, no one pays much attention to the execution and disappearance of heretics, just as the removal of witches and unbelievers was an accepted part of medieval life, reinforcing obedience.'

Revelation 13 speaks of Two beasts: One is this fourth empire – the 'feet and toes' of the Roman Empire and the second beast appears like a saviour, who performs incredible signs in support of the first beast. The first beast holds authority for forty-two months, Rev 13:5; 11:2, this period of time is also read as 'one thousand two hundred- and sixty-days' Rev 11: 3; 12:6, and 'time, times and half a time' Rev 12:14. This text could also be considered as a symbolic period of time describing the whole span of time from the church's inception to the return of the Messiah.

Michael Wilcock in his 'The Message of Revelation' writes, '... to the human readers of Revelation a number *is* given, as a kind of code: *Three and a half years = forty-two months = one thousand two-hundred and sixty days =* the length of the church age. It may be that this was thought an appropriate 'human' number because it corresponded to the length of Christ's ministry. If it was reckoned that sometime over three years elapsed between his baptism and his ascension, then 'three and a bit years', or three and a half years, would be an excellent symbol for the period between the church's 'baptism' at Pentecost and her 'ascension' to meet the Lord when he returns.'[95]

What is to happen in the future? This question was on the minds of the disciples as they left the splendid buildings of the Temple complex and walked up the slope of the Mount of Olives. From their vantage point they looked across at the golden tops of the temple and the white marble which shone under the bright sunshine. Building work was still going on at that time and Jesus had just told

---

[95] Wilcock, p.130.

them that these incredible buildings that they were understandably admiring would all be demolished. This stark announcement shocked the disciples and they asked him, "Tell us when this will happen and what will be the sign of your coming and the end of the age?"

"Watch out that no-one deceives you," Jesus answered.

"For many will come *in my name* claiming I am the Messiah and will deceive many. You will hear of wars and rumours of wars but see to it that you are not alarmed. Such things must happen, but the end is still to come. Nation will rise against nation and kingdom against kingdom. There will be famines and earthquakes in various places. All these are the beginning of birth-pains."[96]

The hope of many Christians is that through the spread of the gospel eventually peace will come to earth, or at least where they live. But others consider that the only real peace that they will experience will be theirs after they die and are finally in heaven. Both these assumptions are unbiblical and are arrived at because the true message of God's empire has either not been heard or has not been believed.

---

[96] Matt 24: 1-8.

Jesus never said that his message will bring peace or that the spread of Christianity will, given enough time, and enough revivals, bring peace. What he said was the opposite. World conditions will get worse and his followers would be persecuted. There were tyrants before Jesus and there are tyrants today. Each of the four empires described by Daniel, either as a statue or as four wild beasts, were tyrannies. That evil will continue and intensify as we move closer to the end of this age.

"I am not praying for the world," Jesus said, "but for those you have given me, for they are yours."[97] Paul wrote of Jesus, 'who gave himself for our sins to rescue us from the present evil age.'[98]

Charles Freeman, in his important book, 'AD 381' writes, 'In 527, the greatest emperor of late antiquity, Justinian, came to the throne of the eastern empire. He was backed by his determined wife Theodora, whom he had raised from a dubious past as a circus artiste. Justinian tried to find a solution to the theological controversy that was splitting the empire [it concerned the nature of Jesus: was he fully divine or half divine: did he have two natures or one? It would have taken a brave person to say

---

[97] John 17:9.
[98] Gal 1:4.

that Jesus was a *man* accredited by God[99]]. Justinian believed in religious unity under the auspices of an emperor appointed by God. His famous laws which brought together a thousand years of Roman law into a coherent body of interlocking texts, were issued in the joint names of Lord Jesus Christ and the emperor himself.

'In one of his laws of the 530s, he ordered all to come forward for Christian baptism. 'Should they disobey, let them know that they will be excluded from the state and will no longer have any rights of possession, neither goods or property; stripped of everything, they will be reduced to penury, without prejudice to the appropriate punishments that will be imposed on them,' The death penalty was decreed for all who followed pagan cults.

'The Trinity was embedded at the core of church doctrine and was upheld in secular and ecclesiastical courts alike. The threat of prosecution for denying the Trinity continued in legal systems for centuries. 'It is striking to note,' writes the scholar Jaroslav Pelikan, 'that the unchallenged theological hegemony of the doctrine of the Trinity, beginning in the fourth century and ending in the eighteenth and nineteenth century, was basically coextensive with the willingness and ability of civil

---

[99] Acts 2:22. My addition to the quote from 'AD 381'.

authorities to go on enforcing it.' Even the Act of Toleration, passed by the English Parliament in defiance of the Anglican Church in 1689, did not extend to tolerating arguments against the Trinity. The scientist Isaac Newton worked assiduously to demolish the scriptural arguments for the Trinity, but he could never publish what he had written.'[100] When the authority of the Roman Catholic Church broke down in the sixteenth century, there was a revival of alternative formulations of the Trinity, including Docetism (that Jesus was completely spiritual – a divine being clothed in the form of a man) and Unitarianism (the belief that there is only one person in the Godhead rather than three). However, most of the Protestant churches maintained the orthodox doctrine of the Trinity. In the Thirty-Nine Articles of the Church of England, finalised in 1571 during the reign of Queen Elizabeth, the Nicene Creed, Athanasius' Creed and the Apostle's Creed are listed together in Article Eight as acceptable statements of faith. Catholicism as such could be condemned, but the core doctrine of orthodox Catholicism was absorbed into Protestantism.'

Some of what Jesus said to his disciples as they sat on the Mount of Olives directly concerned the

---

[100] Charles Freeman, 'AD 381', pp, 153-154; 193-194.

nation of Judea. About forty years later the Roman army under Titus, son of the new emperor Vespasian, destroyed Jerusalem. Jesus gave specific warnings for those who would be living through that siege but then he moved on to an even greater fulfilment of his words when he said, "Immediately after the distress of those days 'the sun will be darkened, and the moon will not give its light; the stars will fall from the sky, and the heavenly bodies will be shaken.'[101]

"At that time the sign of the Son of man will appear in the sky, and all the nations of the earth will mourn. They will see the Son of Man coming on the clouds of the sky, with power and great glory. And he will send his angels with a loud trumpet call, and they will gather his elect from the four winds, from one end of the heavens to the other."[102]

There is no word here of 'the elect' leaving earth and going to heaven, although some have used a text from Paul's first letter to the Thessalonians which concerns those who had 'fallen asleep' (died). He writes that 'we do not want you to be ignorant about those who have fallen asleep … we believe that Jesus died and rose again and so we believe that

---

[101] See Isa 13:10, 13; 34:4; Ezek 32:7-8; Joel 2:10; Amos 8:9; Rev 6: 12-13.
[102] Matt 24:15-31.

God will bring with Jesus those who have fallen asleep in him. According to the Lord's own word, we tell you that we who are still alive, who are left till the coming of the Lord, will certainly not precede those who have fallen asleep. For the Lord himself will come down from heaven, with a loud command, with the voice of the archangel and with the trumpet call of God, and the dead in Christ will rise first. After that, we who are still alive and are left will be caught up together with them in the clouds to meet the Lord in the air. And so we will be with the Lord forever.'[103]

Those 'in Christ' who have died will be collected by the angels and taken to where his descent to earth will be. Those 'in Christ' who are alive will be changed from mortal to immortal at the same time and taken to the same geographical area so that they are all together as they touch down on earth. Where will that be?

The Old Testament speaks about the first coming of the Messiah and of how he was to suffer by taking 'our infirmities and carrying our sorrows, yet we considered him stricken by God, smitten by him, and afflicted. But he was pierced for our transgressions, he was crushed for our iniquities; the punishment that brought us peace was upon

---

[103] 1 Thes 4:13-17.

him, and by his wounds we are healed. We all, like sheep, have gone astray, each of us has turned to his own way; and the Lord has laid on him the iniquity of us all.'[104]

The Old Testament also speaks, in many places, of his second coming to establish God's Empire. The expression, 'on that day,' is used repeatably in the 13th and 14th chapter of Zachariah to emphasise the dramatic importance of that day. Verse three has, 'Then the Lord will go out and fight against those nations, as he fights in the day of battle. *On that day* his feet will stand on the Mount of Olives, east of Jerusalem, and the Mount of Olives will be split in two from east to west … *On that day* there will be no light, no cold or frost. It will be a unique day, without day-time or night-time – a day known to the Lord … *On that day* living water will flow out from Jerusalem … The Lord will be King over the whole earth. *On that day* there will be one Lord, and his name the only name.'

We all die – tragedy surrounds us on every side. Death is inescapable.

After death we come face to face with judgement – a calling to account for how we lived our lives. Both death and judgement are unavoidable.[105]

---

[104] Isa 53:4-6.
[105] Heb 9:27-28.

If you are part of the family of God that judgement is happening now; (It is important to realise that we can lose that divine relationship)[106] if you are outside of that relationship the judgement will come later.[107] What is of vital importance is that we are reconciled to God now.[108] Through repentance (a radical change of mind) and faith (trust in who God is and what the Messiah Jesus accomplished in reconciling us to God) we become citizens of God's empire now; even before it has arrived.

There will come a time when it is too late. We will either be inside or outside of that empire. Those excluded will experience great grief and rage at being found in opposition to God. There is what the Bible calls; 'the second death'[109]

The question of reconciliation is addressed to us personally. What will you and I do with this call to turn to him?

Making the right decision is crucial.[110]

---

[106] Heb 2:1; 3:12; 4:11; 6:4-8; 10:26-31; 12:16-17.

[107] 1 Peter 4:17.

[108] 2 Cor 5:17-21.

[109] Rev 2:11; 20:6,14: 21:8

[110] In proclaiming 'an eternal gospel' Rev 14:6, we find that same message both in the OT and the NT. See Deut 10: 12-15, Acts 14:15-17. The eternal message is the necessity of repentance in light of the imminent judgement.

Access to God is not a wide-open, take-any-route-you-want-affair.

Many mistakenly assume they will be saved because of their frequent use of the name of Jesus yet Jesus himself warned about those who really did not know him.[111]

The Messiah Jesus, or Joshua, as he was named, was uncompromising in his teaching and confrontational in his honesty.

As Jesus went through the towns and villages on his way to Jerusalem, someone asked him, "Lord, are only a few people going to be saved?"

Jesus avoided giving a percentage answer and focused on what was more important: the individual's personal response to his message.

"Make every effort (strive – whole-hearted action) to enter through the narrow door," Jesus answered, "because many, I tell you, will try to enter and will not be able to. Once the owner of the house gets up and closes the door, you will stand outside knocking and pleading, 'Sir, open the door for us.'

---

[111] Matt 7:21-23.

"But he will answer, 'I don't know you or where you came from.'

'We ate and drank with you, and you taught in our streets,' they responded.

"I don't know you or where you came from," Jesus repeated. He then adds his total rejection of these people, "Away from me, all you evildoers!"[112]

That narrow door is still open, but it will be a struggle to get through.

That door will be closed.

There is no automatic entry.

The time to respond is short.

Outward contact with the message and the person of Jesus counts for nothing.

Inward reception is everything.[113]

---

[112] Luke 13: 22-27.
[113] The last two lines come from Darrell L. Bock's commentary on Luke. Vol 2. P.1237. Permission given.

Acknowledgements

Being surrounded by books of all sizes and types, both fiction and factual, I am acutely grateful for having the resources at hand to reread both historical and theological works from various perspectives that have provided the backbone for me to add the sinews and hopefully a few muscles to enable all of us to see and understand how the doctrines and teachings of present-day Christianity vary greatly from the so-called primitive church of almost two thousand years ago.

Bibliography

Karen Armstrong   *The Spiral Staircase*

_____,   *Through the Narrow Gate: A Nun's Story*

Andrew Atherstone   *The Reformation: Faith & Flames*

C. K. Barrett   *Essays on John*

_____,   *The Gospel according to John*

Timothy D. Barnes   *Athanasius and Constantius*

E. W. Bullinger   *Companion Bible*

Anthony Buzzard   *Focus on the Kingdom 10 Sept 2014*

John Calvin   *quoted in 'The Jewish Christian Theology'*

Stuart Clark   *The Sensorium of God*

Eric H.H. Chang   *The Only True God*

Kegan A. Chandler   *The God of Jesus*

Winston S. Churchill   *Thoughts and Adventures*

Larry Collings & Dominigue   *Is Paris Burning?*

John Mark Comer   God has a name

Ivor J. Davidson   *A Public Faith & The Birth of the Church*

Dale Ralph Davis   *The House that Jesus Built*

_____,   *Commentary on the book of Judges*

James Dunn	*Christology in the Making*
Will Durant	*The Story of Civilisation, quoted in 'The God of Jesus'.*
Brian Edger	*The Message of the Trinity*
Mary J. Evans	*Commentary on 1 Samuel*
Charles Freeman	*AD 381*
Edward Gibbon	*The Decline and Fall of the Roman Empire*
Anthony Tyrell Hanson	*The Image of the Invisible God*
Thomas Jefferson	*Quoted in 'heretics' Jonathan Wright*
Christopher B. Kaiser	*The Doctrine of God*
Martin Kiddle	*The Revelation of St. John*
Derek Kidner	*Commentary on Genesis*
Jon Krakauer	*Under the Banner of Heaven*
Paul Kriwaczek	*Babylon*
Peter Lewis	*The Message of the Living God*
John A. Lynn	
Mark H. Graeser	*One God & One Lord.*
John W. Schoenheit	
Candice Millard	*Destiny of the Republic*
Bruce Milne	*Know the Truth*
Ellen MacArther	*Taking on the World*
Ben Macintyre	*The Times, 16 June, 2015*

Leon Morris	*Commentary on Luke*
J. Alec Motyer	*Commentary on Isaiah*
Catherine Nixey	*The Darkening Age*
Dr A. Nyland	*The Source New Testament*
R. Joseph Owles	*The Didache: The Teaching of the Twelve Apostles*
Nick Page	*A Nearly Infallible History of the Reformation*
_____,	*The Wrong Messiah*
Meic Pearse	*The Great Restoration*
_____,	*The Gods of War*
Oliver Rice	*Calvin: Evangelicals Now. July 2009*
Reader's Digest	*After Jesus: The Triumph of Christianity*
Cyril Richardson	*The Doctrine of the Trinity*
J. A. Robinson	*In the End God*
Richard E. Rubenstein	*When Jesus became God*
John Stott	*The Message of Ephesians*
_____,	*The Message of Galatians*
_____,	*The Message of Romans*
_____,	*Commentary on 1 Timothy & Titus*
Frank Stagg	*The Holy Spirit Today*
_____,	*The Lutterworth Dictionary of the Bible: Article on the Holy Spirit*
Michael Wilcock	*The Message of Revelation*